Emotional Intelligence

Copyright © KR Publishing and Annette Prins, Eugene van Niekerk and Annette Weyers

All reasonable steps have been taken to ensure that the contents of this book do not, directly or indirectly, infringe any existing copyright of any third person and, further, that all quotations or extracts taken from any other publication or work have been appropriately acknowledged and referenced. The publisher, editors and printers take no responsibility for any copyright infringement committed by an author of this work.

Copyright subsists in this work. No part of this work may be reproduced in any form or by any means without the written consent of the publisher or the author.

While the publisher, editors and printers have taken all reasonable steps to ensure the accuracy of the contents of this work, they take no responsibility for any loss or damage suffered by any person as a result of that person relying on the information contained in this work.

All cases are for illustrative purposes only and the intent is not to evaluate the performance of an organisation.

First published in 2011
Second updated edition in 2018

ISBN: 978-1-86922-712-8 (Printed)
ISBN: 978-1-86922-713-5 (ePDF)

Published by KR Publishing
P O Box 3954
Randburg
2125
Republic of South Africa

Tel: (011) 706-6009
Fax: (011) 706-1127
E-mail: orders@knowres.co.za
Website: www.kr.co.za

Printed and bound: Tandym Print, 1 Park Road, Western Province Park, Epping, 7475
Typesetting, layout and design: Cia Joubert, cia@knowres.co.za
Cover design: Marlene de'Lorme, marlene@knowres.co.za
Editing and proofreading: Jennifer Renton, jenniferrenton@live.co.za
Project management: Cia Joubert, cia@knowres.co.za

Emotional Intelligence

Tipping Point in Workplace Excellence

By

Dr Annette Prins
Dr Eugene van Niekerk
Dr Annette Weyers

2018

CONTENTS

ABOUT THE AUTHORS	iii
ACKNOWLEDGEMENTS	v
PREFACE	vi
STANDARD ICONS USED	viii
PART 1: OPENING DOORS TO A BETTER LIFE WITH EMOTIONAL INTELLIGENCE	**1**
Chapter 1: Introduction	2
Chapter 2: Emotional Intelligence	5
PART 2: ACQUIRING EMOTIONAL INTELLIGENCE SKILLS	**34**
SECTION A: SELF-PERCEPTION	**35**
Chapter 3: Self-regard	36
Chapter 4: Self-actualisation	49
Chapter 5: Emotional self-awareness	65
SECTION B: SELF-EXPRESSION	**87**
Chapter 6: Emotional expression	88
Chapter 7: Assertiveness	103
Chapter 8: Independence	123
SECTION C: INTERPERSONAL	
Chapter 9: Interpersonal relationships	136
Chapter 10: Empathy	153
Chapter 11: Social responsibility	169
SECTION D: DECISION-MAKING	**179**
Chapter 12: Problem-solving	180
Chapter 13: Reality testing	197
Chapter 14: Impulse control	209

SECTION E: STRESS MANAGEMENT 227

Chapter 15: Flexibility 228
Chapter 16: Stress tolerance 245
Chapter 17: Optimism 269

SECTION F: WELL-BEING 285

Chapter 18: Well-being and happiness 286
Chapter 19: Concluding remarks 301

INDEX 306

ABOUT THE AUTHORS

Dr Annette Prins

Dr Annette Prins, a senior counselling psychologist, involves herself with developing human capital. She lectured at and was sub-head of Psychology at the Bloemfontein campus of Vista University. She held several leadership positions, then opted for a position as student counsellor, one she enjoyed tremendously.

She subsequently moved to the University of the Free State to become involved in postgraduate teaching and staff development. Later, in response to a need, she initiated and headed the Staff Wellness Programme. She, along with her staff, hosted bi-annual conferences on work wellness.

Annette was the CEO and co-owner of the company Talent and Wellness Management, she developed and presented an array of workshops in the people skills arena within the tertiary sector and the corporate environment. She has run a part-time private practice since 1992, and full time since 2015, where she specialises in stress management, anxiety, mood disorders and trauma counselling.

Annette co-edited *Counselling in Southern Africa: A Youth Perspective* and authored three chapters in the 2009 updated reprint, entitled *Handbook on Counselling Youth*. At the request of an international publishing house, her PhD appeared in print in 2010 under the title *Emotional Intelligence and Leadership: A Work Wellness Perspective*. She was editor to *Emotional Intelligence: Tipping Point in Workplace Excellence* (2011) published by Knowres. Annette has also published articles in a number of accredited and non-accredited journals, and has presented papers at both national and international conferences.

She obtained her Master's degree in Counselling Psychology cum laude, and in her final year of study she received the top achiever award.

Dr Eugene van Niekerk

Eugene C. van Niekerk BA (SA) (Hons) MSc (psychol.) (UCT) D.Litt et Phil (UFH) is a former Associate Professor in Psychology at Vista University - subsequently incorporated into the University of the Free State. He has taught psychology at both the under-graduate and post-graduate levels, including lecturing to psychiatric registrars in the Faculty of Medicine at Free State University. With numerous publications to his credit, Eugene is author and lead editor to a number of books, including, amongst others, *Paradigms of Mind – Personality Perspectives in Context* (1997) published by Oxford University Press; *Counselling in Southern Africa: A Youth Perspective* (2001) and *Handbook of Youth Counselling* (2009), both published by Heineman; and *Emotional Intelligence: Tipping Point in Workplace Excellence* (2011), published by Knowres. His academic background is also complemented by his work as a psychotherapist and corporate consultant. Eugene's interests include emotional intelligence; mind-body medicine; mental health in an information society; and how affective neuroscience is able to improve individual and organisational performance. Eugene is presently working on a manuscript, *Mind Alive*, which essays how the mind can better buttress and even flourish in modern times. He currently lives in Cape Town.

Dr Annette Weyers

Annette Weyers (PhD) is a senior social worker registered with the South African Council of Social Service Professions (1003918). As a consultant social worker she has been part of the wellness industry for 15 years. She was co-founder of the Centre for Talent and Wellness Management, an organisation that offered professional services to develop human talent and promote wellness. Services to employees included support and interventions through counselling, coaching, inspirational talks and workshops. In 2015 she resigned from the Centre for Talent and Wellness Management to pursue her interest in assisting women in their psychological and spiritual quest for wholeness and meaning.

Annette's interest in the search for meaning stemmed from her work with the personal development of employees, and served as inspiration for her PhD study. As part of her research she attended various international conferences and workshops, and gained valuable experience in various approaches and techniques that support the pursuit for wholeness and meaning. Further to her studies, she also explored feminine psychology, as well as the work of C.G. Jung on the proses of individuation, relative to the quest for wholeness.

ACKNOWLEDGEMENTS

The authors hereby wish to sincerely thank the following people for their support in the completion of the revised text:

- As always, our families who frequently had to take a back seat while our time was directed towards revising this text.

- Knowledge Resources for requesting a revised edition, and Ms. Cia Joubert (project manager) in particular, for competently assisting us in preparing the text for publication, with the help of her team of language editors and cover designers.

- The many researchers who enthusiastically researched the construct of emotional intelligence. Many different opinions set the scene for ongoing discourse, creating a dynamic field of interest. More specifically, we wish to acknowledge Reuven Bar-On, the Mayer and Salovey team, and Daniel Goleman, who popularised the concept of emotional intelligence.

- We also wish to thank the large numbers of delegates who attend our workshops on acquiring emotional intelligence competencies – they help shape our thinking through their feedback and enthusiastic participation.

- Lastly, we wish to thank God, who created us as people to be the wonderful beings we are, by differentiating us from other creatures through our ability to know, feel and act in an informed and civil manner – especially when our emotional intelligence skills have been somewhat sharpened!

PREFACE

In this book the authors serve as a guide to foster deeper insights into human emotions and how they shape and influence our everyday living. The tenor of the present work has been framed against the backdrop of positive psychology. As we will subsequently learn, positive psychology (still in its infancy yet growing in influence and showing great promise) saw the light at the turn of the present century. This meta-model views the psyche through the prism that allows for identifying strengths (rather than pathology), highlighting such notions as happiness, optimism, and human health.

Amongst others, the voyage invites the reader to better understand human emotions and how EQ can improve an individual's social and work effectiveness. The authors make the case that those who are literate in EQ will shape behaviours critical to work success and human interaction. The authors aim at the following outcome: to better understand EQ and bring intelligence to emotion. There exists a widely-held view that those who master emotional intelligence are rendered less likely to fall victim to debilitating anxiety, job disengagement and depression, and are more able to enjoy life.

The text applies adult learning principles as a conduit to absorb and integrate the acquisition of emotional intelligence skills. The following learning experiences will be included:

- Introductory perspectives describing the constructs involved and reflections on how they interact.
- Case studies.
- Role-play.
- Self-reflective exercises.
- Group work and discussions.
- Own work for personal growth.

Other participatory exercises will also be included, in order to interface theory and practice.

Our journey begins in **Part One**, which provides an overview of the theory informing this book. It elucidates, amongst others, affective neuroscience and the intricacies involved in the development of emotional intelligence. Readers will develop a deeper understanding of the effect and advantages of emotional intelligence on personal and organisational behaviour. Outcomes reflect the ability to do the following:

- Critically reflect on the changing world of work and the new requirements for successful functioning at work.
- Explain how brain plasticity allows for the acquisition of such skills as those propagated by emotional intelligence theorists.
- Discuss the important role of affect (both in mood and emotion) in human behaviour.
- Describe the historical roots of EI and its related concepts.

- Reflect on the development of EI.
- Enhance knowledge of the emotional intelligence construct.

The next stop in our journey, **Part Two**, documents the EI skills according to the revised Bar-On model EQ-i 2.0. Readers will be coached through various steps that will empower them to do the following:

- Develop skills and competencies related to the emotional intelligence construct.
- Manage personal and inter-personal relationships effectively over life domains.

Authors:

Annette Prins
Eugene van Niekerk
Annette Weyers
Bloemfontein, January 2018

STANDARD ICONS USED

 Case studies

 Final word

 Group activities

 Individual activity

 Outcomes

 Self tests

 Self-reflection

PART 1

OPENING DOORS TO A BETTER LIFE WITH EMOTIONAL INTELLIGENCE

Part 1 includes the first two chapters:

Chapter 1: Introduction

Chapter 2: Emotional Intelligence

Chapter 1

INTRODUCTION

Eugene van Niekerk

Jason Jacobs, an otherwise intelligent man, is a domineering boss who intimidates those who work for him. The problem seems to lie in his inability to manage emotions effectively; he is quick to anger, lacks patience, and is an indifferent listener at best, abandoning his staff to a toxic environment. The outcome: declining levels of motivation and morale. When assistant manager Dora brings up the problem of his less than polite behaviour, Jason simply shrugs his shoulders, dismissing her with an offhand retort: "I'm not angry – just doing my job".

The rules of work are changing. We are being judged by a new yardstick: not just how smart we are, or by our training and expertise, but how we handle ourselves and each other. This yardstick is increasingly applied in choosing who will be hired and who will not, and who will let go and who retained, who will be passed over and who promoted…who is most likely to become a star performer and who is most prone to derailing.[1]

Organisations are for the most part social settings that call for sound people skills. It is in such an environment that emotion and its intelligent application plays a major role. Success in the workplace is associated with, amongst others, emotional self-awareness, empathy, impulse control, stress tolerance, optimism and other emotional intelligence skills, which form the centrepiece of this book.

During the first half of the 20th century a one-life-one-work ethos reflected a typical career, but this is hardly the case today. The shelf life of captains of industry has undergone a sea change; consider for a moment that the tenure of a Fortune 500 CEO is down to less than four years. This seems to reflect at all organisational levels, undermining job security.[2,3]

The invasion of technology seems to leave its footprints everywhere. An American study recently found that 34% of managers had their vacation leave interrupted to attend to work-related matters. Even the sanctity of private life is apparently not respected – whether a family is enjoying a cosy supper or a picnic, technology is an unwelcome intruder. A French survey tapping into 2.5 billion TV viewers in 72 countries revealed that the average person spends 3 hours and 39 minutes in front of the box every day. A recent book penned by New York psychologist Dr. Daniel Goleman provides us with a taste of present day teenage behaviour. According to Goleman, "…the average …teen gets and sends more than a hundred texts a day, about ten every hour. I've even seen a kid texting while he rode his bike". Goleman continues "[teens] …are constantly checking their iPhones for who had texted them, what had updated on Facebook, or they were lost in some video game. They're totally unaware of what's happening around them and clueless about how to interact with for any length at time."[4]

Jack Block, a psychologist at the University of California at Berkley, is author to a study that highlights qualities in men who reflect high levels of emotional intelligence. His findings? High EI men present with a profile that include the following attributes: somewhat outgoing and cheerful; not prone to worry and rumination; socially poised; a tendency to community involvement; inclined to invest in social and inter-personal relationships; a somewhat rich and variegated emotional life; and above all, self-regard and an inclination to altruism.[5]

Research further suggests that those who experience high levels of emotional intelligence experience other advantages in life, including:

- Higher levels of satisfaction in the workplace.
- Higher probability of promotion.
- Higher earning capacity.
- Higher standard of living.
- Reduced levels of family conflict.
- Reduced vulnerability to cardio-vascular or immune-related disorders.
- A more fulfilled life.

What are emotions?

The word 'emotion' comes from the Latin word 'emovere', which means 'to move'. (Janet was moved by tears, anger etc.). Psychologists inform us that emotions are typically short lived - rarely more than five to ten minutes. Imagine a typical day at the office. An uncalled for slight from a colleague may provoke anger, a well-received presentation may elicit joy, while a confrontation with a teammate may cause distress. We also experience emotion when something meaningful happens to us. Cindi, an ardent stamp collector, is overjoyed when, on her birthday, she receives a set of rare and interesting stamps. Emotions also allow for visceral responses. When Susan receives some bad news it reflects in her physiology – her heartbeat, pulse rate and blood pressure escalate.[6]

What are moods?

Moods lack a clear eliciting stimulus, are less intense and longer lasting. Moods typically last for hours or days, and in exceptional cases weeks or longer. Psychologists inform us that we can elevate our mood by physical exercise, meditation, yoga, and even medication. While emotions and moods are to a greater or lesser extent short-lived, temperament enjoys a higher degree of permanency. When psychologists refer to an individual's temperament they describe traits that for the most part demonstrate more consistency over the life span. Consider, for instance, that some people are more placid by nature, others are quick to anger, while others are given to a cheerful disposition. On the other side of the spectrum we find individuals who typically present with anxiety or a depressive temperament.

Emotion and mood in the workplace

Studies indicate that when employees experience a positive mood, productivity increases due to higher levels of efficacy and flexibility. This in turn leads to better decision-making skills. An optimistic mood seems especially important in respect to team work.[7]

On the other hand, negative emotion, including anger and anxiety, can adversely impact work performance. As David Rock (2009) noted, even moderate levels of anxiety can interfere with the mind to optimally process information.[8]

An adverse organisational climate may lead to more negative outcomes. Goleman elaborates that "…a sour relationship with the boss can leave a person captive to stress, with a mind preoccupied and a body unable to calm itself". Distress, Goleman continues, not only erodes mental abilities, but also makes people less emotionally intelligent. People who are upset have trouble reading emotions accurately in other people, decreasing the most basic skill needed for empathy, and as a result impairs their social skills. In this sense, leaders who spread bad moods are simply bad for business, while those who pass on good moods help drive business success.[9]

A discussion of Emotional Intelligence follows in the next chapter.

REFERENCES

Block, J. (1995). *IQ vs Emotional Intelligence*. Unpublished Manuscript. University of California at Berkeley.
Goleman, D. (2006). *Working with emotional intelligence*. London: Bantam Books, p. 4.
Goleman, D. (2013). *Primal Leadership*. London: Little Brown.
Goleman, D. (2013). *Primal Leadership*. London: Little Brown, p. 14.
Goleman, D. (2014). *Focus: The hidden driver of excellence*. London: Bloomsbury, p. 5.
Rock, D. (2009). *Your Brain at Work: Strategies for Overcoming Distraction, Regaining Focus, and Working Smarter All Day Long*. New York: HarperCollins Publishers.
Van Niekerk, E.C. (2017). *Mind Alive*. Manuscript in progress. Cape Town.
Wikipedia. (2017). *Information overload* [Available Online]. Org/wiki/information overload [Accessed 5 September 2016].
Winston, R. (2004). *How the mind works*. London: Doring Kindersley.

ENDNOTES

1. Goleman, 2006.
2. Van Niekerk, 2017.
3. Wikipedia, 2017.
4. Goleman, 2014.
5. Block, 1995.
6. Winston, 2004.
7. Goleman, 2013.
8. Rock, 2009.
9. Goleman, 2013.

Chapter 2

EMOTIONAL INTELLIGENCE

Annette Prins

After completing this chapter, you should be able to:

- explain the historical roots of emotional intelligence;
- reflect on the different definitions of emotional intelligence;
- discuss the different concepts related to emotional intelligence competencies;
- differentiate between emotionally intelligent approach and avoidance behaviours;
- critically discuss the Bar-On model;
- describe the influencing factors in the healthy development of emotional intelligence;
- describe the abnormal development of emotional intelligence; and
- reflect on some benefits of emotional intelligence.

INTRODUCTORY PERSPECTIVES

Trevor Noah is a well-known South African comedian who took a quick rise to stardom. Noah is known for his quick wit and challenging approach to the unseen 'elephant in the room'. He is socially and emotionally highly skilled and holds his audience captive. He is, one could therefore assume, emotionally highly intelligent.

Emotional intelligence has increasingly come under scrutiny within the popular media and psychological literature after the publication of Goleman's[1] best seller on the topic. Although some perceived it as a "new" idea, scholars have actually studied this construct "for the greater part of the twentieth century".[2] Its historical roots may indeed go as far back as the work of Charles Darwin (1872/1965) on "emotional expression in survival and adaptation".[3]

During the previous century, scarce research funding led to the medical model dominating psychology, with a primary focus on curing the ill. This narrow focus on mental illness contributed to essentially excluding other areas of importance in human coping seen as difficult to identify, measure and understand. These areas included behaviour, emotions and cognition. Focus thus fell on "scientific data and rationalism".[4] Meanwhile, the Positive Psychology movement (evolving from the humanistic movement and its interest in normal and optimal growth) became interested in human strengths and skills that contribute to coping, adapting well and flourishing. This was in opposition to the medical model with its narrow focus on psychopathology. Coinciding with this development, Reuven Bar-On,[5] an

Israeli clinical psychologist (at the time involved in a PhD. at Rhodes University in South Africa), became interested in why some people thrive despite stressors, whilst others fail to do so. He was first to coin the term "EQ".

At present, researchers are conducting studies that are guided by the developing body of knowledge in the area of emotional intelligence, including tracing the historical roots of EI; investigating the normal and abnormal development of the construct; and relating EI to other psychological theories such as social and practical intelligence, related competency constructs, and a variety of outcome variables such as mental and physical health, the quality of interpersonal relations, etc. Furthermore, new findings in neuroscience offer insights into the workings of emotions and bear implications for the emotional intelligence construct, while studies on particular psychological disorders highlight deficits in emotional intelligence abilities.

The current section serves to review important perspectives and more recent models of the emotional intelligence construct; link it to the work environment; and review criticism that has been levelled in this regard.

When and where did you first encounter the term 'emotional intelligence'?

....

....

What is your view on 'emotional intelligence'?

....

....

HISTORICAL ROOTS OF EMOTIONAL INTELLIGENCE

The term 'intelligence' first appeared in literature during the 20th century;[6] prior to that period, even books of good standing on psychology did not mention the word. Since then, psychologists have tried to define intelligence, with the narrow view that intelligence is only cognitive in nature, soon starting to be challenged and slowly broadened.[7] As early as 1920, Thorndike[8] argued in favour of social ability as an important component of intelligence. He defined social intelligence as the ability to act or behave wisely in relation to others, and distinguished social intelligence from the mechanical and abstract forms of intelligence.

The study of emotional intelligence also ties in with the writings of Wechsler,[9] who referred to the non-cognitive intellective aspects of general intelligence. He subsequently defined intelligence as "the aggregate or global capacity of the individual to act purposefully, to think rationally, and to deal effectively with his (or her) environment".[10] This concept clearly involves more than mere cognitive intelligence, and implicates those abilities required to adapt to new situations and cope successfully with life.

These early thoughts were succeeded by the ideas of Professor Howard Gardner from Harvard University,[11] half a century later. He proposed a theory of multiple types of intelligence that included, in addition to the recognised forms of cognitive intelligence, kinaesthetic, practical, musical and personal intelligence, thereby expanding on Wechsler's concept of general intelligence.

Identify individuals in whom you can notice the types of intelligence recognised by Gardner.
....
....

Gardner conceptualised the personal intelligences as an intrapsychic capacity and an interpersonal skill. According to him, intrapersonal intelligence constitutes the ability to understand oneself, including knowing how one feels about things and understanding one's range of emotions, as well as having insight into the way one acts. Intrapersonal intelligence assists one to act in ways that are appropriate to one's needs, goals and abilities. Interpersonal intelligence, conversely, includes the ability to read the moods, desires and intentions of others, and to act on this knowledge.

On a continuum from one to ten, where would you place Trevor Noah and Donald Trump if one means no emotional intelligence and ten means a perfect level? Discuss.

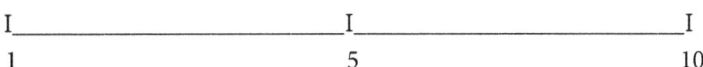

```
I_____I_____I
1                       5                      10
```

The concept of EI has emerged, adding depth to the concept of human intelligence in an attempt to expand the ability to evaluate overall intelligence.[12] Bar-On contends that general intelligence may be conceived of as including both cognitive and emotional intelligence, and views the personal intelligences as the precursors of emotional intelligence. EI speaks to the emotional, social, personal, and survival dimensions of intelligence, rated by some as more important for daily functioning than the renowned aspects of cognitive intelligence. Bar-On assumes that emotional intelligence is tactical and aimed at immediate functioning, while cognitive intelligence is more strategic, with long-term capacity. Emotional intelligence reflects one's ability to manage the immediate situation successfully by applying available knowledge. EI therefore measures a person's 'common sense' and ability to adapt to the world's demands.

DEFINITIONS OF EMOTIONAL INTELLIGENCE

Bar-On (whose model is followed in Part 2 of the current text) defined EI as "an array of non-cognitive capabilities, competencies, and skills that influence one's ability to succeed in coping with environmental demands and pressures".[13] He argues that emotional intelligence is an important predictor of success in life and directly influences an individual's general psychological well-being and health. Bar-On views emotional intelligence in combination with other important determinants as a basis for success in life. These include an individual's biomedical predisposition and conditions, cognitive intellectual capacity, and the limitations and realities of the changing context in which he or she lives. Goleman[14], meanwhile, defines EI as "a learned capability based on emotional intelligence that results in outstanding performance at work". Mayer, Salovey and Caruso[15] argue that emotional intelligence represents a set of mental abilities, including the ability to perceive emotions, access and generate emotion to assist thought, understand and reason about emotion, and reflectively regulate emotions to promote emotional and intellectual growth.

Before EI is discussed in more depth, related competency constructs and the non-intellective intelligences are discussed.

CONCEPTS RELATED TO EMOTIONAL INTELLIGENCE COMPETENCIES

Social competence (SC)

Socially competent behaviour may be defined as "...the behaviour of a person that leads in a specific situation to the achievement of a person's goals while at the same time guaranteeing the social acceptance of the behaviour".[16] Emotional intelligence and social competence are highly interrelated,[17] and emotional intelligence feeds into social competence.[18]

Socially competent people select and control which behaviours to apply in pursuing a given objective, either set by them or prescribed by others, within a given context. Within the work context, such an individual may therefore be self-assertive without being aggressive, thereby regulating the environment to his advantage. Social competence is important since it is a factor in resilience, and the socially competent and integrated individual seems more likely to withstand life stressors and temptations such as involvement in self-damaging behaviours, which may including drug-taking. Given the importance of flexibility in our rapidly changing society, socially competent individuals have been found to be better able to adapt efficiently, responsively and productively to change.[19]

Emotional competence (EC)

EC[20] refers to an individual's ability to identify, respond to, and manage his/her own and others' emotions. The emotionally competent individual shows self-efficacy in emotionally provocative situations. Think here, for example, of individuals who have to negotiate in hostage type situations. EC relates to "...how individuals apply the skills of emotionally competent behaviour in their emotionally evocative transactions with the environment".[21] For example, when a taxi nonchalantly swerves in front of one, one would expect an adult to manage it without undue road rage and "constructively regulate their evoked emotion".[22] For youths, a lack of emotional competence relates to and is predictive of problems in social communication[23] and social anxiety.[24] However, all individuals will at some stage experience some emotional incompetence when unprepared for or overextended within a particular social context.

Where did you experience this?

....

....

Culture is also influential because individuals immerse themselves in their cultural beliefs, attitudes and assumptions, most often communicated by means of narrative and discourse.

Consequences of emotional competence (EC)

Higher EC is, *inter alia*, associated with greater occupational success.[25] EC is important in outcomes that are functional for the individual, including the making and maintaining of friends, for academic success, as well as for community integration.[26] EC is also a strong predictor of subjective health and happiness.[27] In the workplace employee, EC is found to be a crucial predictor of customer loyalty and satisfaction.[28]

In summary, both social and emotional competence seem to feature in the broader EI construct and its competencies. The problem with definitively measuring these two constructs seems to resonate with what was found in the establishment of psychometric measures for emotional intelligence.

NON-INTELLECTIVE INTELLIGENCE

How important is academic intelligence (doing well academically) for successful living?

....

....

Reflect first individually and then in groups on individuals who are known to be successful. How would you typify such an individual in terms of intelligence?

....

....

Could a person be socially intelligent, yet have a low score on a traditional intelligence test? Discuss.

....

....

Emotional, social, practical intelligence and the likes are referred to as non-academic or non-cognitive intelligence,[29] or the non-intellective intelligences.[30]

Social intelligence (SI)

SI is defined as an individual's ability to be aware in and of social situations, being able to effectively manage presenting challenges, and understanding other people's feelings and concerns together with the ability to build and maintain relationships within social settings.[31] Socially intelligent individuals apply this knowledge in order to manage their emotions and direct their behaviour toward desired outcomes.

Researchers have found it difficult to determine with certainty that social intelligence is distinct from academic intelligence. This may, in part, be attributed to the variety of ways in which social intelligence has been defined and measured, a problem that seems to have been repeated in the EI literature.[32]

Practical intelligence

Practical intelligence is essential to successful living.[33] Successful intelligent people recognise and capitalise on their strengths to solve practical problems while compensating for weaknesses. A practically intelligent lawyer will, for example, be able to provide guidance with regard to conduct as it relates to real problems confronting individuals. He might be well suited to translate general principles and laws into concrete guidance for action.[34]

Provide an example from your own life where you have applied this principle.

....

....

Practical intelligence allows for adapting to the environment, shaping (or changing) it, or selecting a new environment in an attempt to attain personally-valued goals. A number of researchers have demonstrated practical intelligence to be distinct from academic intelligence.[35]

Individuals who are adept at solving academic problems are not necessarily equally adept at solving practical problems.[36] Below follows a brief overview of the difference between academic and practical, everyday problems.

Table 2.1: Academic versus practical problems

	Academic problems tend to be:	Practical everyday problems tend to be:
1	formulated by others;	unformulated;
2	well defined;	poorly defined;
3	complete in the information they provide;	lacking in information necessary for a solution;
4	characterised by having only one correct answer;	characterised by multiple "correct" solutions, each with liabilities and assets;
5	characterised by having only one method of obtaining the correct answer;	characterised by multiple methods for picking a problem solution;
6	disembedded from ordinary experience; and	related to everyday experience; and
7	of little or no intrinsic interest.	of personal interest.

Discuss in your group examples which demonstrate the principles in Table 2.1 above.

Interest in these two types of non-intellective intelligences precedes the interest in emotional intelligence, another form of non-intellective intelligence.

SUMMARY

As discussed in the previous section, researchers have attempted to define and understand competencies that relate to successful everyday living, and to discern their contribution relative to that of so-called academic intelligence.[37]

A number of competing EI models have been developed and are briefly discussed.

MODELS OF EMOTIONAL INTELLIGENCE (EI)

EI stands at the nexus between the intelligence and emotion disciplines.[38]

Introductory perspectives

Emotional intelligence is a much-debated topic. The sustained interest in the concept was initiated by two 1990 articles in academic journals.[39] This was followed by the popular best-selling book entitled *Emotional Intelligence* by Goleman.[40] Despite these articles presenting a mixture of sensationalism and science, the concept had great appeal. Since its inception, opposing views with different definitions and models of EI have come into being. "Different conceptualisations of EI are reflected in the broad array of available instruments".[41]

Consensus, however, seems to exist that an awareness of personal emotions is particularly important for emotional intelligence, as it provides the foundation for the successful implementation of the other components of emotional intelligence.[42] Emotionally intelligent behaviour includes impulse control, persistence, zeal and self-motivation, empathy, and social deftness.[43] These behaviours aim at either approach or avoidance, depending on the individual's interpretation of the possible consequences of such actions.[44] The following insights into such behaviours are provided:

- **Emotionally intelligent approach and avoidance behaviours**
  Impulse control, for example, involves refraining from taking a particular action that provides short-term gratification in an attempt to avoid possible negative long-term consequences. An example may be refraining from attacking the person who accidently drove into your car at an intersection. In order to manage such an impulse, a mental representation anticipating possible negative future consequences for self or others needs to be held in the working memory to prevent the action from occurring. Such consequences may, for example, include being convicted. Impulse control therefore involves a **suppression of approach behaviour**. By contrast, persistence is about managing negative emotional reactions when obstacles present whilst you are pursuing your goals. You may be working on a report, feel tired and want to sleep. Instead, you make coffee and get back to the report. Persistence assumes an awareness of negative emotions and **refraining from acting on them**, i.e. it involves the suppression of avoidance responses.

Provide examples of approach and avoidance behaviour. Are you acquainted with the "marshmallow" experiment? Give details. (See Chapter 14.)

....

....

Zeal and self-motivation, on the other hand, have to do with consciously creating a positive affect in order to motivate yourself to achieve your personal goals. A prerequisite is to recognise the absence of positive affect, initiate positive affect, and then monitor and sustain it. An example may be completing a performance management document you may not feel like making the effort, but thoughts of the potential reward that may follow, for example a merit bonus, may inspire you to plough through all the detail. This behaviour therefore entails the enhancement of approach behaviour.

Provide an example of your own.

....

....

Finally, **social deftness** implies the ability to negotiate social interactions skilfully in pursuit of achieving your goals within a particular social context. Successful negotiation is effected when you carefully monitor your own together with others' interests and concerns, and integrate them for suitable action. An example may be when management and unions enter into salary negotiations working towards a win-win situation. Important in this regard is to avoid creating negative responses and rather enhance positive responses in others[45] in order to augment the process.

Provide an example of your own.

....

....

Accurate empathy forms another cornerstone in anticipating whether a particular behaviour will evoke positive or negative responses in others.[46]

Against the background of differing definitions of emotional intelligence, a number of competing models have evolved and are now discussed.

COMPETING MODELS OF EI

A number of emotional intelligence models have been put forward. However three models dominate and the others essentially offer derivatives of these.[47] The first model, developed by Peter Salovey and John Mayer, views EI as cognitive ability, i.e. a form of pure intelligence, while a second model, conceptualised by Reuven Bar-On, views E.I. as a mix of cognitive ability and personality factors. This model places emphasis on how general well-being is influenced by both cognitive and personality factors. The third model, developed by Daniel Goleman, also views E.I. as a mixed intelligence that involves both cognitive ability and aspects of personality, however contrary to Reuven Bar-On, Goleman's model focuses on how these factors influence workplace success.

Bar-On's model is the authors' model of choice and forms the basis for the current text, and more specifically Part 2. It is now further explained.

BAR-ON'S MULTI-FACTORIAL MODEL

Bar-On[48] was intrigued by the fact that some people seemingly enjoy better emotional well-being and are more successful in life than others. He argued that many highly intelligent individuals are unsuccessful despite their obvious cognitive intelligence, while others with less cognitive intelligence are indeed highly successful.

What is your opinion on the above argument?

....

....

Bar-On subsequently investigated social and emotional competencies as underlying constructs for emotional and social intelligence.[49] He sketched emotional intelligence as "an array of non-cognitive capabilities, competencies, and skills that influence one's ability to succeed in coping with environmental demands and pressures".[50] He adopted the term 'emotional intelligence' since it reflects an aggregate of abilities, competencies and skills that are necessary to cope successfully with life's demands (similar to Wechsler's 1940 term 'intelligence'), while the adjective 'emotional' differentiates it from cognitive intelligence. Bar-On has broadened the view of the factors or emotional skills involved in emotional intelligence. He holds the opinion that the factorial components of emotional intelligence resemble personality and are open to change throughout life. He refers to Wechsler,[51] who stated that he was "convinced that intelligence is most usefully interpreted as an aspect of the total personality".

Bar-On's line of thinking, argument and research builds and expands on a number of theorists' work, such as that of Wechsler, Doll, Leeper, Maslow, Gardner, Mayer and Salovey, and others.[52] Despite his working independently of them, the theory he developed and the resulting research has much in common with their research findings.

Much of the research on EI flows from measurements; assessments are continually researched and adapted reflecting new information. Multi Health Systems (MHS) set themselves the task of adhering to such principles when they introduced the new revised EQ-i 2.0 (based on the input of numerous professionals working with the EQ-i) and accumulated new research in the field.[53] The EQ-i 2.0 thus follows from a reconceptualisation of the initial model.

The emotional intelligence definition was slightly adapted as part of the revision and is seen as "a set of emotional and social skills that collectively establish how well we perceive and express ourselves, develop and maintain social relationships, cope with challenges and use emotional information in an effective and meaningful way".[54]

New scales were added and the model was adapted accordingly, as per Figure 2.1 below.

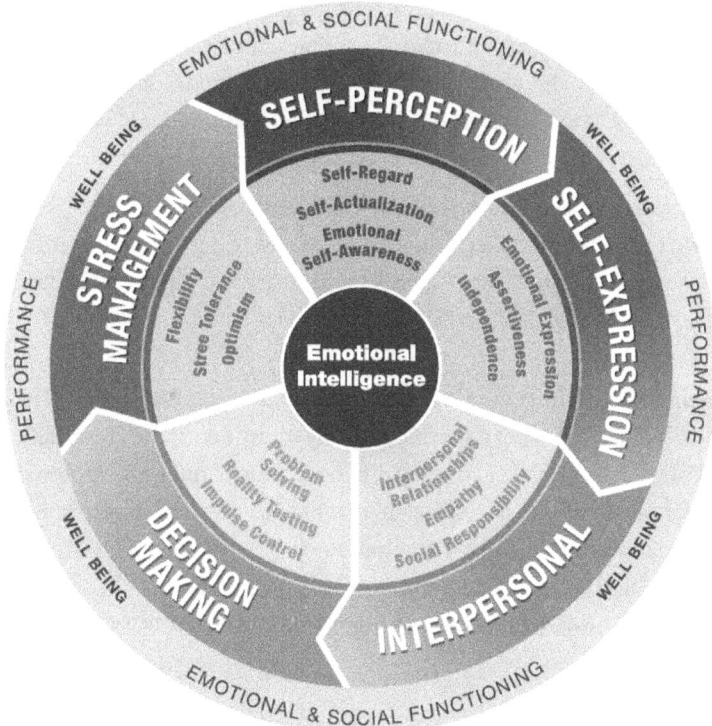

Figure 2.1: The new EQ-i2.0 Model (With permission from Multi-Health Systems Inc. (MHS))[55]

Below please find an overview of the **composite scales.**

Self-perception focuses on the "inner self", and aims to measure feelings of inner strength and self-confidence, as well as perseverance in pursuing personally relevant and meaningful goals, while having an understanding of what, when, why and how different emotions influence thinking and behaviour. Subscales include assertiveness, self-actualisation and emotional self-awareness.

Self-expression offers an extension of the self-perception scale and pays attention to the external expression or action component of a person's internal perceptions. It assesses the person's ability to be self-directed and openly express thoughts and feelings, whilst these feelings are expressed in a constructive and socially acceptable manner. Subscales include emotional expression, assertiveness and independence.

Interpersonal represents the ability to build relationships based on trust and caring; to express an understanding of a different perspective; and to act responsibly while caring for others, the team and the larger organisation/society of which they form part. Subscales include interpersonal relationships, empathy and social responsibility.

Decision-making refers to the manner in which a person applies emotional information and the extent to which they understand the impact that emotions have on decision-making. This includes the ability to withstand or postpone impulses, and to remain objective and thus prevent rapid actions together with ineffective problem solving. Subscales include problem solving, reality testing and impulse control.

Stress management refers to how well one copes with emotions that come with change and unknown and unpredictable circumstances, whilst being hopeful regarding the future and resilient when confronted by setbacks and obstacles. Subscales include flexibility, stress tolerance and optimism.

The instrument further allows for a ***wellness indicator.*** Happiness is indicative of emotional health and well-being, and is not a specific subscale of any one of the areas. It is characterised by feeling satisfied and the ability to enjoy different facets of one's life. It does not contribute directly to the total EI score. Associated subscales include assertiveness, optimism, interpersonal relationships and self-actualisation.[56]

Please see Table 2.2 below for an overview of the subscales.

Table 2.2: Composite subscales

Self-Perception Composite	**Includes**
Self-Regard	Respecting oneself; confidence
Self-Actualisation	Pursuit of meaning; self-improvement
Emotional Self-Awareness	Understanding own emotions
Self-Expression Composite	
Emotional Expression	Constructive expression of emotions
Assertiveness	Communicating feelings, beliefs; non-offensive
Independence	Self-directed; free from emotional dependency
Interpersonal Composite	
Interpersonal Relationships	Mutually satisfying relationships
Empathy	Understanding, appreciating how others feel
Social Responsibility	Social consciousness; helpful
Decision-Making Composite	
Problem Solving	Find solutions when emotions are involved
Reality Testing	Objective; see things as they really are
Impulse Control	Resist or delay the impulse to act

Stress Management Composite

Flexibility	Adapting emotions, thoughts and behaviours
Stress Tolerance	Coping with stressful situations
Optimism	Positive attitude and outlook on life

Well-being Indicator

Happiness: satisfied with life, content

Influential subscales include:

Self-Regard	Optimism
Interpersonal relationships	Self-Actualisation

Happiness both contributes to, and is a product of, emotional intelligence.[57]

Bar-On developed an initial assessment tool that he named the Emotional Quotient Inventory.

- **Assessment: Emotional quotient inventory (EQ-i and EQ-i2.0)**
  Since Bar-On's[58] definition of emotional intelligence, which is similar to Goleman's, includes a broad array of factors, he finds it virtually impossible to distinguish between the various forms of 'non-cognitive' intelligences (such as social and practical intelligence), and includes most factors associated with these forms of intelligence. Bar-On continued to develop a first assessment measure, the Emotional Quotient Inventory (EQ-i), which proved to have good psychometric properties that were supportive of its reliability and validity etc.[59] From this followed the EQ-i 2.0, as referred to earlier on.

Reliability and validity

"Based on results from numerous statistical analyses, users of the EQ-i 2.0 can be confident that the scores generated by this assessment will be consistent and reliable. Results also revealed that the EQ-i 2.0 very accurately measures emotional intelligence".[60] "Decades of research demonstrated the effectiveness of the EQ-i in measuring emotional intelligence, related concepts, and relevant outcomes. We found a very strong relationship between the scores on the original EQ-i and the EQ-i 2.0".[61]

DEVELOPMENT OF EMOTIONAL INTELLIGENCE

"Healthy individuals spontaneously model and respond to the mental states of other people (their knowledge, intentions, beliefs, and desires) to guide their own interpersonal behaviour. The ability to make inferences about what is going on in another person's mind is a cognitive skill called theory of mind."[62] This ability is essential for any form of EI.

Our attention now turns to the normal development of EI, before we highlight the abnormal development.

Healthy development of EI

Neurological substrates in support of EI are discussed first, because research in the emerging field of affective neuroscience[63] offers an interesting view of neural substrates supportive of an EI-based range of behaviour.

Neurological underpinnings of EI

Emotional intelligence, which is essentially about emotions and the concept of emotional intelligence, has its foundations in "the modern understanding of the role of emotional circuits in the brain".[64] Affective neuroscience seems to indicate that "the determining boundary in brain activity between emotional intelligence and cognitive intelligence is the distinction between capacities that are purely (or largely) neocortical and those that integrate neocortical and limbic circuitry".[65] Traditional IQ abilities (verbal fluency, spatial logic, and abstract reasoning) are primarily based in specific areas of the neocortex. Damage to these areas influences the corresponding intellectual ability. As far as emotional intelligence is concerned, the limbic centres, which project into the cortex or thinking brain, are the main areas involved with emotion. Research data informs us that "unique brain centers govern emotional intelligence".[66] Brain researchers including Bar-On and Damasio[67] have, via lesion studies, identified a distinct circuitry involved in emotional intelligence. These areas are separate from those involved in IQ. Individuals with an injury to the right amygdala, for example, experienced a loss in emotional self-awareness (Bar-On in Goleman[68]).

The somatosensory cortex in the right hemisphere is involved in both self-awareness and empathy, while empathy also depends on the insula, which "senses our entire bodily state and tells us how we are feeling".[69] The anterior cingulate, again, is involved in managing impulse control, which influences our ability to manage a range of distressing emotions. The ventral medial strip of the pre-frontal cortex is equally important, as the pre-frontal cortex contains the executive centre of the brain that we use to solve problems of both a personal and an interpersonal nature. This circuitry is essential for the development of skills in each of the four main domains of emotional intelligence.[70] It was found that lesions in these areas produce deficits in the hallmark abilities of emotional intelligence, namely self-awareness, self-management (including motivation), social awareness skills such as empathy, and relationship management. For further elaboration, the interested reader is referred to Goleman's *The brain and emotional intelligence: New insights*.

Next, attention turns to the neurology of decision-making, since what we observe in individuals' behaviour is frequently a demonstration of decisions that influence their behaviour.

The neurology of decision-making

(This is intended for the more advanced reader)

Twenty years of research in two very different fields — neuroscience and behavioural economics — has established quite clearly that people base their decisions on a complicated mixture of emotion and reason. Indeed, recent work suggests that emotions may play a larger role than analysis. "Individuals may think that their behaviour is purely rational, it rarely is.")[71]

Decision-making constitutes a bioregulatory response that aims to ensure survival.[72] Patients with (ventromedial prefrontal) lesions were found to develop serious impairments in personal and social decision-making, despite otherwise largely preserved intellectual abilities. These patients were, prior to the lesion, intelligent and creative, but the choices they made after sustaining these lesions were remarkably different and much less advantageous than before the brain injuries, as well as repeatedly being against their own best interests.

Damasio,[73] a neuroscientist, believes that the neural basis of the decision-making impairment characteristic of these patients is the defective activation of somatic states or emotional signals that attach value to particular options and scenarios that function as covert, or overt, biases in guiding decisions. Emotions help to influence decisions via memories of past events, eliciting positive or negative emotions, reward or punishment, pleasure or pain, happiness or sadness. "Whether these emotions remain unconscious or are perceived consciously in the form of feelings, they provide the go, stop and turn signals needed for making advantageous decisions."[74] The activation of somatic states therefore provides biasing signals that assist in the selection of advantageous responses from among an array of available options. The ventromedial prefrontal cortex directly or indirectly receives projections from all sensory modalities. In addition, it has extensive bi-directional connections with the amygdala, which is important for emotion. When a person is confronted with a decision, different chains of physiological events take place, informing the decision-making process.[75] If the underlying neurology is not functioning, the individual cannot make well-informed decisions that may bias behaviour in an emotionally intelligent manner. This research provides consistent and strong support for the main concept of emotional intelligence, namely a collection of emotional abilities that constitute a form of intelligence that is different from cognitive intelligence or IQ.[76]

The next component discussed in the normal development of EI is the role of the primary caregiver.

The role of the primary caregiver

An infant's healthy emotional development is strongly dependent on the emotional state of the mother or caregiver.[77] Of importance is the caregiver's ability and willingness to regulate emotional distress in the child,[78] as well as for reflective self-awareness and the ability to transmit this capacity to the infant. Both fathers and mothers exhibiting a self-reflective capacity had a three to four times greater chance of having securely attached children.[79] Research has also established that maternal EI, and especially a mother's accurate emotional perception, correlates highly with empathy, prosocial peer relations and relatedness in the child. The mother's EI also correlates with secure infant attachment, as per objective classification.[80]

While a caregiver's emotional interactions influence the development of certain mental capacities in an infant, evidence is mounting that the caregiver also exerts "a regulatory influence on the maturation of parts of the brain that are involved in emotional awareness and emotion regulation".[81] It is possible to identify an infant's attachment style reliably at approximately one year of age.[82]

Attachment behaviour is of importance with regard to establishing significant interpersonal relationships in adulthood.

Next, the role of emotional awareness in support of the normal development of EI is examined.

The role of emotional awareness

The ability to be aware of one's own emotional state is fundamental to the key features of emotional intelligence. "Emotional awareness is conceptualized as a domain of cognitive development that unfolds in a manner parallel to that of intelligence in the usual cognitive sense."[83] This developmental process is similar to that which Piaget described for cognition in general.[84] A fundamental principle of this approach is that variations will be reflected in individual differences in levels of emotional awareness. There are five levels of emotional awareness sharing the structural characteristics of Piaget's stages of cognitive development. In ascending order, these are: representing physical sensations; action tendencies; single emotions; blends of emotions; and blends of emotional experience. These levels influence the ability to recognise complexity in the experiences of the self and others, and to use this information as a guide in order to act adaptively.

Successful social adaptation requires a duel task ability, namely to consider one's own and others' needs simultaneously.[85] A prerequisite for optimal social adaptation is the appreciation of the differentiated feelings of the self and others. This information needs to be integrated into actions that lead to the attainment of personal goals that harmonise with the social context.[86] Higher levels of emotional awareness are supportive of learning from the modelling of appropriate behaviour or in emotional skills training.

Another influential aspect in the normal development of EI is language.

The role of language in emotions

Theorists,[87] in attempting to conceptualise stages in the normal development of the representations of emotions, have proposed that the acquisition of progressively complex language skills link with the development of increasingly complex cognitive schemata.

These schemata "gradually elevate the conscious experience of emotions from an awareness of peripheral manifestations of emotional arousal only (namely, undifferentiated bodily sensations and/or a tendency to action), to an awareness of blends of feelings, an ability to make subtle distinctions between nuances of emotions, and a capacity to appreciate the emotional experience of others".[88] (See Figure 2.2 below.).

Level of abstraction	Increased complexity	Increased differentiation
Language skills	Cognitive schemata	Conscious experience of emotion

Figure 2.2: Stages in the normal development of representations of emotions

> Things in the world become known to an observer by how they are represented symbolically. This perspective is consistent with the theory of Karmiloff-Smith,[89] who was a successor of Piaget. She believes that cognitive development occurs through a process she named **representational redescription**, which assumes the transformation of knowledge from implicit (procedural, sensorimotor) to explicit (conscious thought) representations by means of the use of language or another symbolic mode. This makes thought more flexible, adaptable, and creative. "Higher levels of representations of emotions in the working memory and associative memory systems not only enhance the conscious appraisal and self-regulation of states of emotional arousal (the latter via neural pathways from the prefrontal cortex and hippocampus to the amygdala) but also enable the person to intentionally communicate feelings to others via language and images."[90] Furthermore, symbolic imagery representing affective other-self interactions contributes to the development of memories, fantasies and dreams which help in containing and modulating states of emotional arousal.[91] Symbolic representation such as language is therefore a prerequisite for the normal development of EI.

To summarise, it is therefore important that a number of factors effectively interface to orchestrate the normal development of EI. These include an intact neurological system, an emotionally effective caregiver, appropriate levels of emotional awareness and language abstraction, together with the duel task ability of simultaneously considering one's own and others' needs.

We now look at factors impeding the healthy development of EI.

ABNORMAL DEVELOPMENT OF EI

In discussing the abnormal development of EI, two aspects receive attention, namely early childhood trauma and alexithymia.

Childhood trauma

Evidence demonstrates that the development of parts of the neocortex may be impeded by emotional trauma. Investigators of school-aged children with histories of psychological, physical or sexual abuse found evidence of a greater prevalence of left-sided fronto-temporal electroencephalogram (EEG) abnormalities than in non-abused children, while a higher prevalence of right-left hemispheric asymmetries were also prevalent.[92] Atypical development affecting cortical maturation and laterality was demonstrated in children who had experienced severe physical or psychological abuse.[93] (Children who had suffered head trauma were excluded from the study.) Further studies using PET scans indicate possible abnormalities of the corpus callosum for traumatised children, therefore it is apparent that early childhood trauma may impede the normal development of EI.

Alexithymia

Alexithymia means "no words for feeling", and is viewed as a stable personality trait.[94] Alexithymia (inversely) relates and exhibits considerable overlap with Gardner's[95] conception of personal intelligences, and more specifically intrapersonal intelligence, particularly the ability to identify, label and discriminate among feelings and to represent them symbolically. According to Gardner,[96] the core capacity of intrapersonal intelligence involves the accessing of one's emotional life – one's range of affect or emotions: "... the capacity to instantly effect discrimination among these feelings and, eventually, to label them, to enmesh them in symbolic codes, to draw upon them as a means of understanding and guiding one's behaviour". Conversely, the interpersonal intelligence ability to pick up on others' feelings and to act sensitively in accordance is known as empathy. These two forms of intelligence flow from attending to one's subjective emotional experience.

Alexithymia (in working age populations) appears to occur in 9-17% of men and 5-10% of women. As a result of their lack of social skills, alexithymic individuals tend to feel uncomfortable in social situations; they find it difficult to protect themselves from the potentially harmful influences of stressful events via social support, as they struggle to build and maintain close relationships with others.[97] Evidence is furthermore accumulating that suggests that extreme degrees of alexithymia may result from early trauma and emotional deprivation or neglect, as discussed. These environmental influences appear to stunt the maturation of particular brain structures and the mental capacities associated with emotional processing and emotional intelligence. Alexithymic individuals are, therefore, more inclined to, for example, use substances as a coping mechanism, and their behaviour is guided by rules and regulations rather than feelings. Treatment has been reported as challenging due to their lack of emotional awareness and externalised style of living, and they are poor candidates for insight oriented therapies.

It is therefore apparent that the bi-directional influence of environment and neurobiology determines the individual's level of EI. When an individual is exposed to a climate that is supportive of the development of EI, it is indeed possible (given the plasticity inherent in our neurology) for changes to take place in the individual's level of EI. It is, however, important to consider early trauma that may have had an irreversible influence on the level of EI sensitivity.

Next, we reflect on some of the benefits assumed to flow from emotional intelligence.

BENEFITS OF EMOTIONAL INTELLIGENCE

Emotional intelligence has been studied in relation to a vast number of outcomes, a few of which are highlighted here.

Relationships

The positive effect of emotional intelligence on relationships is well documented. Emotional intelligence and the ability to perceive one's own and others' emotions has, for example, shown to significantly predict increases in trust, which positively impacts relationships.[98]

Mental and physical health

"As such, EI intuitively offers a window into mental health, since the ability of individuals to recognize, use, and understand their own emotional states or emotional problems is considered an important indicator of healthy mental functioning."[99] "Emotionally intelligent people can cope better with life's challenges and environmental demands, and control their own emotions more effectively, contributing to good psychological and physical health."[100]

Workplace benefits

Numerous benefits have been linked to an increased EI. EI has, indeed, consistently demonstrated a highly significant relationship with occupational performance,[101] flourishing in the workplace[102] and leadership.[103] A meta-analysis of research on the relationship between individual emotional intelligence and workplace performance suggest that individual emotional intelligence can effectively predict workplace performance.[104] EI is used to predict work success in numerous careers, from the military to banking, sports, medicine, journalism, collection agencies and teaching.[105] The development of emotional intelligence increases the bottom line via occupational performance, leadership and organisational productivity.[106] Emotional intelligence has furthermore demonstrated a statistically significant effect on motivation,[107] again influencing performance.

EI significantly relates to better mental health, higher levels of work engagement, heightened satisfaction with social support, as well as more perceived power in the workplace. A positive significant relationship has also been established in the teaching environment between emotional intelligence and job satisfaction, and between emotional intelligence and organisational commitment.[108]

Prins,[109] after having extensively reviewed the literature, is in support of the important and leading role of emotions with regard to human functioning, and the neural plasticity that allows for lifelong learning and adaptation, also in the affective realm. Her empirical research clearly demonstrates a significant positive relationship between employee EI, experienced psychological (work) climate, experienced job affect, and a number of indices of wellness. (See Figure 2.4 below.)

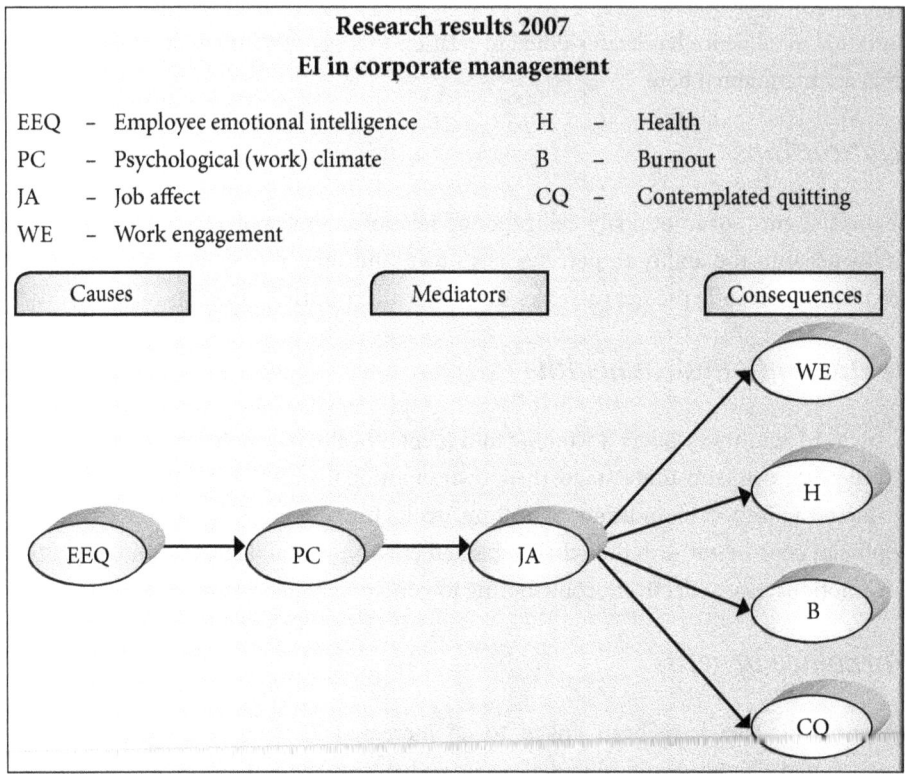

Figure 2.4: Employee emotional intelligence and its relation to workplace wellness (Prins, 2007)[110]

MAKING SENSE OF THE EVOLVING EI CONSTRUCT

Psychologists have, of late, proposed that "understanding emotions in oneself and others is the key to a satisfying life. Those people who are self-aware and sensitive to others manage their affairs with wisdom and grace, even in adverse situations. On the other hand those who are emotionally illiterate blunder their way through lives marked by misunderstandings, frustrations and failed relationships".[111]

"There is a compelling need for innovative approaches to the solution of many pressing problems involving human relationship in today's society."[112] In this regard, EI is an exciting and developing research area related to organisational behaviour and the growing interest in the role of emotions within organisations.[113] Research is proceeding vigorously – in searching the web via Google on 16 March 2017, over 11,600,000 results were found with regard to emotional intelligence. EI is a tool to be applied by I/O psychologists and scholars of organisational behaviour in understanding and predicting behaviour in the workplace, however researchers should not make unsubstantiated claims but rather follow rigorous research practices.

A FINAL WORD ON PART 1

Bar-On believes that EI is made up of a series of overlapping but distinct skills and attitudes that may be grouped together under five general themes (as discussed previously), and further subdivided into 15 distinct skills. This is the model of choice for the authors because of its accuracy in defining and measuring the construct; its wide and extensive use across the globe (66 countries, translated into 45 languages, administered to more than a million people); and being the most widely-applied EI test in the world.[114]

After reviewing the importance of emotional intelligence in Part 1, it is equally important to turn now to developing the related skills in Part 2, empowering us to function more effectively at work, at home and in our communities. Emotional intelligence is believed to be a flexible set of skills that can be acquired and improved with practice.[115] Experiential practice is crucial in order for us to acquire new skills, and each skill is therefore carefully reviewed, with supportive individual, group and extended self-exercises provided.

REFERENCES

Arghode, V. (2013). Emotional and social intelligence competence: Implications for instruction. *International Journal of Pedagogies & Learning, 8*(2), 66-77.

Ashkanasy, N.M. & Daus, C.S. (2005). Rumors of the death of emotional intelligence in organizational behavior are vastly exaggerated. *Journal of Organizational Behavior*, 26, 441–452.

Bar-On, R. (1997). *Bar-On emotional quotient inventory (EQ-i): Technical manual.* Toronto: Multi-Health Systems.

Bar-On, R. (2002). *Bar-On emotional quotient inventory: A measure of emotional intelligence.* New York: Multi-Health Systems.

Bar-On, R. (2004). The Bar-On Emotional Quotient Inventory (EQ-i): Rationale, description and summary of psychometric properties. In G. Geher (Ed). *Measuring emotional intelligence: Common ground and controversy.* Hauppauge, NY: Nova Science.

Bar-On, R. (2006). The Bar-On model of emotional-social intelligence (ESI) 1. *Psicothema, 18*(Suplemento), 13-25.

Bar-On, R. (2010). Emotional intelligence: an integral part of positive psychology. *South African Journal of Psychology, 40*(1), 54-62.

Bechara, A., Tranel, D. & Damasio, A.R. (2000). Poor judgement in spite of high intellect: Neurological evidence for emotional intelligence. In R. Bar-On & J.D.A. Parker (eds.). *The handbook of emotional intelligence: Theory, development, assessment, and application at home, school, and in the workplace.* San Francisco: Jossey-Bass, p. 195.

Bharwaney, G., Bar-On, R. & MacKinlay, A. (2011). *EQ and the Bottom Line: Emotional Intelligence Increases Individual Occupational Performance, Leadership and Organisational Productivity.* Bedfordshire, UK: Ei World Limited, p. 1-35.

Bhootrani, M.L. & Junejo, J. (2016). Emotional Intelligence is a Key to Success. *Liaquat University of Medical and Health Sciences, 15*(3), 108-9.

Boyatzis, R., Goleman, D. & Rhee, K. (2000). Clustering competence in emotional intelligence: Insights from the emotional competence inventory. In R. Bar-On & J.D.A. Parker (eds.). *The handbook of emotional intelligence: Theory, development, assessment, and application at home, school, and in the workplace.* San Francisco: Jossey-Bass, p. 343–362.

Boyatzis, R. (2007). *The creation of the emotional and social competency inventory (ESCI).* Boston: Hay Group.

Brackett, M.A. & Salovey, P. (2006). Measuring emotional intelligence with the Mayer-Salovey-Caruso Emotional Intelligence Test (MSCEIT). *Psychothema,* 18, 34-41.

Brown, D. (1993). Affective development, psychopathology, and adaptation. In S.L. Ablon, D. Brown, E.J. Khantzian & J.E. Mack (eds.). *Human feelings: Explorations in affect development and meaning.* Hillsdale, NJ: Analytic Press, p. 5–66.

Cantrell, D.J. & Sharpe, K. (2015). *Practicing Practical Wisdom.* Boulder, CO: University of Colorado Boulder.

Cheung, C., Cheung, H. & Hue, M. (2015). Emotional intelligence as a basis for self-esteem in young adults. *Journal of Psychology, 149*(1), 63-84.

Christie, A.M.H., Jordan, P.J. & Troth, A.C. (2015). Trust antecedents: Emotional intelligence and perceptions of others. *International Journal of Organizational Analysis, 23*(1), 89-101.

Conte, J.M. (2005). A review and critique of emotional intelligence measures. *Journal of Organizational Behavior.* 26, 433–440.

Damasio, A. (1999). *The feeling of what happens: Body and emotion in the making of consciousness.* New York: Harcourt.

Damasio, A.R. (1994). *Descartes' error: Emotion, reason, and the human brain.* New York: Grosset/Putnam.

Darwin, C. (1872). *The expression of the emotions in man and animals.* Chicago: University of Chicago Press.

Darwin, C. (1965). *Expression of the emotions in man and animals.* New York: Philosophical Library.

Davidson, R.J., Jackson, D.C. & Kalin, N.H. (2000). Emotion, plasticity, context, and regulation: perspectives from affective neuroscience. *Psychological Bulletin, 126*(6), 890–909.

De Cuyper, N., Sulea, C., Philippaers, K., Fischmann, G., Iliescu, D. & De Witte, H. (2014). Perceived employability and performance: moderation by felt job insecurity. *Personnel Review, 43*(4), 536-552.

Delcourt, C., Gremler, D.D., van Riel, A.C. & van Birgelen, M.J. (2016). Employee Emotional Competence: Construct Conceptualization and Validation of a Customer-Based Measure. *Journal of Service Research, 19*(1), 72-87.

Di Fabio, A. & Palazzeschi, L. (2012). Organizational Justice: Personality Traits or Emotional Intelligence? An Empirical Study in an Italian Hospital Context. *Journal of Employment Counselling, 49*(1), 31-42.

Di Fabio, A. & Bar-On, R. (2013). The application of emotional intelligence in the reduction of risk factors: New perspectives in career counselling and development. *Counseling, 6*(1), 7-23.

Di Fabio, A. & Kenny, M.E. (2015). The contributions of emotional intelligence and social support for adaptive career progress among Italian youth. *Journal of Career Development, 42*(1), 48-59.

Downey, L.A., Johnston, P.J., Hansen, K., Schembri, R., Stough, C., Tuckwell, V. & Schweitzer, I. (2008). The relationship between emotional intelligence and depression in a clinical sample. *European Journal of Psychiatry, 22*, 93–98.

Fleming, J.H., Coffman, D. & Harter, J.K. (2005). Manage your human sigma. *Harvard Business Review, 83*(7), 106–114.

Flowers, L.K., Thomas-Squance, R., Brainin-Rodriguez, J.E. & Yancey, A.K. (2014). Interprofessional social and emotional intelligence skills training: study findings and key lessons. *Journal of Interprofessional Care, 28*(2), 157-159.

Gardner, H (1983). Can Piaget and Levi-Strauss be reconciled? *New Ideas in Psychology,* 1, 187–189.

Gardner, H. (1983/1993). *Frames of mind: The theory of multiple intelligences.* New York: Basic Books.

Gardner, H. (1999). Are there additional intelligence in the case for naturalist, spiritual, and existential intelligences? In J. Kane (ed.). *Education, information, and transformation.* Upper Saddle River, NJ: Prentice-Hall, p. 111–131.

Goldberg, S., McKay-Soroka, S. & Rochester, M. (1994). Affect, attachment and maternal responsiveness. *Infant Behavior and Development,* 17, 335–339.

Goleman, D. (1995a). *Emotional intelligence: why it can matter more than IQ.* New York: Bantam Books.

Goleman, D. (1998). What makes a leader? *Harvard Business Review,* 776 (6), 93–103.

Goleman, D. (2001). An EI-based theory of performance. In C. Cherniss & D. Goleman (eds.). *The emotionally intelligent workplace.* San Francisco: Jossey Bass, p. 27–44.

Goleman, D. (2011). *Leadership: The Power of Emotional Intelligence.* Northampton, MA: More than Sound.

Goleman, D., Boyatzis, R. & McKee, A. (2013). *Primal Leadership unleashing the power of emotional intelligence.* Boston: Harvard Business Review Press.

Hay Group. (2005). *Emotional Competence Inventory: Technical Manual: Hay Group Web Products ESCI.* [Online] Available: http://www.haygroup.com/leadershipandtalentondemand/ourproducts/index.aspx [Accessed] March 22, 2017.

Hay Group. (2011). *Emotional and social competency inventory (ESCI): A user guide for accredited practitioners.* [Online] Available: http://www.eiconsortium.org/pdf/ESCI_user_guide.pdf [Accessed April18, 2017]

Ito, Y., Teicher, MH., Glod, C.A. & Acerman, E. (1998). Preliminary evidence for aberrant cortical development in abused children: A quantitative EEG study. *Journal of Neuropsychiatry and Clinical Neuroscience, 10,* 298-307.

Itzkoff, D. (2015, March 30). Trevor Noah to Succeed Jon Stewart on 'The Daily Show. *The New York Times.*

Kewalramani, S., Agrawal, M. & Rastogi, M.R. (2015). Models of emotional intelligence: Similarities and discrepancies. *Indian Journal of Positive Psychology, 6*(2), 178-181.

Khraisat, A.M., Abdul Rahim, A.F. & Yusoff, M.S.B. (2015). Emotional Intelligence of USM Medical Students. *Education in Medicine Journal, 7*(4), 420-430.

Krystal, H. (1974). The genetic development of affects and affect regression. *Annual of Psychoanalysis, 2,* 98–126.

Lanciano, T. & Curci, A. (2015). Emotional Intelligence as a predictor of academic success: A study of an Italian University sample. *Health Communication, 30*(11), 1112-1121.

Lanciano, T. & Curci, A. (2015). Does Emotions Communication Ability Affect Psychological Well-Being? A Study with the Mayer–Salovey–Caruso Emotional Intelligence Test (MSCEIT) v2.0. *Health Communication, 30*(11), 1112-1121.

Landy, F.J. (2005). Some historical and scientific issues related to research on emotional intelligence. *Journal of Organizational Behavior, 26,* 411–425.

Lane, R.D. & Schwartz, G.E. (1987). Levels of emotional awareness: A cognitive developmental theory and its application to psychopathology. *American Journal of Psychiatry, 144,* 133–143.

Lane, R.D. (2000). Levels of emotional awareness: Neurological, psychological, and social perspectives. In R. Bar-On & J.D.A. Parker (eds.). *The handbook of emotional intelligence: Theory, development, assessment, and application at home, school, and in the workplace.* San Francisco: Jossey-Bass, p. 186.

Mahmut, A. & Oğuz, I. (2012). Effects Of Emotional Intelligence Levels' Health Employees On Their Motivation. *Dumlupinar University Journal of Social Science, 1*(32), 109-123.

Mayer, J.D., DiPaolo, M.T. & Salovey, P. (1990). Perceiving affective content in ambiguous visual stimuli: A component of emotional intelligence. *Journal of Personality Assessment, 54,* 772–781.

Mayer, J.D. & Salovey, P. (1993). The intelligence of emotional intelligence. *Intelligence, 17,* 433–442.

Mayer, J.D. & Salovey, P. (1995). Emotional intelligence and the construction and regulation of feelings. *Applied and Preventive Psychology, 4,* 197–208.

Mayer, J.D., Caruso, D. & Salovey, P. (2000). Selecting a measure of emotional intelligence: The case for ability scales. In R. Bar-On & J.D.A. Parker (eds.). *The handbook of emotional intelligence: Theory, development, assessment, and application at home, school, and in the workplace.* San Francisco: Jossey-Bass, p. 320–342.

Mayer, J.D., Salovey, P. Caruso, D.R. & Sitarenios, G. (2003). Measuring emotional intelligence with the MSCEIT V2.0. *Emotion, 3*(1), 97.

Mayer, J.D., Salovey, P. & Caruso, D.R. (2008). Emotional intelligence: new ability or eclectic traits? *American Psychologist, 63*(6), 503.

Mayer, J.D., Salovey, P. & Caruso, D.R. (2012). The validity of the MSCEIT: Additional analyses and evidence. *Emotion Review, 4*(4), 403-408.

Mayer, R.E. (2002). Multimedia learning. *Psychology of Learning and Motivation, 41,* 85-139.

Mayes, L.C. & Cohen, D.J. (1992). The development of a capacity for imagination in early childhood. *Psychoanalytic Study of the Child, 47,* 23–47.

Mersino, A. (2013). *Emotional Intelligence for project managers* (2nd ed.). New York: Amacom.

Moreno-Manso, J.M., Garcia-Baamonde, M.E., Guerrero-Barona, E. & Pozueco-Romero, J.M. (2017). Emotional competence disorders and social communication in young victims of abuse. *Journal of Child and Family Studies, 26*(3), 701-708.

Mikolajczak, M.A., Hervè, V.S., Verniest, R., Callens, M., Van Broeck, N., Fantini-Hauwel, C. & Mierop, A. (2015). A nationally representative study of emotional competence and health. *Emotion, 15*(5), 653-667.

Multi-Health Systems Inc. (2011). *The complete EQ-i 2.0 experience.* Toronto: Multi-Health Systems Inc.

Multi-Health Systems Inc. & Jopie van Rooyen Psychometrics. (2011). *The complete EQ-i 2.0 experience.* Toronto: Multi-Health Systems Inc.

Murphy, K.R. (ed.). 2013. *A critique of emotional intelligence. What are the problems and how can they be fixed?* New York: Routledge

Naderi Anari, N. (2012). Teachers: emotional intelligence, job satisfaction, and organizational commitment. *Journal of Workplace Learning, 24*(4), 256-269.

Nehra, D.K., Kumar, P., Sharma, V. & Nehra, S. (2013). *Alexithymia and emotional intelligence among people with cannabis dependence and healthy control: a comparative study.* [Online] Available: https://www.researchgate.net/profile/Dharmender_Nehra. [Accessed August 05, 2013].

Na, J., Wilkinson, K., Karny, M., Blackstone, S. & Stifler, C. (2015). A synthesis of relevant literature on the development of emotional competence: Implications for design of augmentative and alternative communication systems. *American Journal of Speech-Language Pathology, 25*(3), 1-12.

Nozaki, Y. & Koyasu, M. (2016). Can we apply an emotional competence measure to an eastern population? Psychometric properties of the Profile of Emotional Competence in a Japanese population. *Assessment, 23*(1), 112-123.

Palmer, B.R., Gignac, G., Manocha, R. & Stough, C. (2005). A psychometric evaluation of the Mayer-Salovey-Caruso Emotional Intelligence Test Version 2.0. *Intelligence, 33*(3), 285-305.

Piaget, J. (1981). *Intelligence and affectivity.* Palo Alto, CA: Annual Reviews.

Prins, A. (2007). *Emotional intelligence and leadership in corporate management: A fortigenic perspective.* (Unpublished PhD Thesis). Bloemfontein: University of the Free State.

Prins, A. (2010a). *Emotional intelligence and leadership: A work wellness perspective.* Saarbrücken: VDM Verlag Dr Müller.

Rahim, M.A., Psenicka, C., Polychroniou, P., Jing-Hua Zhao, Yu, C.S., Chan, K.W., Kwok Wai Yee, S., Alves, M.G., Lee, C., Ralunan, S., Ferdausy, S. & van Wyk, R. (2002). A model of emotional intelligence and conflict management strategies: a study in seven countries. *The International Journal of Organizational Analysis, 10*(4), 302 – 326. DOI: 10.1108/eb028955.

Reitz, S. (2012). *Improving Social Competence Via E-learning? The Example of Human Rights Education.* Peter Lang Gmbh, Internationaler Verlag Der Wissenschaften.

Saarni, C. (1999). *The development of emotional competence.* New York: Guilford Press.

Saarni, C. (2000). Emotional competence: A developmental perspective. In R. Bar-On & J.D.A. Parker (eds.). *The handbook of emotional intelligence: Theory, development, assessment, and application at home, school, and in the workplace.* San Francisco: Jossey-Bass, p. 72-73, 85.

Saarni, C. (2007). The Development of Emotional Competence: Pathways for helping children to become emotionally intelligent in R. Bar-On, J.G. Marais & M. J. Elias. *Educating People to be emotionally intelligent.* Johannesburg, Heinemann Publisher Pty.

Saarni, C., Mumme, D. & Campos, J. (1998). Emotional development: Action, communication, and understanding. In W. Damon & N. Eisenberg (eds.). *Handbook of child psychology. Vol. 3: Social, emotional and personality development* (5th ed.). New York: Wiley, p. 237–309.

Salovey, P. & Mayer, J.D. (1990). Emotional intelligence. *Imagination, Cognition, and Personality, 9*, 185–211.

Salovey, P., Bedell, B.T., Detweiler, J.B. & Mayer, J.D. (2000). Current directions in emotional intelligence research. In M. Lewis & J.M. Haviland-Jones (eds.). *Handbook of emotions* (2nd ed.). New York: Guilford Press, p. 504–522.

Schore, A.N. (1994). *Affect regulation and the origin of the self: The neurobiology of emotional development.* Hillsdale, NJ: Erlbaum.

Schore, A.N. (1996). The experience-dependent maturation of a regulatory system in the orbital prefrontal cortex and the origin of developmental psychopathology. *Development and Psychopathology,* 8, 59–87.

Schutte, N.S. & Loi, N.M. (2014). Connections between emotional intelligence and workplace flourishing. *Personality and Individual Differences,* 66, 134-139.

Spearman, C. (1927). *Abilities of man.* New York: The Macmillan Company.

Stein, J.S. & Book, H. (2011). *The EQ Edge: Emotional intelligence and your success* (3rd ed.). San Francisco: Jossey-Bass.

Sternberg, R.J. (1985). *Beyond IQ: A triarchic theory of human intelligence.* New York: Cambridge University Press.

Sternberg, R.J. (1997). *Successful Intelligence.* New York: Plume.

Sternberg, R.J., Wagner, R.K. & Okagaki, L. (1993). Practical intelligence: The nature and role of tacit knowledge in work and at school. In H. Reese & J. Puckett (eds.). *Advances in lifespan development.* Hillsdale, NJ: Erlbaum, p. 205–227.

Sternberg, R.J., Wagner, R.K., Williams, W.M. & Horvath, J.A. (1995). Testing common sense. *American Psychologist,* 50, 912–927.

Taylor, G.J. & Bagby, R.M. (2000). An overview of the alexithymia construct. In R. Bar-On & J.D.A. Parker (eds.). *The handbook of emotional intelligence: Theory, development, assessment, and application at home, school, and in the workplace.* San Francisco: Jossey-Bass, p. 3.

Teicher, M.H., Ito, Y., Glod, C.A., Schiffer, F. & Gelbard, H.A. (1996). Neurophysiological mechanisms of stress response in children. In C.R. Pfeffer (ed.). *Severe stress and mental disturbance in children.* Washington, DC: American Psychiatric Press, p. 59–84.

Van Zyl, C.J. (2014). The psychometric properties of the Emotional Quotient Inventory 2.0 in South Africa. *South African Journal of Industrial Psychology,* 40(1),1-8.

Wagner, R.K. & Sternberg, R.J. (1986). Tacit knowledge and intelligence in the everyday world. In R.J. Sternberg & R.K. Wagner (eds.). *Practical intelligence: Nature and origins of competence in the everyday world.* New York: Cambridge University Press, p. 51–83.

Sternberg, R.J., Wagner, R.K. & Okagaki, L. (1993). Practical intelligence: The nature and role of tacit knowledge in work and at school. *Advances in Lifespan Development,* 205-227.

Webb, C.A., Schwab, Z.A., Weber, M., DelDonno, S., Kipman, M., Weiner, M.R. & Killgore, W.D.S. (2013). Convergent and divergent validity of integrative versus mixed model measures of emotional intelligence. *Intelligence,* 41, 149–156.

Wechsler, D. (1940). Non-intellective factors in general intelligence. *Psychological Bulletin,* 37, 444–445.

Wechsler, D. (1958). *The measurements and the appraisal of adult intelligence* (4th ed.). Baltimore, MD: Williams & Wilkins.

Wikipedia. (2014). *Emotional Intelligence.* [Online] Available: from https://en.wikipedia.org/wiki/Emotional_intelligence [Accessed March 21, 2017].

Wikipedia. (2007). *Psychometrics.* [Online] Available: https://en.wikipedia.org/wiki/Psychometrics [Accessed March 21, 2017].

Wong, R.J., Aguilar, M., Cheung, R., Perumpail, R.B., Harrison, S.A., Younossi, Z.M. & Ahmed, A. (2015). Non-alcoholic steatohepatitis is the second leading etymology of liver disease among adults awaiting liver transplantation in the United States. *Gastroenterology,* 148(3), 547-555.

Ybarra, O., Kross, E. & Sanchez-Burks, J. (2014). Symposium. The "Big Idea" that is yet to be: Toward a more motivated, contextual, and dynamic model of emotional intelligence. *The Academy of Management Perspectives,* 28(2), 93-107.

Zhang, H.H. & Wang, H. (2011). Conflict Engagement: Emotional and Social Intelligence. *Acta Psychologica Sinica,* 43(2), 188-202.

ENDNOTES

1. Goleman, 1995.
2. Bharwaney, Bar-On & MacKinlay, 2011.
3. Bar-On, 2010:54.
4. Stein & Book, 2011:18.
5. Bar-On, 2010.
6. Spearman, 1927.
7. Bar-On, 1997; Mayer & Salovey, 1993; 1995.
8. Prins, 2007.
9. Wechsler, 1940.
10. Wechsler, 1958:7.
11. Gardner, 1983; 1993; 1999.
12. Bar-On, 1997.
13. Bar-On, 1997:14.
14. Goleman, 2001:27.
15. Mayer, Salovey & Caruso, 2000.
16. Reitz, 2012:7.
17. Arghode, 2013.
18. Kraisat et al., 2015.
19. Flowers et al., 2014.
20. Na et al., 2016.
21. Saarni, 2007:19.
22. Saarni, 2007:18.
23. Moreno-Manso et al., 2017.
24. Cheung et al., 2015.
25. Mikolajczak et al., 2015.
26. Na et al., 2016.
27. Nozaki et al., 2016.
28. Delcourt et al., 2016.
29. Bar-On, 1997; Sternberg, 1985; 1997.
30. Wechsler, 1940.
31. Rahim et al., 2015.
32. Prins, 2007; 2010.
33. Sternberg, 1985; 1997.
34. Cantrell et al., 2016.
35. Sternberg, Wagner & Okagaki, 1993; Sternberg, Wagner, Williams & Horvath, 1995; Sternberg et al., 2000.
36. Wagner & Sternberg, 1986.
37. Prins, 2007; 2010.
38. Mestre et al., 2016.
39. Mayer, DiPaolo & Salovey, 1990; Salovey & Mayer, 1990.
40. Goleman, 1995a.
41. Webb et al., 2013.
42. Lane, 2000.
43. Goleman, 1995a; Mayer, Salovey & Caruso, 2000.
44. Lane, 2000.
45. Lane, 2000.
46. Lane, 2000.

47 Di Fabio & Bar-On, 2013.
48 Bar-On, 1997.
49 Bar-On, 2000.
50 Bar-On, 1997:14.
51 Wechsler, 1958:vii.
52 Bar-On, 1997.
53 Stein & Book, 2011.
54 MHS, 2011:6.
55 MHS, 2011:12.
56 MHS & JvR, 2011:7-10.
57 MHS, 2011:18.
58 Bar-On, 1997.
59 Bar-On, 2002.
60 MHS, 2011:7.
61 MHS, 2011:7.
62 Lane, 2000:182.
63 Davidson, Jackson & Kalin, 2000.
64 Mayer, 2000; Ashkanasy & Daus, 2005:445.
65 Goleman, 2001:30.
66 Goleman, 2011:14.
67 Goleman, 2011.
68 Goleman, 2011.
69 Goleman, 2011:16.
70 Goleman, 2011.
71 Fleming, Coffman & Harter, 2005:107.
72 Bechara, Tranel & Damasio, 2000.
73 Damasio, 1994.
74 Bechara et al., 2000:195.
75 cf Bechara et al., 2000.
76 Bechara et al., 2000.
77 Goldberg, MacKay-Soroka & Rochester, 1994.
78 Gray & Webb, 2013.
79 Fonagy et al., in Taylor & Bagby, 2000.
80 Marsland & Likavec in Brackett & Salovey, 2006.
81 Taylor & Bagby, 2000:57.
82 Schore, 1994.
83 Lane, 2000:186.
84 Lane & Schwartz, 1987.
85 Baddeley & colleagues in Lane, 2000.
86 Lane, 2000.
87 Taylor & Bagby, 2000; Piaget, 1981; Krystal, 1974; Lane & Schwartz, 1987.
88 Taylor & Bagby, 2000:52.
89 Lane, 2000.
90 Taylor & Bagby, 2000:52.
91 Brown, 1993; Mayes & Cohen, 1992.
92 Teicher, Ito, Glod, Schiffer & Gelbard, 1996.
93 Ito, Teicher, Glod & Ackerman, 1998.
94 Sifneos in Nehra & Kumar, 2013.

95   Gardner, 1983.
96   Gardner, 1983:239.
97   Nehra & Kumar, 2013.
98   Christie et al., 2015.
99   Downey et al., in L. & A. Curci, 2015:1118.
100 L. & A. Curci, 2015:1118.
101 Bar-On, 2010.
102 Schutte & Loi, 2014.
103 Mersino, 2013; Goleman, 2013.
104 Zhang et al., 2011.
105 Stein & Book, 2011:15.
106 Bharwaney, Bar-On & MacKinlay, 2011.
107 Akbolat & Işik, 2012.
108 Anari, Nahid & Naderi, 2012.
109 Prins, 2007.
110 Prins, 2007.
111 Kewalramani, Agrawal & Rastogi, 2015:178.
112 Murphy, 2013:ix.
113 Ashkanasy & Daus, 2005.
114 Stein & Book, 2011:15.
115 Bhootrani & Junejo, 2016.

PART 2

ACQUIRING EMOTIONALLY INTELLIGENT SKILLS

Part 2 includes five sections that focus on the acquisition of emotionally intelligent skills according to the Bar-On model of emotional intelligence. This section takes cognisance of the changes to the first instrument (EQ-i) that emanated from research. The follow-up instrument, EQ-i 2.0, builds on the EQ-i, and introduces some differences that stem from changes (based on extensive feedback) to assessment items, updated norms, and rigorous reliability and validity studies.[1] The model presented in this text honours these changes.

Section A: SELF-PERCEPTION

Section B: SELF-EXPRESSION

Section C: INTERPERSONAL

Section D: DECISION-MAKING

Section E: STRESS MANAGEMENT

SECTION A: SELF-PERCEPTION

According to the introduction to the new EQ-i 2.0,[2] self-perception has to do with the inner self and aims to assess an individual's feelings of inner strength, confidence and persistence, whilst pursuing goals that are both relevant and meaningful for the individual. This also assumes that the individual understands 'what', 'when', 'why' and 'how' different emotions influence thoughts and actions. Individuals who are on average well-developed in this area are in touch with their inner feelings, feel good about themselves, and are positive about their lives. Well-developed individuals are competent at expressing their feelings, and are independent, strong, and confident in expressing their ideas and beliefs.[3]

The following skills are discussed:

Chapter 3: Self-regard

Chapter 4: Self-actualisation

Chapter 5: Emotional self-awareness

ENDNOTES

1 MHS, 2011.
2 MHS & JvR, 2011:7.
3 Prins, 2007.

Chapter 3

SELF-REGARD

Eugene van Niekerk

Willingness to wrestle with your demons will cause your angels to sing .
                                                               –August Wilson

SECTION 1: OVERVIEW

In the practice of counselling and psychotherapy, anecdotal evidence seems to suggest that low self-regard is deeply interwoven into the fabric of contemporary society. It seems that most of us find it less of a challenge to forgive others their blunders and blotches than it is to forgive ourselves. Could this be because the taproot of the innermost chambers of the psyche is judged unworthy and doesn't deserve to be forgiven? We urge the reader to ponder on this as we are about to journey through psychic terrain called the mind.

Given the spirit of the times (*zeitgeist*), self-regard has gained a newfound urgency. The world of work presents new challenges – including our need to negotiate steep learning curves, make appropriate choices, and above all, manage change. In this respect, self-regard takes centre stage.

Why is self-regard important? Bar-On[1] cites self-regard as one of the most important predictors of successful behaviour. Self-regard further enjoys a deep interrelationship with the other EI skills dealt with in this volume. For example, self-regard allows for a greater degree of personal flexibility, self-confidence and happiness. Self-regard is often viewed as a synonym for self-esteem, hence for the purposes of this chapter, 'self-esteem' and 'self-regard' are used inter-changeably. As we will learn, this is in line with the thinking of Carl Rogers, a pioneer in self-theory.

 After completing this chapter, you should be able to:

- define self-regard;
- understand some theory informing self-regard;
- reflect on low self-regard;
- understand ways to develop self-regard;
- assess your own level of self-regard; and
- implement individual and group activities to enhance self-regard.

SELF-REGARD DEFINED

In essence, self-regard reflects how we feel about ourselves. This includes our ability to accept ourselves - including our strengths and weaknesses. The dictionary of psychology authored by Ray Corsini[2] defines self-regard as "that aspect of the self-concept that develops from the esteem or respect accorded to the self".

Building healthy self-regard allows for ongoing exploration and probing our psychological landscape (often referred to as the universe within) that allows for greater insight into who we are – our sense of self-identity. A healthy self-regard reflects - at least in part - our ability to give expression to the 'self' - our desires, values, beliefs, interests and the like. Other examples that illustrate this deep interconnectedness includes how self-regard is, for example, related to problem solving and self-assertiveness. Cultivating assertiveness is critical to self-regard; if we are unable to clearly articulate our needs and wants to others, we are bound to end up frustrated, helpless and powerless. If we do nothing else, the practice of assertive behaviour in and of itself can increase our feeling of self-respect. Honouring your own needs with other people in an assertive manner also increases their respect for you, and quickly overcomes any tendency on their part to take advantage of you.[3]

It is useful to reiterate that individuals who experience self-regard demonstrate deeper knowledge and insight into their strengths and shortcomings. Positive self-regard also reflects elevated feelings of self-adequacy, self-confidence, and personal happiness. In contrast, individuals at the opposite end of the self-regard spectrum are liable to fall victim to bouts of feelings of inferiority and increasing levels of feelings of personal inadequacy.

Closely associated to self-regard is self-esteem. Self-esteem reflects our attitude to the self that may turn out to be positive, neutral or negative. Self-esteem is also viewed as an attitude of self-acceptance and self-respect. Needless to say, a feeling of self-worth is an important ingredient in well-being. On the extreme opposite end of the self-regard spectrum we find individuals given to self-loathing, often referred to as self-hate.

Those who view themselves in a negative light are also fraught with self-doubt and self-criticism. Such individuals are often subject to negative self-talk such as "I'm unlovable", "I'm not good enough", or "I'll never amount to anything". Frequently, such thoughts give rise to painful emotions including worthlessness, anger, fear, and more seriously, depression. Individuals who experience low self-esteem similarly find it more difficult to make decisions because they doubt their own abilities. On the other hand, people with high self-esteem report higher levels of subjective well-being and happiness.

THEORY INFORMING SELF-REGARD

Carl Ransom Rogers, the American pioneer and founder of humanistic psychology, "placed the need for self-esteem at the centre of inter-personal relations, only he called it self-regard…".[4] Rogers[5] theorised that when children/youth experience unconditional positive regard (from significant others) it serves as a solid foundation in respect to their personal development. The foundation to self-regard is formed early on in life, for example, when children experience love and affection and their needs for love and acceptance are satisfied, basic trust ensues. A child's self-worth is further nourished when the parents respond to the child with appreciation and praise.

Self-regard is ongoing – it manifests itself throughout life. At first its building blocks are inauspicious – overcoming small obstacles – learning to walk, becoming potty trained and later acquiring the necessary skills to negotiate more complex social environments. When this foundation is flawed, low self-regard is often a likely outcome. It is also important to note here that when parents feel the urge to over-protect their child from the unhappy consequences of life, personal growth may be stunted and hence the ability to build a healthy sense of self-regard is compromised.[6]

WHEN SELF-REGARD IS WANTING

Low self-regard is often associated with both mental and physical disorders including depression, insomnia, headaches, poor appetite, and in extreme cases, suicide. People who experience low levels of self-regard feel vulnerable and anxious when they compare themselves to others. Those who think of themselves as not quite good enough are vulnerable to low self-regard. Such individuals are prone to developing an inferiority complex – basic feelings of inadequacy and insecurity which originate in childhood dependence and helplessness.

How adequate or inadequate we feel about ourselves is often associated with what psychologists refer to as "interior speech" or "self-talk". The inner critic is often referred to as a form of self-talk that reminds us of our failures, imperfections, and inadequacies – our need to be 'perfect'. When the inner critic gets its way, it lowers self-regard and makes us more vulnerable to stress and depression. The inner critic is fond of having us compare ourselves to others, and to overlook our positive qualities while highlighting our deficiencies and perceived inadequacies. The inner critic may be embodied in our dialogue as a voice of a significant other – such as a parent, teacher, or some other authority figure - who has hurt or aggrieved us in the past with their criticism. Does the following sound familiar: "What a disappointment you are!", 'That was stupid', "You could have done better", or "Can't you ever get it right?"

Inadequate self-regard is further associated with:

- overly critical parents;
- significant childhood loss including divorce or the death of a parent;
- parental abuse;
- parental alcoholism or drug abuse;
- parental neglect;
- parental rejection;
- parental over-protectiveness;
- learners with disabilities including dyslexia, ADHD etc;

- career indecision – inability to make realistic career choices;
- inability to advance in one's career; and
- marital instability including divorce.

DEVELOPING POSITIVE SELF-REGARD

Self-talk

As already mentioned above, negative self-talk (inner critic) is associated with low self-regard. Negative thinking is particularly active when the mind is racing or we are tired. In this respect, any form of meditation that slows down a racing mind and elicits the alpha response (wakeful relaxation) can be effective (cf. chapter 16 on stress tolerance).

Affirmations are effective in countering negative self-talk. You may begin by writing self-affirmations on cards that you carry in your pocket or handbag. Use self-affirmations to interrupt and replace self-critical thought patterns. Examples include: "I accept myself exactly as I am", "I am successful", "mistakes are my opportunity to learn", "I am not here to live up to the expectations of others", and "I am strong, capable and confident".

When you find yourself getting embroiled in self-critical dialogues consider trying the following:

- Break the chain of negative thought by redirecting attention to some other activity:
    - Practice brief meditation (see chapter 15 on stress tolerance).
    - Practice a technique known as 'thought stopping' - every time you encounter self-limiting thoughts say "stop" silently to yourself.
    - Snap a rubber band against your wrist – this is a behavioural technique operating on the principle of negative reinforcement (see the works of B.F. Skinner on the internet).

Self-acceptance

There appears to be general agreement amongst health professionals that self-blame and a negative inclination is a default setting in our psychological makeup. Joan Borysenko, a Harvard-trained psychologist, opines that it is as though we all more or less suffer from a chronic virus of self-doubt.[7] Yet exactly how pervasive this is, is not known. What is more certain is that without self-acceptance, self-regard is impossible. Self-acceptance implies the recognition of personal abilities and achievements, as well as an acknowledgement and acceptance of personal limitations.

We promote self-acceptance when we acknowledge what is presently 'right' about ourselves. For many this is difficult because habits of negative thinking make it easier to identify what is wrong, thereby activating the 'virus' of self-doubt. While we concede the obvious benefits to acknowledging shortcomings and weaknesses, when this becomes the dominant focus, self-regard suffers.

Many people are unaware of their lack of self-acceptance. Becoming more aware that we are judging ourselves too harshly sets the stage for greater self-acceptance. We should also realise that comparing ourselves to others is counter-productive and may lead to ever greater personal insecurity and greater self-disconnect. On the other hand, acknowledging our strengths and achievements often dissolves anger and resentment. We also need to remind ourselves that we are not perfect and must learn to practice the art of self-forgiveness. We should also bear in mind that failing at something does not suggest that we are indeed failures. Affirming the good and attractive in ourselves while accepting compliments from others will go a long way to engendering a greater degree of personal acceptance. This provides a solid foundation on which positive self-regard can be built. Additionally, consider the following pointers which may enhance self-acceptance.

- Accept compliments from others.
- Find the good and attractive points in yourself.
- Compliment yourself on a task well done.
- Reassure yourself that you are a good person.
- Stop criticising yourself.
- Affirm that you are blessed with good health and a sound mind and are physically healthy.
- Let go of your constant need for approval from others.

Physical well-being and self-regard

It is difficult to feel good about yourself when you are following an unhealthy lifestyle. Aerobic exercise, sufficient sleep, and sound eating habits serve to establish a firm basis on which to build positive self-regard. The development and maintenance of healthy self-regard is ongoing. From the moment we are born, we refine and change our sense of personal identity and self-acceptance. As with any skill, self-regard takes time to achieve and practice to maintain.

Scientific consensus suggests that one's body/mind is intimately connected. If you want to experience positive mental health, you need to take good care of your body. People neglect to care for their bodies by having unhealthy eating habits, following a sedentary lifestyle, experiencing sleep deprivation, abusing alcohol, and often feeling stressed, fatigued and mentally rundown. The point is that you cannot neglect your body and expect to feel good. As Shiraldi[8] insists: "Time invested in physical health is a wise investment indeed [and] …improves mental health". While most people are intuitively aware that caring for their body is good for them, few realise that aerobic exercise also improves self-regard. It is unnecessary to spend hours in the gym to experience good health; investing in aerobic exercise for 20 to 30 minutes every other day is sufficient, provided we adhere to the routine. If time allows, working out anaerobically confers additional benefits.

THE HEALING POWER OF MEDITATION AND DEMOCRATIC SELF-LOVE

Meditation is an invaluable resource for individuals who need to better their self-regard, as it melts away layers of anxiety, sadness, depression, shame and addiction (see also chapter 16 on stress tolerance). It is also time to be gentle with yourself and simultaneously unearth the deeper recesses of your psyche. Meditation further allows the mind/brain to re-programme thoughts so that positive feelings can, in the final analysis, carry the day. One further thought. A fine line exists between narcissism (self-absorption) and the individual who praises him/herself with 'democratic' self-love, i.e. a love of self and a love of others. American existentialist psychologist Rollo May refers to this kind of love as *Agape* – a love for the other's welfare beyond any gain one can get out of it – including the love of God for humankind.[9]

You can't reach out to others unless you feel comfortable with yourself. Low self-regard is rooted in beliefs you have about yourself and negative impulses that cloud the mind. When we are at war with ourselves, we are more likely to engage in damaging behaviours that harm our bodies or spirits and our relationship with others.[10]

Finally, Selzer offers sage advice. To become more self-accepting, we must start telling ourselves (repeatedly and ***hopefully***, with ever increasing conviction) that given all our negative self-referencing beliefs and biases, we've done the best we could. In this light, we need to re-examine residual feelings of guilt as well as our many self-criticisms and put-downs. We must ask ourselves specifically what it is we do not accept about ourselves and – as agents of our own healing – bring compassion and understanding to each point of self-rejection. By doing so we can resolve exaggerated feelings of guilt based on standards and expectations that simply don't mirror what was possible from us at the time.[11]

Dealing with setbacks

Loss and suffering is an inevitable part of life. In a fast-paced and volatile society, people need to deal with setbacks, transitions, and an uncertain future. Yet a setback may serve as an opportunity to build mental muscle and regroup inner resources. Consider some of the following:

- Take care of yourself physically and emotionally.
- Develop a network of friends, peers and business associates.
- Develop problem-solving skills.
- Develop a sense of humour.
- Learn to embrace change.

Further pathways to enhance self-regard

Finally, consider other pathways to self-regard:

- Take an inventory of your strengths.
- Celebrate progress and small victories.
- Stop putting yourself down.
- Practice gratitude.
- Learn from your mistakes.
- Give yourself credit.
- Take calculated risks.
- Outline your personal goals.
- Imagine your goals achieved.
- Associate with people who are supportive and positive.
- Don't compare yourself to others.
- Focus on your positive qualities.
- Learn the power of saying no.

Social support and self-regard

People are social animals who need love and affection. When cut off from human contact and support, they soon experience alienation. While it's true that self-regard is cultivated from within, it is also true that social support feeds and nourishes our sense of self-regard. While others cannot validate us, they can strengthen the positive feelings we have of ourselves.

It is true that friends and social support serve as an essential ingredient to health and happiness, including healthy self-regard. Friends are particularly important in times of personal transition such as divorce, death in the family, illness, or being retrenched. Do you experience loneliness? If so, consider how you would go about acquiring friends. (See also chapter 9, interpersonal relationships.)

Individuals epitomising self-regard

Dr Frederick van Zyl Slabbert (politician)
Roger Federer
Margaret Thatcher
Eva Peron
Desmond Tutu
Others?

> # A FINAL WORD
>
> From self-esteem scholar and author Nathaniel Brandon,[12] a last word. He has called self-esteem [self-regard] "… the immune system of the mind. Just as a healthy immune system does not guarantee that one will never become ill, but makes one less vulnerable to disease and better equipped to overcome it, so a healthy self-esteem does not guarantee that one will never suffer anxiety or depression in the face of life's difficulties, but makes one better equipped to cope, rebound and transcend".

SECTION 2: ACTIVITIES FOR SKILLS DEVELOPMENT

Self-assessment

Individual activities

Spend a few moments assessing your self-regard skills. Answer the following questions honestly. Assign a number to each item, using this scale:

1 = Very seldom or not true of me
2 = Seldom true of me
3 = Sometimes true of me
4 = Often true of me
5 = Very often true of me

I feel good about my achievements in life.				
1	2	3	4	5

I accept myself warts and all.				
1	2	3	4	5

I feel good about myself.				
1	2	3	4	5

When people praise me I deserve it.

| 1 | 2 | 3 | 4 | 5 |

Multiply the total by 5 to arrive at a total out of 100.

Skills development scale

| 10 | 20 | 30 | 40 | 50 | 60 | 70 | 80 | 90 | 100 |

 **Activity 2**

How would you describe your relationship with yourself? Do you like yourself? Are you your own greatest critic?

....

....

What are your strengths and weaknesses?

....

....

How have these strengths and weaknesses influenced your life?

....

....

Could you improve further on these strengths?

....

....

Has there been a time when your self-regard took a nosedive? What were the factors that led to negative self-regard? What were the consequences of negative self-regard?

....

....

Name ten personal qualities you are particularly proud of. (See also Chapter 17 on happiness.)

....

....

Group activity

 Activity 3

Discuss how positive self-regard can be useful to your career.

....

....

Own work for personal growth: a to-do list for the next fortnight

 Activity 4

Parental messages

When you were a child, what was the predominant tone of the messages (in respect to self-worth) that you received from your parents/caregivers or significant others? Did they enhance self-regard, or were they put-downs? Did these messages enhance or influence the development of your adult self-regard positively or negatively? Explain.

....

....

Self-improvement exercise

Consider particular area(s) in your life you would like to improve. Find a comfortable chair and sit in a position that supports your back. Close your eyes and initiate the meditation process (follow the instructions on page 259). Once you experience a deeply relaxed state, consider a major goal(s) in life you would like to attain. In your relaxed state, you may want to break down your goal into a number of sub-goals.

What are the most important things you want out of life?

....

....

What are you doing about these goals right now? To answer the first question you need to define what your goals are. If this is presently unclear, thinking about what you want in each of the areas below may help you to be more specific:

- Physical health
- Psychological well-being
- Finances and money
- Intimate relationships
- Family
- Friends
- Career
- Education
- Personal growth
- Recreation and leisure
- Spiritual life

What are my most important personal goals:

- for the next month;
- for the next six months;
- for the next year; and
- for the next three years?

Identify your needs

Identify three or four needs from the list below to which you would like to give special attention. Then take action to do something about meeting the needs you have singled out. What specifically will you look at?

- Financial security
- Friendship
- Intimacy
- Sexual expression
- A sense of accomplishment
- A sense of progress towards a goal
- Spiritual awareness
- Creativity
- Feeling complete and masterful in some area
- Fun and play

Moral compass

Our moral compass and personal character are supportive of our self-regard. Below is a list of a number of qualities that could be considered moral strengths. Circle an item if developing it more fully could further your personal growth and self-regard.

- Forgiveness
- Trust
- Knowledge
- Honesty
- Integrity
- A sense of duty
- Respect for the self
- Thriftiness
- Consideration/thoughtfulness
- Humility
- Tolerance for diversity

Characteristics reflecting healthy self-regard

Listed below are a number of characteristics that are typical of people who harbour high self-regard. Circle those items that may further enhance the level of your self-esteem.

- Avoid belittling others.
- Ability to grow in the face of setbacks.
- Ability to learn from mistakes – experience a learning curve in every given situation.
- Confident without coming across as arrogant or conceited.
- Ability to deal with criticism in a mature way.
- Ability to communicate your needs to others.
- Not obsessed with failure or looking foolish.

Maintenance of self-regard

Are you mindful of maintaining positive self-regard? Circle an item that could further contribute to the maintenance of a healthy self-regard.

- Not allowing yourself to dwell on (real or imagined) personal weaknesses and past failures.
- Forgiving yourself for your weaknesses and past failures.
- Treating yourself with loving kindness.
- Judging yourself against realistic and reasonable standards.
- Changing the way you talk to yourself.

REFERENCES

Anon (2016). *Self-esteem*. [Online] Available: https://en.wikipedia.org/wiki/Self-esteem [Accessed 8 December, 2016].

Anon. (2017). *The healing power of meditation*. [Online] Available: https://mail.google.com/mail/u/o [Accessed 3 January, 2017].

Bar-On, R. (2002). *Bar-On emotional quotient inventory. A measure of emotion*. New York: Multi-Health Systems.

Borysenko, J. (2007) *The power of the mind to heal*. [Online] Available: www.hayhouse.com. [Accessed 8 December, 2016].

Brandon, N. (1994). *The six pillars of self-esteem*. New York. Bantam Press.

Corsini, R. (2002). *The Dictionary of Psychology*. New York: Brunner_Routledge.

Hergenhahn, B.R. (1976). *An Introduction to theories of personality*. London: Prentice-Hall.

Prochaska, J. & Norcross, J. (2007). *Systems of psychotherapy*. Belmont: Thompson/Brooks Cole.

Rogers, C.R. (1965). *Client-centred therapy*. London: Constable.

Seltzer, L. (2008). *The path to unconditional self-acceptance*. [Online] Available: https://www.psychologytoday.com/blog/evolution-the-self/200809/the-path-unconditional-self-acceptance [Accessed 17 December, 2016].

Shiraldi, G. (2005). *The self-esteem workbook*. Oakland: New Harbinger Publications.

Stein, S. & Book, H. (2011). *The EQ edge. Emotional intelligence and your success*. Toronto: Stoddard Publishing Company Ltd.

ENDNOTES

1   Bar-On, 2002.
2   Corsini, 2002.
3   Stein & Book, 2011.
4   Prochaska & Norcross, 2007.
5   Rogers, 1965.
6   Anon, 2016.
7   Borysenko, 2007.
8   Shiraldi, 2005.
9   Hergenhahn, 1976.
10 Anon, 2017.
11 Seltzer, 2008.
12 Brandon, 1994.

Chapter 4

SELF-ACTUALISATION

Annette Weyers

Man's main task in life is to give birth to himself, to become what he potentially is.
–Erich Fromm

SECTION 1: OVERVIEW

Self-actualisation is the fulfilment of the inborn need for personal growth. This need inspires the lifelong quest to realise the full scope of your latent capabilities. The actualisation of your talents, abilities and deeply held values produces a feeling of gratification, of meaningfulness of being intensely alive – a feeling that this is who you really are and who you are meant to be.[1]

After completing this chapter, you should be able to:

- define self-actualisation;
- understand the theory informing self-actualisation;
- reflect on the benefits of self-actualisation;
- understand ways to improve self-actualisation;
- identify self-actualised individuals;
- assess your own level of self-actualisation; and
- implement individual and group activities to enhance self-actualisation.

DEFINITION OF SELF-ACTUALISATION

Self-actualisation can be defined in a number of ways. For example, self-actualisation is:

- the process of striving to actualise one's potential capacities, abilities, and talents. It requires the ability and drive to set and achieve goals, and is characterised by being involved in and feeling committed to various interests and pursuits. Self-actualisation is a lifelong effort leading to the enrichment of life;[2]

- the process of living up to one's potential. It involves the full use and exploitation of talents, capacities and potentialities;[3]

- the process of being true to one's own nature and fully committed to developing one's capacities. It includes the concepts of growth, motivation, and meeting one's 'being' needs;[4]

- the ability to realise one's potential capacities. This component of emotional intelligence is manifested by becoming involved in pursuits that lead to a meaningful, rich and full life;[5] and

- an inner-directed process, by means of which an individual expresses and fulfils his or her inner self.[6]

Note: Self-actualisation should not be confused with self-indulgence, self-absorption or excessive individualism.[7]

THEORY INFORMING SELF-ACTUALISATION

The German psychiatrist, Kurt Goldstein, first conceptualised the term 'self-actualisation', however it was Carl Rogers and Abraham Maslow, two of the pioneers of humanistic psychology, who brought new meaning to the term. In response to the mostly pessimistic stance of psychoanalysis, Rogers and Maslow supported a more positive approach, which emphasised developmental processes that resulted in healthier personal functioning. Their research identified self-actualisation as a key factor that is vital in the campaign for optimum functioning.

For Rogers, the "single master motive in the life of the individual" is the self-actualising tendency, referring to an inherent tendency of living beings to develop all their capacities.[8] Drawing inspiration from Rogers' work, Maslow in turn explored self-actualisation as a source of human motivation. His work on human motivation culminated in his classic conception of a hierarchy of human needs.[9] The model originally described five needs, but was later expanded to include eight needs considered universal to all humans.

The systematic arrangement of core needs is portrayed as a pyramid comprising eight levels. Physiological and safety needs or lower needs are referred to as *deficiency needs* or *basic needs,* while the higher needs are termed *growth needs* and are associated with psychological needs.[10]

THE HIERARCHY OF NEEDS

Basic physiological needs – these are the basic needs for survival, including food, water, oxygen and sex.

Safety – the need for security such as the need for a safe environment.

Belonging/Love – the need to form attachments to others (family, friends), the need for intimacy and love.

Self-esteem/Status – the need for recognition, approval, respect, self-esteem and to be treated with dignity.

> ***Cognitive needs*** – the need to be informed and to understand the intricacies of the world; self-understanding and the need for knowledge.
>
> ***Need for beauty*** – people need beauty in their lives. At one level, this is the natural beauty of parks, forests, mountains and rivers. At another level, we need beautiful things like music and works of art to uplift the human spirit.
>
> ***Self-actualisation*** – the need for personal growth and fulfilment.
>
> ***Transcendence*** – the spiritual need to find an overarching purpose in life.

Although Maslow's model reflects a linear pattern of growth, where basic needs have to be met before higher-order needs can be fulfilled, Maslow conceded that they do not have to be fully satisfied before higher order needs are considered.[11] Thus, self-actualisation is not necessarily a mechanistic step-by-step process, but can proceed in a non-sequential manner.

Assess which of the needs described above are not adequately met in your life. How does this influence your life?

....

....

Recent history witnessed the emergence of positive psychology, an orientation in psychology that is strongly associated with the humanistic school of thought. Positive psychologists are encouraged to focus on positive human functioning.[12] Emotional intelligence can be considered an integral part of positive psychology, as it also focuses on enhancing human functioning[13] (see Chapter 1).

The legacy of Maslow and Roger is evident in positive psychologists' recognition of the positive correlation between self-actualisation and subjective well-being, as aptly corroborated in the observation that "happiness results from realisation of our potentials. We are happiest when we follow and achieve our goals and develop our unique potentials".[14] Therefore, a wise course of action is to focus on the personal growth of all one's capacities, talents and abilities.

The quest to fulfil one's potential is never fully satisfied, and one is continually challenged by opportunities for further growth and to reach for higher goals.[15] Accordingly, self-actualisation is not an end that one achieves; rather, it is a dynamic, lifelong undertaking – it is always a work in progress!

Self-actualisation and emotional intelligence

The inclusion of self-actualisation as a competency in the Bar-On model constitutes the recognition that self-actualisation is foundational to being successful in life and to experience life satisfaction. In addition, self-actualisation is one of the subscales (the others are optimism, self-regard and interpersonal relationships) most associated with well-being. High scores in these scales suggest that one experiences feelings of contentment and happiness and that one enjoys the many aspects of one's life. Recent research results, which corroborate that self-actualisation plays a vital role in the subjective experience of well-being, lend further credence to the argument for the development of self-actualisation.[16]

Self-actualisation is recognised in people who are excited about life, open to new experiences, keen to learn new things, self-motivated, and relentlessly confront obstacles in the pursuit of self-improvement. They display a willingness to pursue personally important and meaningful goals actively and intentionally. According to Hughes and Terrel,[17] self-actualised people move beyond emotional intelligence to achieve a higher level of human effectiveness.

The reciprocal relationship between the various emotional intelligence competencies implies that advancement in one competency can affect another competency positively. The emotional intelligence competencies that are supportive of self-actualisation include:

- *self-awareness* – vital for understanding oneself, what one is feeling and why. It enhances a greater sense of what is personally significant, thus it is helpful in setting meaningful goals;
- *self-regard* – self-actualisation is dependent on a well-developed sense of identity;
- *independence* – helps to pursue self-generated goals, rather than goals one is coerced into following;
- *problem-solving skills* – effectively address developmental challenges;
- *assertiveness* – empowering one to follow through on personal decisions; and
- *optimism* – reinforces the possibility to actualise one's potential.

One of the most effective ways to assist people to activate the best in themselves and to strengthen the potential to succeed in their personal goals is to follow a holistic approach that harnesses all relevant EI competencies.

The benefits of being self-actualised

There is ample evidence that the intentional and persistent pursuit of personal growth yields many rewards, not only in the personal domain but also in the workplace.

Personal excellence

A review of the literature reveals that self-actualisation provokes a combination of positive emotional, psychological, social and spiritual consequences that enhance one's overall sense of well-being.[18] For example:

- *Emotional well-being* is promoted by an increase in positive affect, including happiness, life satisfaction, inner peace, feelings of fulfilment and optimism.
- *Psychological well-being* is advanced by a greater sense of autonomy and efficiency, a notable increase in creativity, greater levels of independence, a sense of environmental mastery and greater success with the integration of their personality.
- *Social well-being* is bolstered by rewarding interpersonal relationships, social contribution (feeling one's life is useful to society), social integration (feeling a sense of belonging to the community), greater success at work, gratification with one's lifestyle, and the evolution of expertise in one's field of interest.
- *Spiritual well-being* incorporates realising personally expressive goals, not only providing the pathway for self-realisation and self-fulfilment, but also bestowing a powerful sense of meaning and life purpose. What the individual experiences is the sense that, "This is who I am and this is what I am meant to do".[19]

The contribution of self-actualisation to enhancing one's overall sense of well-being is significant. In turn, a higher sense of well-being is associated with improved functioning, greater success in life, increased resilience, and a deeper sense of fulfilment. The person who experiences high levels of self-actualisation finds life richer and more enjoyable.

Maslow identified 15 personality traits which are typical of self-actualisers:

MASLOW'S HEALTHY PERSONALITY

- An individual well grounded in reality.
- Self-acceptance and acceptance of others.
- Spontaneity, simplicity and naturalness – a lack of artificiality.
- An orientation to something they must pursue as a mission.
- A certain level of detachment - the need for privacy.
- Autonomy - independence from culture and the environment.
- Continued freshness of appreciation.
- Mystical and peak experiences.
- Social interest – empathy, compassion and identification with the human race.
- An intimate group of close friends.
- A democratic character structure – a lack of pretence and hypocrisy.
- An ability to discern the good from the bad.

> **MASLOW'S HEALTHY PERSONALITY (continued)**
>
> - A philosophical, non-hostile sense of humour.
> - A balance between polarities in personality, e.g. the ability to be playful, but also the ability to be serious when the situation calls for it.
> - Creativity.
>
> These personality traits influence the way in which people interact with the world and themselves. The traits described here are "ideal typical"; very few people will reflect all these attributes.[20]

How would you describe yourself in relation to these characteristics?

....

....

One of the core qualities of self-actualising individuals is an openness to experience, particularly to that which is *good* for them and which resonates with their core selves.[21]

Success in the workplace

Self-actualisation is at the heart of organisational prosperity; it is the one factor of emotional intelligence that consistently shows up as a predictor of success, regardless of job type. By the same token, high-performing leaders consistently produce high scores on the competency of self-actualisation.[22] The performances of self-actualised employees are testament to the link between self-actualisation and success. These are the employees who are more likely to be:

- engaged in what they do;
- satisfied with their jobs and finding pleasure in their work;
- motivated to succeed;
- committed;
- interested in problem solving;
- innovative;
- productive; and to
- have good relationships with co-workers.

Perceptive organisations realise that employees' motivation, commitment and job satisfaction are directly linked to the extent to which they find purpose in their work. These organisations create the conditions and offer opportunities for employees to grow and expand their capabilities and talents. Predictably, job satisfaction is a significant contributor to employees' overall sense of well-being.

STRATEGIES FOR DEVELOPING SELF-ACTUALISATION

As a point of departure for the improvement of self-actualisation, it may be helpful to:

- identify your talents and the activities you enjoy doing;
- assess the extent to which you achieve a work life balance; and
- set growth goals that are personally meaningful.

Identify activities you enjoy doing

All emotional intelligence skills advance the development of self-actualisation, however emotional self-awareness is essential for this undertaking. The drive for self-actualisation is highly individualised, therefore self-knowledge is a key factor when identifying what you enjoy doing. Emotional self-awareness provides the information about your deepest motivations and longings; it guides you to pinpoint that which you find exciting, meaningful and are passionate about. For one person it may be the desire to be an effective parent; for another it may be expressed through excellence in dancing, poetry or music.[23] Self-actualisation invites you to become the author of your own life as you proceed to identify and develop your unique capabilities and talents.[24]

Use the table below to help you identify what you enjoy doing. It is by no means an exhaustive list, however it may inspire further exploration of activities you find enjoyable. When you do something and it is accompanied by emotional experiences such as contentment, joy, satisfaction, animation, or a sense of accomplishment, it may indicate that you are expressing a talent or natural capability.

Categories	Activities	Emotional Experience
Sport/Outdoor activities		
Hobbies		
Spending time with friends and family		
Working		
Being alone		
Spirituality		
Community service		
Your own category		

It is not always immediately obvious what your talents are and it may require quite an effort to unearth them. The following questions may be helpful:

What do you do that comes most naturally to you?

What is it that you do that feels like an expression of your authentic self?

What did you take pleasure in doing in the past?

When as a child you had the time of your life, what did you do?

What activities engage you to the extent that you forget time?

The times you were successful, what were you doing?

Note: It is important to be open to all possibilities and to try things you have never done before. You may be pleasantly surprised!

Work-life Balance

One of the most rewarding experiences in life is to be engaged in work that is a source of personal fulfilment. Although your work may be highly significant, when it becomes all-consuming it leaves no room to pursue personal interests or develop talents in other areas of your life. An equitable distribution of time in the spheres of life and work (for many of us an elusive ideal!) allows for a more even-handed development of capacities in all areas of life. A wholesome work-life balance is thus beneficial in one's quest for self-actualisation.[25]

One of the ways to achieve more balance in your life is to be clear about your priorities. What matters most? Identify the areas in your life (e.g. family, health, fitness or leisure) where you need to invest more time. Do you have enough time for your personal life, according to your own standards? Use the diagram below to identify areas of your life you would like to develop. Single out the activities you wish to attend to in each area, then set long- and short-term goals with manageable steps to achieve your goal.[26]

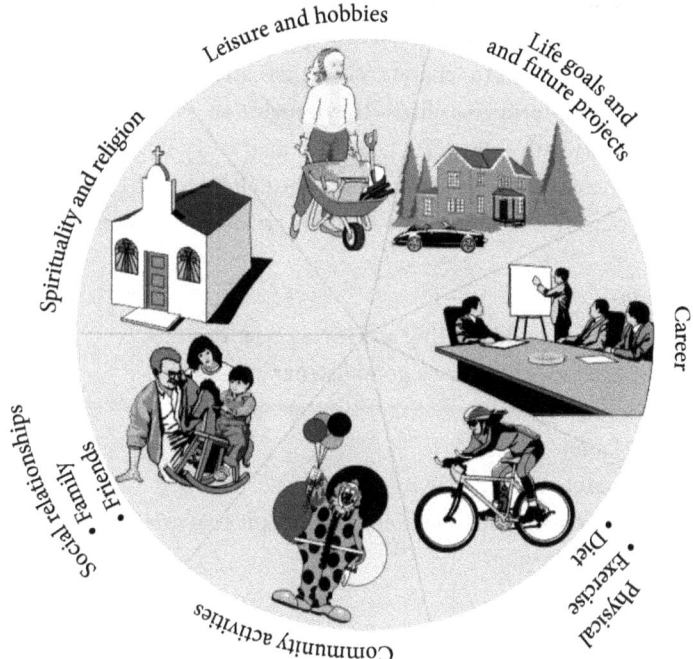

Figure 4.1: Work-life balance

Setting Growth Goals

Most people have aspirations of how they want to live and what they want to accomplish in life; they commit to goals that would allow them to fulfil these intentions. The right goals inspire the thoughts, emotions and behaviour that enable you to fulfil your ambitions; they give direction and purpose to life. Moreover, they provide meaning as they explain why you are doing what you do.[27] Evidently, goals lend form and order to life and are regarded by some as a key element of psychological organisation.[28]

Self-actualisation goals are coloured by each person's unique qualities, personality and circumstances. It is generally accepted that intrinsically based goals are the most effective to promote self-actualisation. These are goals that serve an intrinsic need, such as the need for self-actualisation. Intrinsic goals are self-generated, inspired by what you believe to be important, emanate from developing interests, are aligned with your core values, and reflect important aspects of yourself.[29] In addition, positively framed goals are more effective than those set to avoid the negative (e.g. I should avoid being alone at all costs).[30] Thus you are more likely to achieve optimal personal growth when your goals are autonomous and intrinsically oriented.

Not all goals are created equal, thus they do not hold equal value.[31] This is also true of personal growth goals. For example, the goal to master a computer programme may enhance a capability, but it may not be especially meaningful to you. In contrast, the goal of having a personal relationship with the Divine may have immense significance for you. Self-actualisation goals will include more trivial as well as deeply meaningful goals.

A constructive approach is to separate self-actualisation goals into long-term and short-term goals. Set your long-term goals first - they provide an overall vision of what you want to achieve. Follow these with short-term goals that map every stage of the progression. This may seem an overwhelming task, therefore it may be helpful to use Figure 7.1 to identify the different areas in your life where there is a need for growth. For example:

Social relationships
Long-term goal: I want to build trusting and loving relationships.
Short-term goal: I want to learn to be a good listener.

Spirituality and religion
Long-term goal: I want to seek the Divine every day.
Short-term goal: I must schedule time every day for spiritual practices.

Career
Long-term goal: I want to be an inspired leader.
Short-term goal: I need to know my own limitations and strengths (as a point of departure).

Goals need to be evaluated on a regular basis to ascertain that you are still on the right track.

Note: It is important to know which goals serve your best interests and which goals are simply foolish or utterly unattainable. Pursuing the wrong goals can cause misery and distress.

Individuals epitomising these skills

Nelson Mandela
Sir Richard Branson
Abraham Lincoln
Viktor Frankl
Others?

A FINAL WORD

The great tragedy of our time is that so many people simply follow the script handed to them by society about who they should be and how they should live. This is counterintuitive to the hardwired need for self-actualisation; the summons to honour your distinctive potential, to give voice to your true self, and to share your unique gifts with others. You will be petitioned to move beyond your comfort zone; to face your fears unflaggingly; to lay your vulnerabilities bare sometimes; to take risks and often oppose the existing norm. However, the bounty of your efforts will be a fulfilling and meaningful life. Accept as a gracious gift the ability to create yourself according to your distinctive blueprint.

SECTION 2: ACTIVITIES FOR SKILLS DEVELOPMENT

Self-assessment

Individual activities

Activity 1: Test your own level of self-actualisation

Spend a few moments assessing your level of self-actualisation. Answer the following questions honestly and assign a number to each item using this scale:

1 = Very seldom or not true of me
2 = Seldom true of me
3 = Sometimes true of me
4 = Often true of me
5 = Very often true of me

I have a clear idea of what I want to accomplish in life.				
1	2	3	4	5

I'm eager to develop my interests and abilities and values.				
1	2	3	4	5

I have a yearning to improve myself.				
1	2	3	4	5

In the past few years, I have accomplished quite a lot.				
1	2	3	4	5

I have a lively interest in a wide range of topics.				
1	2	3	4	5

Multiply the total by 4 to arrive at a total out of 100.

Skills development scale									
10	20	30	40	50	60	70	80	90	100

Group activities

 Activity 2

Group members discuss the opportunities for self-actualisation in their company:

- Pinpoint the barriers to self-actualisation.

....

....

- Submit a proposal on how self-actualisation can be advanced in the company.

....

....

 Activity 3

Read the following case study, and then answer the questions:

James Bradshaw is a 35-year old management consultant at a large multi-national company. He is married and has three children. His wife works as a part-time secretary at a charity organisation.

For the past 10 years, James has worked between 60 and 70 hours per week. He is in his office at seven every day and works until nine at night. Weekends are spent trying to clear his backlog. He has no outside interests or hobbies; he does no physical exercise and he rarely spends time with his family. His wife accuses him of being a workaholic.

As a high-school student, James dreamt of becoming an artist. He was enrolled in the arts programme at school and won several awards for his sculptures. In his final year, he won a scholarship to study art. His father, a successful lawyer, persuaded James to study economics and enter the world of business, as this would afford him the opportunity to earn more money.

Over the past three years, James has increasingly been experiencing feelings of emptiness, depression and frustration. He is unable to meet the challenges at work and constantly feels guilty for neglecting his wife and children.

Would you consider James a self-actualised person? Motivate your answer.

....

....

What, if any, are the barriers that prevent James from becoming a fully actualised person? What would be your advice to James?

....

....

Own work for personal growth: a to-do list for the next fortnight

 Activity 4

Reflect on the following questions:

- What do I want to achieve in life?
- What is my life task?
- How do I want to live?
- Who do I want to be?
- What is holding me back?
- How do I want to continue?

REFERENCES

Bar-On, R. (2010). Emotional Intelligence: An Integral Part of Positive Psychology. *South African Journal of Psychology, 40*(1), 54 – 62.

Bar-On, R. (2001). EI and self-actualisation. In C.J. Forgas and J. Mayer (eds.). *Emotional Intelligence in Everyday Life*. New York: Psychology Press.

Baumgardner, S. & Crothers, M. (2014). *Positive Psychology* (1st ed.). Essex: Pearson.

Bergh, Z. & Theron, A. (2007. *Psychology in the Work Context*. Cape Town: Oxford University Press.

Bernstein, D.A., Penner, L.A., Clark-Stewart, A. & Roy, E.J. (2006). *Psychology* (7th ed.). New York: Houghton Mifflin Company.

Braham, B.J. (1991). *Finding your Purpose; A Guide to Personal Fulfilment*. Menlo Park: Crisp Publications.

Compton, W.C. (2005). *An Introduction to Positive Psychology*. London: Thompson Wadsworth.

Emmons, R.A. (2003). Personal goals, life meaning, and virtue: Wellsprings of a positive life. In C.L.M. Keyes & J. Haidt (eds.). *Flourishing: Positive Psychology and the Life Well-Lived*. (pp.105-128). Washington D.C.: American Psychological Association.

Hughes, M. & Terrel, J.B. (2005). *Emotional Intelligence in Action* (2nd ed.). San Francisco: Pfeiffer.

Merlevede, P.E. & Bridoux, D.C. (2004). *Mastering Mentoring and Coaching with Emotional Intelligence*. Carmarthen: Crown House Publishing.

Newman, M. (2008). *Emotional Capitalists: The New Leaders*. Chichester: John Wiley.

Spence, G., Oades, L.G. & Caputi, P. (2004). Trait Emotional Intelligence and Goal Self-Integration: Important Predictors of Emotional Well-being? *Personality and Individual Differences 37*, 449 - 461.

Stein, S. & Book, H. (2011). *The EQ edge: Emotional Intelligence and your Success* (3rd ed.). San Francisco: Jossey-Bass.

Van Niekerk, E. (1996). *Paradigms of Mind: Personality Perspectives in Context*. Cape Town: Oxford University Press.

Weiten, W. (2002). *Psychology Themes and Variations* (5th ed.). Belmont: Wadsworth.

ENDNOTES

1. Baumgardner & Crothers, 2014:20.
2. Bar-On, 2001:89.
3. Compton, 2005:60.
4. Hughes & Terrell, 2012:41.
5. Stein & Book, 2011:52.
6. Bergh & Theron, 2007:158.
7. Compton, 2005.
8. Van Niekerk, 1996.
9. Bernstein et al., 2006.
10. Bernstein et al., 2006.
11. Compton, 2005.
12. Compton, 2005.
13. Bar-On, 2010:59.
14. Baumgardner & Crothers, 2014:20.
15. Bergh & Theron, 2007.
16. Baumgardner & Crothers, 2014:20.

17 Hughes & Terrel, 2012:42.
18 Weiten, 2002; Bernstein et al., 2006; Bergh & Theron, 2007; Hughes & Terrel, 2012; Baumgardner & Crothers, 2014.
19 Baumgardner & Crothers, 2014:147.
20 Compton, 2005.
21 Mittelman, in Bergh & Theron, 2007.
22 Hughes & Terrel, 2012; Newman, 2008.
23 Compton, 2005.
24 Newman, 2008.
25 Stein & Book, 2011; Newman, 2008.
26 Merlevede & Bridoux, 2004.
27 Baumgardner & Crothers, 2014.
28 Emmons, 2003.
29 Spence et al., 2004.
30 Emmons, 2003.
31 Emmons, 2003.

Chapter 5

EMOTIONAL SELF-AWARENESS

Annette Prins

To be human is to be self-conscious; and to be self-conscious is to bring one's self into the sphere of art, as an object to be judged, altered, improved.
–William Ernest Hocking (in Watson & Idinopulos, 2007:117)[1]

SECTION 1: OVERVIEW

Self-awareness and self-control form the keystones for emotional intelligence, thus a lack thereof is the biggest barrier to developing emotional intelligence.[2] Seligman[3] states that self-awareness involves "reflection and introspection to gain insights into life's pressing questions". These questions relate to fulfilling one's potential and finding meaning in life. It includes one's identity, purpose, being authentic and creating a life worth living.

Furthermore, self-awareness includes the ability to "attune to your own emotions and feel them on a physiological level as well as understand them on a psychological level".[4] This also encompasses an empathic understanding of other individuals. It may contribute to sensitivity and burnout. A heightened insula activation may indicate higher levels of self-awareness.

Emotions are inborn, and are changed and shaped by our personal history; they 'happen' to us rather than our willing them to occur. We therefore have very little direct control over our emotional reactions.[5] (Also refer to Part 1 in this regard.)

Most of us are too busy to pay much conscious attention to our experienced emotions,[6] therefore many of us unfortunately have a limited awareness of our experienced emotions or what triggers them. For emotional literacy, empathy and functional interactive skills to develop, such awareness is a prerequisite.[7]

After completing this chapter, you should be able to:

- define emotional self-awareness;
- understand part of the theory underpinning the self-awareness construct;
- reflect on benefits derived from enhanced self-awareness;
- understand how to develop self-awareness;
- identify individuals epitomising these skills;
- assess your own level of self-awareness; and
- implement individual and group activities to enhance self-awareness.

DEFINITION OF SELF-AWARENESS

Self-awareness constitutes ongoing attention to one's internal state.[8] "In this self-reflexive awareness, the mind observes and investigates experience itself, including the emotions." Self-awareness is therefore being aware of "both our mood and our thoughts about that mood".[9] Emotional self-awareness includes recognising and understanding one's own emotions, as well as being able to differentiate between subtleties in one's own emotions while understanding the cause of these emotions and the impact they have on the thoughts and actions of oneself and others.[10]

Serious deficiencies in this area are found in those with alexithymic conditions (the inability to express feelings verbally).[11] Furthermore, in order to understand others' emotions, it is necessary to understand one's own emotions.

Self-awareness is "one of the most critical components of emotionally effective living" and is associated with our ability to zoom in on others' feelings and why they feel that way.[12] Self-awareness and empathy help us to motivate our own and others' thoughts and actions, helping us succeed in life. Without having a good hold on our own emotions, we would find it difficult to move into the other emotional competencies.

THEORY INFORMING THINKING ON SELF-AWARENESS

The following is a short overview of the self-awareness construct.

Introduction to self-awareness

Self-awareness develops as follows;[13] firstly, emotions manifest in bodily sensations, such as the tightening of muscles when an experience is disturbing and relaxing when we are comforted. We place a value on our sensory experience. Is it pleasant or unpleasant? Following from sensory experience is symbolic awareness, i.e. translating our awareness into language in order to express our needs and wants. The ability to express our emotional preferences relates to our experiencing of pleasant and unpleasant sensations. As alluded to above, self-awareness is the capacity to understand your own emotions and to stay in touch with your feelings. This includes the ability both to recognise your feelings and to understand how they "... influence your personal opinions, attitudes and judgments".[14] These, in turn, exert an obvious influence on your behaviour and the response it elicits from the people with whom you interact. Self-awareness is therefore an important building block in regulating relationships.

A primary building block in developing EI competencies

If "you don't recognize you can't manage or change".[15] If one wishes to improve all areas of emotional intelligence, this is the one overarching skill to master. A strong sense of self-awareness helps one recognise one's range of emotions and how these may affect behaviour that might alienate others. This allows for a degree of control over potentially harmful behaviour. Individuals are often the very last to clearly recognise their own moods, but being aware of one's emotions is the first step in controlling them. When emotions are out of control they tend to sabotage adaptive behaviour and might alienate those whom you wish to draw closer. Therefore, important relationships may turn sour before they are even established.

Emotional awareness is indeed the primary building-block for all people skills.[16] Making insightful decisions and building worthwhile relationships are dependent on your ability to use all your senses and mind to become aware of both the inner and the outer world. It is a prerequisite for empathy, emotional control, and good customer service. It also assists in acting appropriately in tense situations, as well as giving you the ability to persuade and inspire others. Consequently, self-awareness is an important cornerstone of leadership.

We now look at different levels of awareness experienced by individuals.

Levels of self-awareness

Levels of emotional awareness will, of necessity, differ among people. To account for different levels in such awareness, Steiner[17] developed an 'emotional awareness scale'. The scale reflects the following, from the lowest to the highest level of awareness:

- *Numbness* occurs when an individual does not have any awareness of experienced feeling, such as in alexithymia (a lack of emotional awareness), which can cripple relationships and leave us fog-bound about ourselves.

- At the following level, *physical sensations representing emotions are recognised* in an individual (such as in headaches or migraines, also called **somatisation**), but the individual is not aware of the feelings themselves. The feelings present as physical signs as the individual does not have the vocabulary to differentiate and name the experienced feelings.

- *Primal experience of feelings indicates an awareness of emotions*, but the individual is unable to recognise them distinctively and can neither understand nor discuss them.

- *Differentiation* means that the individual has crossed the verbal barrier, can talk about experienced emotions, and is able to differentiate between basic emotions such as anger, love, shame, joy and hatred.

- *Causality* is the next step in the continuum, and allows the individual to identify both the emotion and its causative factor.

- *Empathy* represents a more advanced level of awareness, namely becoming aware of others' emotions.

- *Interactivity* demonstrates the highest form of experienced emotions, allowing for sensitivity to the ebb and flow of emotions and how they relate to one another. Knowledge of one's emotions together with an awareness of one's own and others' emotions constitute a first step towards emotional literacy.

Emotional numbness .... Interactivity

> *Where do you place yourself and your partner or closest friend on this continuum? How does this influence your relationship?*

THE FUNCTION OF SELF-AWARENESS

Personal competence "... is about knowing yourself and doing the most you can with what you have".[18] It is not about having complete control of your emotions or being perfect, but rather about allowing your feelings to guide your behaviour. Helping people enhance their self-awareness is a fundamental goal in coaching; coaching is like holding up a mirror for individuals to view themselves with greater clarity. It helps them understand how their behaviour affects others, which includes identifying strengths and blind spots limiting personal and interpersonal effectiveness. We need to become aware of our feelings and how they drive behaviour, which includes becoming aware of the values, beliefs and assumptions that shape our life experiences. Self-control is instrumental in helping us manage our negative emotions.[19]

Genuine self-awareness:

- provides for a "... steady stream of information you need to understand yourself".[20] EI skills will assist you to become more sophisticated in the ability to recognise and use emotions to your advantage. People who have experienced great challenges and have been able to manage them tend to have higher scores on emotional intelligence inventories;

- opens you up and entices you into wanting to receive feedback;[21]

- opens up an avenue to effective assertiveness, i.e. the ability to communicate your feelings, thoughts and beliefs in an open and authentic or honest manner; and

- is an important ability supporting the development of leadership.

Self-awareness and its associated competencies

Self-awareness is about being mindful of our own emotional state.[22] It entails various competencies, including emotional self-awareness, accurate self-assessment, and self-confidence. These are now briefly discussed.

Emotional self-awareness at work

Managers or leaders could traditionally get away with taking on domineering characteristics including being explosive, results driven, unethical, rigid and ego driven, as well as having weak emotional control and always being right.[23] These characteristics served to ignite fear in employees who would then find it difficult to challenge management. Negative emotions were applied in order to maintain a dominant leadership role. Currently, leaders attempt to manage in the best interests of the team, the organisation, and society. Now, emotional skills including self-awareness and social responsibility are deemed better measures of "cognitive intelligence and critical thinking (knowing when to be strategic and when to be tactical)".[24]

Self-awareness does not aim to rid us of unpleasant feelings that naturally flow from loss, criticism and disappointment. However, increasing consciousness of what we feel assists us to manage internal forces that may otherwise push us into self-defeating behaviour by default.[25]

Emotional [self-]awareness:[26]

- is an important soft skill in both business and the professions, since it alludes to intuition or a gut feeling that offers information on which to base decisions in addition to objective facts. A myriad of studies have described the role of intuition in enabling leaders to make better decisions, as it helps in the successful alignment of actions with values. Much energy is released when an individual works in accordance with his or her values, however burnout may ensue if the opposite is true. Examples of values are provided below:[27]

Acceptance	Admiration	Approval	Attention	Authority
Beauty	Commitment	Communication	Compassion	Competition
Conformity	Co-operation	Education	Efficiency	Entertainment
Equality	Expression	Faith	Fame	Family
Fidelity	Freedom	Friendship	Forgiveness	Gratitude
Happiness	Hard work	Health	Honesty	Humility
Image	Independence	Integrity	Knowledge	Liberty
Logic	Loyalty	Love	Manners	Material wealth
Obedience	Organisation	Others' opinions	Pain avoidance	Peace

Popularity	Politeness	Power	Punishment	Quiet
Reality	Reason	Relationships	Religion	Respect
Security	Self-sacrifice	Self-reliance	Serenity	Status
Success	Tradition	Truth	Wisdom	Other

Identify ten values that are important to yourself and prioritise them in order of importance. Are you living according to these at both home and work?

Home:
....
....

Work:
....
....

Self-awareness may be challenging for the following reasons[28]:

- Emotions are volatile and ever changing, evolving and mixing primary emotions into a range of secondary emotions (which are more difficult to identify correctly). These may all happen within a short time frame. For example, we may feel elated at being promoted, only to feel anxious the next moment about our ability to manage the new position (together with its challenges). We may therefore experience a mix of emotions such as being happy and anxious at the same time.

- We may experience – at any given time – a particular emotion that simultaneously masks another emotion, with the masked emotion frequently being the more important one. An example may be an individual who expresses anger at an unfaithful partner, but who is really ashamed at the thought that the partner had substituted her with a younger and more attractive lady.

- Our personal history may make accessing our emotions difficult as a result of, *inter alia*, trauma that we experienced as a child. An example may be people who grew up in a family where the free expression of emotions was not condoned. If emotions were expressed children might be sent to their room "to get over it". These children learnt, in order to survive, to suppress their emotions, so that accessing them in later years may be quite difficult. We thus have to "unlearn" many unhealthy things that were taught to us as children, and break bad habits.

Accurate self-assessment

A second component of self-awareness is accurate self-assessment.[29] Self-assessment is about viewing ourselves accurately and eliciting feedback from others in order to better our performance.

The following are benefits of accurate self-assessment.[30]

- Being aware of and making an accurate assessment of our own strengths and weaknesses.
- Being conscious of strengths and avoiding dwelling on weaknesses.
- Being reflective and open to gaining and learning from feedback and experience.
- Having an accurate perspective of self.
- Being able to appreciate the humour in situations.
- Continuous improvement as a personal and an organisational priority.
- Self-development that takes place via openness to feedback, learning continuously, and gaining new perspectives.

Accurate self-assessment is associated with superior performance.[31] Finally, the key to developing self-awareness is to focus on how we feel at the present moment.

Self-confidence[32]

The third competency associated with self-awareness is self-confidence. According to Goleman, self-confidence is "a strong sense of one's self-worth and capabilities".[33]

Benefits of self-confidence include:

- presenting with a greater measure of self-assurance, a "presence", and often an inspiring charisma;
- the ability to put forward unpopular views, to have the courage of one's convictions, and to be prepared to stick one's neck out for what is seen as right;
- the ability to act decisively and to make sound decisions despite pressure and uncertainty.

Furthermore, Goleman[34] provides for certain nuances in differentiating between aspects associated with self-awareness. This is now briefly discussed.

Nuancing self-awareness

According to Goleman[35]:

- *being self-aware* is being aware of one's moods as they occur, and being sophisticated about one's emotional life. The clarity experienced with regard to emotions may co-vary with personality traits such as being autonomous, being sure of one's own boundaries, experiencing psychological health, and having a tendency to view life from a positive perspective. Such an individual has presence of mind and is able to disengage sooner from a bad mood rather than brooding on an issue;

- *feeling engulfed* is about feeling overcome by one's feelings and being helpless to escape from them. Such individuals' moods take charge of them; they tend to be lost in their moods since they are unable to take on a meta-perspective by means of a detached view of their feelings. They do little to escape the bad mood since they believe they have little control over such moods, and tend to frequently feel "overwhelmed and emotionally out of control" – as if up against a tsunami; and

- *being accepting* refers to the ability some people have to accept their moods and not attempt to change them. These people may be relatively clear on the emotions they experience and may find themselves in one of two categories. First, there are those who tend to experience generally elated and happy moods and who therefore do not have a need to change their mood, while others, such as depressed individuals, simply and in a *laissez-faire* manner accept bad moods as part of their condition. They are therefore resigned to their despair.

After this short overview of some of the theory related to the construct of self-awareness, our attention turns to benefits derived from self-awareness.

BENEFITS DERIVED FROM ENHANCED SELF-AWARENESS

Without emotional self-awareness, we will simply live a life of reaction rather than taking initiative and steering our own and others' lives effectively.[36] A person communicating from a position of self-awareness may be better at forming productive, meaningful and personal relations.[37] However, in overdrive, self-awareness can make one oversensitive to emotions, believing situations to be emotionally evocative when others do not view them as such.

Self-awareness is valuable since it forms the very core of being human.[38] Emotional self-awareness can present as a gut feeling, indicating that something 'feels' right or wrong. It provides for an additional source of information via an intuitive reaction to stimuli from the environment, and helps us to be more strategic and effective in interacting with the environment.

This skill helps us to know how we are responding to our *umwelt* (environment) via what we are feeling. Are we, for example, happy, loving, sad, angry, apathetic, or perhaps ambivalent in response to what we sense? When the skill of emotional self-awareness is well-developed, it helps us to identify more easily when something is emotionally energising or draining. It also provides us with information on why we are feeling a particular way and assists us to make an informed decision about whether we should continue our involvement with the eliciting person, organisation or activity. It therefore provides for an internal 'radar' that provides us with information to assist us with decision-making. (See Wechsler's definition of intelligence, where one component of intelligence is to "deal effectively with his (or her) environment".)[39]

A family on vacation decides to paint their beach cottage. The eldest brother assists but does so carelessly and is scolded. Inflamed, he throws a paint brush inside and smashes the glass of a loved painting. This elicits a strong reaction of disgust from the family and the incident further taints the already strained relationship. He then realises that his lack of control over his emotional reaction is again detrimental to his relationship and storms off in a huff. Angry at himself, but blaming the family members. Again.

We need not live in a state of emotional numbness, nor are we doomed to live in a negative emotional state such as being perpetually anxious or irritable.[40] Furthermore, we need not be enslaved by others' feelings or subjected to uncontrollable impulses. When used appropriately, emotions should become a source of joy. Within an emotionally-literate environment, a new emotional self can evolve, together with transformed relationships, making a rediscovery or refinement of our emotional self an exciting adventure. Further benefits include that:[41]

- it helps us seek fulfilment of our emotional needs;
- it helps us manage emotions creatively – to know when to let go and when to hold back;
- we learn how to manage emotional numbness or feeling upset;
- it helps us to make meaningful contact with other people and form long-term relationships in different life arenas such as with family, at work, or during leisure periods; and
- we learn how to move from a love-centred approach to personal power in an environment that is becoming increasingly dehumanised.

DEVELOPING SELF-AWARENESS

The pathway to developing self-awareness is multifaceted. A few of these are now briefly discussed, with attention paid first to the physical dimensions of emotion.

Attending to the physical dimensions of emotions

Emotions manifest physically in our bodies. These bodily sensations may be used as a source of information to assist us in recognising our felt emotions. How the physical sensations tend to present may, to some extent, be individualised. Mersino,[42] for example, suggests the following:

- **Sadness** may manifest in tensed muscles in the chest, moist eyes or crying, feeling cold, and perhaps a lump in the throat.
- **Anger** may be recognised by an increased heart rate, clenching of the jaws or fists, stomach pain, an increase in body heat and shouting.
- **Anxiety** may present itself physically in an increased heart-rate, shortness of breath or shallow breathing, sweating, feeling cold, and tension in the neck muscles.
- **Happiness** may be recognised in a faster heartbeat, relaxed muscles, and involuntarily smiling or laughing.
- **Excitement** may manifest in an increased pulse rate, tensing of muscles, restlessness, and yelling.
- **Tenderness** may present in feeling relaxed and warm, having a full sensation in the chest, and wanting close physical contact, such as hugging.

The next aspect that may help with developing self-awareness is facial expressions.

Facial expressions

Facial expressions can provide an additional clue to emotions being experienced by an individual who struggles to recognise and name his or her emotions. Facial expressions flowing from emotions are difficult to fake. Examples include corners of the mouth being turned down in sadness, clenched teeth when angry, etc. If a person is not certain of the emotion he or she is experiencing, the individual may view his or her face in a mirror and learn to track emotions by consulting sources such as Mersino[43] or requesting feedback from others as to emotions being facially displayed. A person can, for example, request feedback on the most dominant emotions reflected on his or her face. In this way, the individual may gradually increase their self-awareness with regard to experienced emotions.

I messages

We can "discover and share" our internal experience by using "I" messages, such as "I feel upset because you are late again" or "I feel excited because it is our Grade 12 farewell tonight". Hughes and Terrell[44] suggest that we learn to regularly "take our emotional pulse" and share it when we feel it is appropriate to do so.

Journalling

- Keep a journal of your feelings: in an attempt to enhance self-awareness, consider keeping a journal of your feelings over a period to check for typical feelings, viewing changes in the pattern of feelings and trying to understand what led to the changes.

Write down what was happening, what you were feeling, and how you reacted. Was there a physical reaction, such as racing heart, sore neck and shoulders?

- Make a list of your roles and write down the feeling connected to each role. You might be a brother, sister, employee, husband, wife, mother, father, sportsman or woman – think of as many as you can. Your feelings for each role might be happy, frustrated, anxious... again, think of as many as you can.
- Predict how you will feel: think about a situation you're going into and predict how you will feel. Practice naming and accepting the feelings. You might say "I may feel angry" or "I may feel frustrated". Naming the feeling puts you in control. Try to choose an appropriate reaction to the feeling rather than just reacting to it.[45]

Values, beliefs and assumptions

Values are the principles, standards, morals, ethics and ideals that guide our lives. Knowing your values is essential to building awareness of yourself; it's like following a well signposted road. You may feel comfortable and secure since you know where you are, and where you're heading. That makes you feel confident, relaxed and happy knowing you're on the right road.[46]

Leaning into one's discomfort

Increased self-awareness comes with discomfort, since it requires admitting to shortcomings.[47] Indeed, "leaning into your discomfort"[48] is the only way to change. Rather than avoiding a feeling, one should move towards it and through it. Even mild emotions such as boredom, anticipation, and confusion need attention. If we ignore such emotions, we miss out on the opportunity to manage them productively; ignoring feelings does not rid us of them, they simply surface again later when least expected. Moving into the feeling allows for change. If ignored, it can lead one down a repetitive, unproductive, and unsatisfying path of behaviour. An example may be a person who has been raped and who subsequently pushes all related memory out of his or her consciousness. This does not solve the problem, and memories may come back to haunt the person when triggered by a related stimulus.

Read the following questions and reflect on them individually.

Ingrid is the incessant livewire at each party ... what might she be hiding?

....

....

And you? What dominant emotion are you running away from?

....

....

Just thinking about something that causes you discomfort sparks change, so don't be afraid of emotional mistakes. They provide information as to what you may contemplate doing differently next time.

ENHANCING EMOTIONAL SELF-AWARENESS

Steiner[49] proposes three routes to enhancing emotional self-awareness. The interested reader is referred to this source for a further refinement of skills. He proposes the following:

Opening the heart

Opening the heart essentially entails the giving and receiving of 'strokes', accepting or rejecting such strokes, and giving ourselves strokes.

> *What strokes do you feel are due to you which you have not been receiving of late? From whom?*

Surveying the emotional landscape

This loosely refers to an action, feeling or statement, where you refrain from specifically blaming another for the effect of their actions on your mood, but instead just state how you have been affected by a particular action. It further entails a verification of your hunches and intuitive feelings about events, situations, or actions.

Taking responsibility

We take responsibility where we sincerely apologise for our mistakes, accept or reject others' apologies, ask for forgiveness, and grant or deny such forgiveness.

Individuals epitomising self-awareness

Oprah Winfrey
President Barack Obama
Dr Phil
Others?

A FINAL WORD

In summary, it seems as if emotions and our differentiated awareness thereof are of much greater importance than previously realised. It is damaging to our existence to ignore the part of ourselves that provides us with information regarding our inner responses to a situation or a person. This skill is a prerequisite to understanding both ourselves and others, and is a core facet in the formation of caring relationships. We need to be aware of the different levels of self-awareness, its function, the benefits arising from being self-aware, and how to develop this core competency.

SECTION 2: ACTIVITIES FOR SKILLS DEVELOPMENT

Self-Assessment

Individual activities

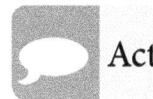 Activity 1

Spend a few moments assessing your emotional self-awareness. Answer the questions below honestly. The point is not to "look good" but to gain an indication of where you stand in terms of emotional self-awareness. Assign a number to each item using this scale:

1 = Very seldom or not true of me
2 = Seldom true of me
3 = Sometimes true of me
4 = Often true of me
5 = Very often true of me or true of me

I can identify my feelings with great accuracy.

1	2	3	4	5

I understand what has caused me to be happy, sad, angry etc.

1	2	3	4	5

It is easy for me to describe my feelings to a loved one.

1	2	3	4	5

I am fully aware of how my feelings change during the day.				
1	2	3	4	5

Multiply your score by 5 to arrive at a total out of 100.

Emotional self-awareness scale

10	20	30	40	50	60	70	80	90	100

 ## Activity 2: Tuning into our inner selves by identifying what we are feeling

What is happening inside me right now? Why?

....

....

How long have I felt this way, and what has triggered the feeling?

....

....

Has it been simmering for some time? When did I first notice the feeling?

....

....

Reflect on the intensity of the feeling.

....

....

What am I thinking or feeling about the current situation?

....

....

What cues can I observe about the emotions and state of mind of the people around me?

....

....

What do I want to gain from this situation?

....

....

Is this emotion part of a typical pattern of emotions that I experience?

....

....

This exercise is also useful in many different situations, including, for example, when chairing a meeting or sitting in a meeting.⁵⁰

 **Activity 3**

We need to pay attention to our thoughts as well as the accompanying physical signs that go with an emotion. These are our perfectly normal responses to situations that prove to be emotionally arousing.⁵¹

> You are tense and strained after a day full of conflict at work. You need to complete an urgent document for the CEO's visit first thing tomorrow. You walk to your PC in your study and turn it on so that you can get it done and have some rest, but all the systems are down. The screen goes blank. Describe your feelings under the following headings:
>
> - Bodily responses ....
> - Emotions ....
> - Thoughts..
> - Behaviour ....

Group activity

 **Activity 4**

What may happen when emotional self-awareness is lacking in the workplace?

Scenario 1

A line manager, Lindy, is highly intelligent, ambitious and very task oriented. She has favourites for whom the rules are bent, upsetting the other staff members. She also does not place much emphasis on keeping to confidentiality, so staff members are unwilling to share information with her. Neither is she really interested in their feedback and holds the opinion that they tend to be overly emotional, which makes her rather curt and dismissive in her interactions with them.

How does Lindy's behaviour influence the office climate?

....

....

How might her reactions influence office politics?

....

....

What implications does Lindy's behaviour have for productivity, staff turnover, job satisfaction, and the profitability of the company?

....

....

How does Lindy's emotional profile influence her staff with regard to productivity and creativity? Why?

....

....

You want to set a meeting to raise issues of concern, but you realise that you may be belittled should you put the concerns on the table. What do you do?

....

....

The admin team has had enough! The working context is toxic. How will you manage the situation and help Lindy become more functional at work?

....

....

Scenario 2

Your peers in your team do not share your value system. They are planning to divulge information to a third party in a competing company for a huge financial gain. In order to access full gain from the *transaction* they want all of the members of the small team to participate. How do you manage the situation when you realise non-compliance threatens your safety? Discuss.

....

....

Scenario 3

Your assistant is very social and talkative. Though she is pleasant, it starts to irritate you that she loses concentration in *meetings* and agenda points have to be returned to. She is insensitive to her effect on the other members. You do not want to dampen the current goodwill. How will you manage this?

....

....

Own work for personal growth: a to-do list for the next fortnight

 **Activity 5**

To enhance your ability to recognise emotions, contemplate the range of emotions people may experience. All emotions are derivatives of a few core emotions, such as happiness, sadness, anger, fear, and shame. However, such emotions differ in intensity, colouring the effect they have on us. (See Chapter 2 in Part 1.)

1. **Pointers to developing self-awareness**[52]

    1.1 Learn to focus, either inwardly or on another individual, so that you can consciously access information from the emotional and mental world, pick up subtleties in the behaviour of another, and use this information to steer your decisions and actions.

    1.2 Stop other activities and reflect inwardly:

      - Search inside with regard to your felt "emotions, intentions, desires, needs, thought patterns and motivations"[53] to help you remain focused, communicate well, and manage frustration.
      - Analyse your thought processes for any preconceived images, ideas, or self-persuasion with regard to, for example, an upcoming meeting or situation. Do you experience repetitive thoughts, especially negative ones that have the ability to sabotage your effectiveness?
      - Be alert to physical signs such as a tenseness in certain parts of your body. Do you experience any other discomfort, such as a clenching of your jaw? Or do you feel energised by what is coming? Your body is likely to provide you with signs that are indicative of your emotional condition.
      - Review recent statements made by you. What have you been telling yourself over the last few days? Is there a pattern to be detected?

- Be alert to both direct and indirect feedback on your responses, for example, "You seem to be preoccupied/not your own self/upset", etc.
- Talk to a good listener – talking it over with someone helps to clarify thinking.
- Record your thoughts in writing. What were your impressions about someone or a specific situation? Were you relaxed or tense about it?
- Speak to others about their awareness of the situation.

2. **Charting your moods**

   Check to see how you are feeling every hour for a week (or longer), allocating a point from 1 to 10 for each emotion, based on the following scale:

Not at all	1	2	3	4	5	6	7	Intense

Appreciated	Apathetic	Bored	Belittled	Busy
Calm	Cared for	Concerned	Confident	Considerate
Curious	Criticised	Delighted	Disappointed	Disrespected
Distressed	Distrusted	Disheartened	Enthusiastic	Encroached upon
Excited	Empty	Forced	Fortunate	Glad
Grateful	Happy	Healthy	Hopeful	Hopeless
Hyperactive	Insecure	Invaded	Invalidated	Interrogated
Imprisoned	Joyful	Judged	Lonely	Loved
Misunderstood	Mocked	Neglected	Optimistic	Passionate
Peaceful	Pleased	Pressured	Proud	Punished
Resentful	Respected	Sad	Satisfied	Scared
Strong	Stressed	Tender	Tearful	Threatened
Uncared for	Understood	Unheard	Unimportant	Unsupported
Unseen	Underestimated	Valued	Warmhearted	Weak
Other?				

– Adapted from Bharwaney[54]

Identify the predominant emotions you tend to experience.

Does your mood shift during the course of the day?

....

....

In the evening, analyse what you have written down during the course of the day.

....

....

Identify the pointers of mood changes.

....

....

What triggered the change? How did it impact on your thoughts and behaviour?

....

....

Search the internet for many more practical exercises to enhance your level of self-awareness.

REFERENCES

Bar-On, R. (2002). *Bar-On emotional quotient inventory: A measure of emotional intelligence*. New York: Multi-Health Systems

Bharwaney, G. (2006). *Emotionally intelligent living. Strategies for increasing your EQ* (Rev ed.). Carmarthen: Crown House Publishing Limited.

Bradberry, T. & Greaves, J. (2005). *The emotional intelligence quick book*. New York: Simon & Schuster.

Cherniss, C. & Adler, M. (2005*). Promoting emotional intelligence in organizations*. Alexandria: ASTD Press.

Connelly, M. (2011). *Kurt Lewin change management model*. [Online] Available at: http://www.change-managementcoach.com/kurt_lewin. html. [Accessed October 3, 2016].

Ferguson, R. & Kelly, M. (2005). *Enhancing emotional intelligence. Leadership tips from the executive coach*. Raleigh, NC: Mark Kelly Books.

Goleman, D. (1995a). *Emotional intelligence: why it can matter more than IQ*. New York: Bantam Books.

Goleman, D. (1995b). What's your emotional intelligence quotient? You'll soon find out. *Utne Reader*, November–December.

Hughes, M., Patterson, L. & Terrell, B.J. (2005). *Emotional intelligence in action: Training and coaching activities for leaders and managers*. San Francisco: Pfeiffer.

Hughes, M. & Terrel, B.J. (2012). *Emotional intelligence in action: training and coaching activities for leaders, managers, and teams* (2nd ed.). San Francisco: Pfeiffer

LeDoux, J.E. (1998). *The emotional brain: The mysterious underpinnings of emotional life*. London: Weidenfeld & Nicolson.

Lomas, T., Hefferon, K. & Ivtzan, I. (2014). *Applied positive psychology: Integrated positive practice*. London: Sage.

Mersino, A.C. (2013). *Emotional intelligence for project managers: the people skills you need to achieve outstanding results* (2nd ed.). New York: American Management Association.

Multi-Health Systems Inc. (2011). *The complete EQ-i 2.0 experience*. Toronto: Multi-Health Systems Inc.

Multi-Health Systems Inc & Jopie van Rooyen Psychometrics. (2011). *The complete EQ-i 2.0 experience*. Toronto: Multi-Health Systems Inc.

Newman, M. (2007). *Emotional capitalists. The new leaders*. Chichester: John Wiley & Sons.

Seligman, M.E. (2011). *Flourish: a visionary new understanding of happiness and well-being*. New York: Free Press.

Stein, J.S. & Book, H. (2011). *The EQ Edge: Emotional intelligence and your success* (3rd ed.). Ontario: John Wiley & Sons.

Steiner, C. (1999). *Achieving emotional literacy. A personal programme to increase your emotional intelligence*. London: Bloomsbury.

Van Niekerk, E.C. (2007). *A neural path less travelled: Why workshops fail*. Paper delivered at Wellness in the Workplace Conference held 17–18 April in Bloemfontein.

Wall, B.L. (2007). *Coaching for emotional intelligence: the secret to developing the star potential in your employees*. New York: Amacom.

Watson, C.E. & Idinopulos, T.A. (2007). *Are you your own worst enemy? The nine inner strengths you need to overcome self-defeating tendencies at work*. Oxford: Greenwood World Publishing.

Wechsler, D. (1958). *The measurements and the appraisal of adult intelligence* (4th ed.). Baltimore: Williams & Wilkins.

ENDNOTES

1. Watson & Idinopulos, 2007:117.
2. Wall, 2007.
3. Seligman, 2011:150.
4. Lomas, Hefferon & Ivtzan, 2014:46.
5. LeDoux, 1998.
6. Mersino, 2013.
7. Steiner, 1999:29.
8. Goleman, 1995:46.
9. Salovey in Goleman, 1995:47.
10. MHS & JvR, 2011:2.
11. Bar-On, 2002:15.
12. Hughes & Terrell, 2011:47.
13. Hughes & Terrell, 2011.
14. Newman, 2007:11.
15. Stein & Book, 2011:43.
16. Ferguson & Kelly, 2005:16.
17. Steiner, 1999:53.
18. Bradberry & Greaves, 2005:91.
19. Wall, 2007.
20. Bradberry & Greaves, 2005:93.
21. Newman, 2007:96.
22. Mersino, 2013.
23. Stein & Book, 2011: 44.
24. Stein & Book, 2011:45.
25. Stein & Book, 2011:46.
26. Cherniss & Adler, 2005:13.
27. Bharwaney, 2006:108; Van Niekerk & Weyers, 2007.
28. Mersino, 2013:35.
29. Mersino, 2013:44.
30. Cherniss & Adler, 2005:14.
31. Boyatzis in Cherniss & Adler, 2005:14.
32. Mersino, 2013:45; Cherniss & Adler 2005:17.
33. Goleman, 1995.
34. Goleman, 1995:48.
35. Goleman 1995:48.
36. Hughes & Terrell, 2011.
37. MHS & JvR, 2011.
38. Hughes et al., 2005:46.
39. Wechsler, 1958:7.
40. Steiner, 1999:54.
41. Steiner, 1999:60.
42. Mersino, 2013:41.
43. Mersino, 2013.
44. Hughes & Terrell, 2012:49.
45. Connelly, 2011.
46. Connelly, 2011.

47 Bradberry & Greaves, 2005:91.
48 Bradberry & Greaves, 2005:92.
49 Steiner, 1999.
50 Hughes et al., 2005; Ferguson & Kelly, 2005.
51 Bradbury & Greaves, 2005.
52 Ferguson & Kelly, 2005:16.
53 Ferguson & Kelly, 2005:17.
54 Bharwaney, 2006:76, 77.

SECTION B: SELF-EXPRESSION

Self-expression offers an extension of the self-perception scale and pays attention to the external expression or action component of a person's internal perceptions. It assesses the person's ability to be self-directed and openly express thoughts and feelings, whilst these feelings are expressed in a constructive and socially acceptable manner.

The following skills are discussed:

Chapter 6:   Emotional expression
Chapter 7:   Assertiveness
Chapter 8:   Independence

Chapter 6

EMOTIONAL EXPRESSION
Annette Prins

Wise men talk because they have something to say: fools, because they have to say something.
–Plato

SECTION 1: OVERVIEW

This work relates to Charles Darwin's interest in the role of "emotional expression in survival and adaptation".[1]

Emotional expression provides a measure of how effective we are at accurately communicating our feelings to others. In the first version of the Bar-On test (EQ-i), this aspect was incorporated in the skill of self-awareness. These are indeed different skills and far better represented in the 2.0 edition. A broad emotional vocabulary assists one to be able to express clearly what one experiences at the emotional, including sensory, level. Both an individual and team require enough feeling words to allow them to differentiate accurately between a range of emotional states, helping them to have a fair grasp of another individual's emotional state/experience, as well as the team climate.[2] To function effectively we need to be able to understand and differentiate both the emotion and the intensity thereof, to enable us to express ourselves with the necessary finesse and empathy. For example, are the staff members *accepting* of a change or *passionately* embracing it…?

After completing this chapter, you should be able to:

- define emotional expression;
- understand some of the theory underscoring emotional expression;
- demonstrate insight into the function of emotional expression, including emotion regulation and verbal and non-verbal forms of expressing emotion;
- have some understanding of how culture influences emotional expression;
- show insight into benefits flowing from an enhanced emotional expression;
- assess your own level of emotional self-expression; and
- implement individual and group activities to enhance your emotional expression.

DEFINITIONS

Emotions are "internal phenomena that can, but do not always, make themselves observable through expression and behavior".[3]

"Emotional expression is openly expressing one's feelings verbally and non-verbally."[4]

We are constantly sending out emotion laden messages to others. These messages are conveyed at various levels, including verbal via tone of voice, meaning and volume; and non-verbally via facial expressions and body language.[5] Most people are intent on picking up these cues accurately to navigate their way in interpersonal negotiations. People who are effective at emotional expression tend to be open and congruent in their communication. Incongruences are picked up and may confuse the receiver of the message.

Emotional expression includes facial expressions such as smiling or scowling, or behaviours such as laughing or crying. The expression of emotion could occur either with or without self-awareness. Individuals supposedly have conscious control over their emotional expressions, but can express emotions without a conscious awareness of their affective or emotional state.[6]

THEORY INFORMING THINKING ON EMOTIONAL EXPRESSION

"Emotional expression is an extension of the Self-Perception Composite scale."[7] It refers to the observed expression or the behavioural component of an individual's internal perception; an individual's inclination to be self-directed and the ability to openly express feelings and thoughts, whilst communicating these in a "constructive and socially acceptable way".

Emotions are value laden. Since we are creatures primed for survival, our emotional response to what we perceive is intended to help us survive. Emotions are therefore evolutionary and come with a physiological response preparing us for fight, flight or freeze in reaction to environmental stimuli. If what we observe is positive, it will enhance our approach behaviour, if negative, it will stimulate avoidance behaviour.

Introduction to emotional expression

Individuals who are effective at emotional expression are able to find both "the words and physical expression to convey their feelings in a way that is not hurtful to others".[8] Emotional expression entails a few steps, including an awareness of the emotion, labelling it and then interpreting it together with its possible impact. Being aware of the emotions initiates a form of controllability.[9]

Effective emotional expression is being comfortable to express both positive and negative feelings via suitable vocabulary and fitting non-verbal expressions. Since the verbal and non-verbal expression of emotion makes the meaning clear, others do not have to guess the individual's feelings; emotions are not bottled up but are expressed and shared in an appropriate and fitting manner. This holds positive implications for relationship building since openness furthers intimacy and meaningfulness in relationships. In the working environment, adaptive emotional expression assists with team communication and decision-making, which may help to resolve conflict and obtain the required resources. However, sharing too much emotion too frequently might be disturbing or even overwhelming for others. One needs to observe the reaction of others (both verbal and non-verbal) and adapt one's expression accordingly. Related subscales include interpersonal relations, assertiveness and empathy.

THE FUNCTION OF EMOTIONAL EXPRESSION

Emotional awareness may enhance social interaction by means of modulating emotional expressions in harmony with the changing demands of the social context. This requires a high level of differentiation and insight in expressing emotion. We need to monitor and modulate how our emotions are outwardly expressed, and consider how a given display may impact others. It is therefore predicted that higher levels of emotional awareness would potentially co-vary with greater appropriateness of emotional expression in social interactions.[10] A cognitive-development approach assumes five levels of interpersonal negotiation strategies. These five levels (in ascending order) may be described as negotiation through:[11]

- physical force;
- implicit power (threat or willpower);
- psychological power (persuasion);
- interpersonal collaboration; and
- integration and synthesis.

Can you think of examples of these negotiation strategies?

....

....

Each successive level is indicative of an increase in the degree to which the other individual is seen as separate, autonomous yet interdependent, and having needs, feelings, and rights that are as legitimate as the individual's own.

Emotional regulation

Emotions are critical for how people relate to each other within interpersonal interactions. How emotional exchanges take place may have important social consequences and contribute to whether relationships are maintained and enhanced, or give rise to interpersonal antagonism and discord.[12] We need to successfully regulate emotions to maintain positive relationships via, for example, cognitive reappraisal within the situation to regulate for negative emotions, and expressive suppression, where appropriate, to mask signs of inner emotional states.[13]

Verbal expression

Verbal expression should be suited to the occasion. It includes using words and sounds to express oneself in contrast to using mannerisms, gestures etc. to convey a message. Clarity, accuracy and honesty are important to promote understanding. "Successful relations flow from a willingness to openly exchange thoughts and feelings."[14] Other factors of importance include being calm and focussed, polite and keeping to basic rules of etiquette. Basic listening skills, reflecting and clarifying, using encouraging words to reinforcement participation, summarising and rounding up the communication are of equal importance. The first few minutes in interpersonal encounters are extremely important, as first impressions have a significant impact on the success of further communication. Communication barriers include a lack of attention, disinterest, distractions, differences in viewpoints etc.

Can you think of incidents where you experienced these? Discuss.

....

....

A strong ability for verbal communication and a feel for an appropriate level of verbal interaction is required if one would like to advance in a career. Workplace communication is critical since it allows companies to be productive and operate effectively. Employees are more likely to experience increased morale, productivity and commitment if the company climate allows for communication up and down the communications chain in an organisation, and when information is shared for commercial benefit. In the work place you may want to energise, engage and motivate co-workers, colleagues etc. In order to do so you need to know your audience and adapt to their needs, for example, noting the needs of different generations. In addressing millennials, for example, steer clear from the "tried and true" approaches. They may find them outdated and stale, seeking creativity embedded in technology they are comfortable with. Millennials want to make informed and educated choices.

When communicating at a personal level, building trust and affection, managing conflict and showing appreciation is important, together with sharing concerns, wishes, hopes and dreams.

Consider using I messages such as:

- I hope…
- I realise…
- I expect…
- I want…
- I am happier when…
- I am puzzled by…
- I am hurt by…
- I am afraid of…
- I notice…
- I assume this means…
- I wonder…
- I believe…
- I am frustrated by…
- I regret…
- I resent…

Transparency in verbal expression refers to a lack of hidden agendas and conditions, providing access to the full information required for collaboration, cooperation, and collective decision-making. Being over emotional, on the other hand, including emotional outbursts, can contribute to overwhelming and alienating partners.[15] A balance between the expression/non-expression of emotions is advisable; always consider how emotional expression may impact others. It may be unconstructive to share your emotions with individuals who have no interest in assisting you or who are uncaring regarding your needs. It may elicit "criticism, avoidance, ridicule and in worst cases manipulation of the exposed vulnerability". It is therefore important to always consider the context and the individuals present before expressing emotions. In this way you may reap the beneficial fruits of emotional expression.

Non-verbal behaviour

Non-verbal behaviour is defined as communicating without words, that is, sending and receiving wordless clues. Communication includes more than just the explicit meaning of the words conveyed - it also carries an implicit meaning which is conveyed intentionally or unintentionally. Non-verbal behaviour can either reinforce the spoken word or negate it. It conveys information about the individual's emotional state, provides additional feedback to the other person, and regulates the flow of communication. Non-verbal communication includes aspects such as facial expressions (smiling, frowning, blinking); eye contact (the amount of eye contact is indicative of the level of trust); frequency of glances; para-language (tone of voice, pitch, speed of talking); handshaking; dress; body language (hand gestures, nodding, shaking the head); posture (how you sit or stand, arms crossed or not); spatial distance kept between individuals (determined by the level of intimacy); and physiological changes (sweating, blinking more). It is general knowledge that good communication provides a foundation for successful relationships, both personal and professional. It's important, however, that it's our nonverbal communication that speaks the loudest.[16] Interpreting non-verbal behaviour is not simple since there is no fixed meaning attached to it. The individuals involved, the context and the culture are all important. Despite non-verbal behaviour being very important, some individuals are unaware of their non-verbal behaviour and its impact.

Have you had someone squashing your hand bones when meeting?

....

....

Someone sweating profusely when they tell you all is fine with your investment?

....

....

Facial expressions

Facial expressions convey information of one's internal state. These expressions are unique to each emotion and the information is used in coordinating social interactions.[17]

Smiling, for example, is not a single class of behaviour. Ekman and Friesen describe the appearance of "false smiles", which are to purposefully convince someone that enjoyment is taking place when it is not; "masking smiles", which are employed to conceal negative emotions experienced; and "miserable smiles", where the individual willingly endures an unpleasant circumstance. This is in opposition to the so called "Duchess smile", which is related to real enjoyment.[18]

> Humans are quick to identify happy facial expressions, whereas the disgust expression takes them longer to identify.[19]

How easy do you find it to identify such a false smile? How does it make you feel?

....

....

How does a Duchess smile make you feel?

....

....

Look in the mirror and try to convey the following emotions or role play these in a group, and try and identify what the person is trying to project.

Adoration Affection Agitation Agony Amusement Anger Anguish Annoyance Anxiety Apathy Arousal Attraction Awe Boredom Calmness Compassion Contempt Contentment Defeat Depression Desire Disappointment Disgust Ecstasy Embarrassment Empathy Enthrallment Enthusiasm Envy Euphoria Excitement Fear Frustration Gratitude Grief Guilt Happiness Hatred Homesickness Hope Horror Hostility Humiliation Hysteria Infatuation Insecurity Insult Interest Irritation Isolation Jealousy Joy Loneliness Longing Love Lust Melancholy Neglect Nostalgia Panic Passion Pity Pleasure Pride Hubris Rage Regret Rejection Remorse Resentment Sadness Sentimentality Shame Shock Shyness Sorrow Spite Stress[20]

EMOTIONS AND CULTURE

Emotional expression and culture

Darwin[21] was interested in the relationship between culture and emotions, and argued that emotions and their expressions are universal. Since then, this topic has elicited much interest among researchers of human behaviour and the possible universality of the *six basic emotions* (i.e. happiness, sadness, anger, fear, disgust, and surprise). Some theorists believe that emotions are universal phenomena but are affected by culture. *Emotions* identified to be universal are indeed experienced in similar ways, eliciting similar reactions in response to comparable events across different cultures. Other emotions, however, exhibit substantial cultural differences in the way they are experienced, the eliciting reactions, and how they are perceived in the surrounding context. Some theorists (social constructionists) believe emotions are more deeply influenced by culture. Therefore, the components of emotions are universal, but the patterns are social constructions. Culture thus provides a framework for understanding human behaviour by means of structure, guidelines, expectations and rules. These are learned through socialisation. Unwritten/meta-rules lay the foundations of how emotions may be expressed.[22]

Individualistic vs. collectivistic cultures

Culture provides the conduit whereby emotions are both moulded and expressed; it influences both emotional values and how emotion is regulated. Emotion has widely been studied in relation to individualistic and collectivistic cultures. Collectivistic cultures seek social harmony and promote the interdependence of its members; focus falls on the collective needs, wishes, and desire of their collectives. Any emphasis on individuality is either absent or minimised in this cultural model.[23] On the contrary, individual autonomy and independence is emphasised in individualistic cultures. Personal attainment, together with individual needs, wishes, and desires, are promoted. Africa, Asia and Latin America constitute collectivistic cultures, whilst North America and Western Europe are typically seen as individualistic cultures.

Emotional expression is informed by culture. Within more collectivistic cultures, emotions are conceived of in relation to the group and occurring between individuals rather than within an individual.[24] Japanese school students, on being asked, would reply that their emotions come from their outside social surroundings, rather than from within.[25] Students in individualistic cultures such as America, when questioned, view emotions as occurring within, constituting independent internal experiences. Americans therefore consider emotions to be personal, experienced internally and independently. Emotions including friendliness and shame that underscore interconnectedness are dominant in Asian culture. Individualistic European-American cultures exhibit more individualistic emotions, such as pride or anger.[26]

Emotion suppression

Individuals within collectivistic cultures may be less inclined to express emotions and are careful not to upset social harmony. The Japanese, for example, tend to be more inhibited when it comes to emotional expression in both verbal and non-verbal self-disclosure.[27] This is attributed to their collectivistic orientation. Emotional moderation is more expected in collectivist cultures due to the possibility of strong emotions and emotional expression being disruptive of smooth social functioning and interpersonal relations.[28]

People in individualistic cultures are more inclined to freely express emotions, seek emotional closeness with a selected few, and more openly express negative emotions.[29] Their research indicated that non-responsive reactions and hostility were elicited when the suppression of emotions occurred for those with European Americans values. The opposite held for people with bicultural Asian-American values; they were seen as less hostile and more engaged when they chose to suppress their emotions. Since negative emotions are viewed as disruptive of social harmony, Asian-Americans may more often habitually engage in suppression.

BENEFITS DERIVED FROM ENHANCED EMOTIONAL EXPRESSION

EI is the ability to effectively respond to emotions in daily life.[31] One benefit of the expression of emotions is that it enhances a sense of intimacy and helps us connect to others. "Expression of emotion involves revealing part of the self. It enables the development of emotional ties with others and the ability to let others get to know our real self."[32] This obviously strengthens relationships.

How we manage strong emotions[33] affects both our physical and emotional health. When we actively hold back on strong emotions, we tax the body's defences, including the immune system, cardio-vascular system etc. Confronting and expressing deep-set thoughts and feelings positively contributes to health.

Thus, emotional competence is a core competency associated with health benefits when individuals are able to effectively communicate their emotions. Individuals adept at communicating their emotions "should be able to give and receive emotional support more effectively than those with low levels of emotions communication abilities".[34] This includes the ability to give and receive emotional support, to initiate and maintain emotional conversations, and to express emotions and feelings clearly.[35] Individuals' psychological well-being is influenced by their level of interpersonal relationships, which, in turn, is influenced by how well they can communicate their feelings. Overall, the present findings seem encouraging regarding the value of EI ability as a possible psychological health correlator or predictor.

Another benefit includes increased self-awareness, as by expressing emotions it helps clarify them.

Humans are motivated by four main drivers - fear, desire, anger and altruism.[36] These drive us to take action, i.e. we move away from things that create fear (or dislike), such as a fire or an unpleasant bossy person. If we desire something we will move toward it, such as a meaningful relationship or further education. If we are obstructed in our pursuit of what we desire, we may move against the policies, people and structures that obstruct us, such as was the case with the 'Fees must fall' campaign at universities across South Africa in 2016, which brought education to a standstill with much destruction taking place at tertiary institutions. If people are driven by altruistic emotions, they move towards those people and situations requiring assistance, such as Doctors without Borders, the Red Cross, and other volunteers during earthquakes and other crises following natural disasters. As for anger, people may fiercely defend themselves when they are of the opinion that they are being wrongly accused or when their reputation is being tainted.

In the workplace,[37] resonant leaders can attune to the emotional register of their employees. If an incident occurred that saddens or angers them, the resonant leader can both empathise and express emotions on behalf of their employees. This reinforces synchrony in the same manner as does passion and enthusiasm, since it leaves people feeling both understood and cared for. When people connect at an emotional level they tend to stay focussed and get things done, even within uncertainty and profound change. Connecting with others at an emotional level makes work more meaningful. It is here that appropriate emotional expression plays a critical role.

DEVELOPING EMOTIONAL EXPRESSION

Our emotional literacy and vocabulary are key elements to enhancing our emotional expression. If we need others to take proper cognisance of what we are experiencing at the emotional level, we need to be able to provide them with a nuanced insight to enable them to effectively respond. We need to also be aware of our non-verbal communication and whether it supports what we express verbally. If not, we will confuse others and not come over as authentic. We therefore need to take a bird's eye view of how we come across – does the other individual seem to understand the meaning of what we had tried to get across? If not, check the person's understanding.

In order to express ourselves accurately and openly at the emotional level, we need to have the necessary confidence flowing from a positive self-regard, together with the courage to act assertively.[38] Enhanced emotional intelligence flows from the intertwining of various skills that act as support for the other skills. Any one skill does not make an individual emotionally intelligent, but rather enhances the range of skills in support of one another.

We need to take greater cognisance of and sharpen our non-verbal skills. We may inadvertently discount our verbal message by using a posture, tone of voice, volume, facial expression or gesture that does not support the message we want to send. It is common knowledge that non-verbal communication accounts for about 90% of a message sent, with the words accounting for as little as 7%.[39] Thus, if our non-verbal message, stemming primarily from the unconscious, unintentionally radiates our internal judgement, anger, fear etc., it may make our communication inauthentic and dismissible, thereby decreasing our impact or ability to secure cooperation from those we need to influence.

Individuals epitomising emotional expression

Barack Obama – recall the speech he delivered at Madiba's funeral or his inaugural speech.
Madiba – emotional contagion inspiring others.
Ronald Reagan – influencing American citizens' opinion with his charisma.

A FINAL WORD

When we are adept at emotional expression, we tend to express our feelings and thoughts with the necessary finesse and empathy, taking cognisance of the possible impact on others and modulating the expression in harmony with the requirements of the changing social context. This includes being comfortable expressing positive and negative feelings via suitable vocabulary and fitting non-verbal expressions. The ultimate aim is to communicate clearly and openly in order to create intimacy and meaningfulness in relationships.

Self-assessment

Individual activities

 Activity 1

Spend a few moments assessing your emotional expression. Answer the questions below honestly. The point is not to 'look good', but to gain an indication of where you stand in terms of emotional expression. Assign a number to each item using this scale:

1 = Very seldom or not true of me
2 = Seldom true of me
3 = Sometimes true of me
4 = Often true of me
5 = Very often true of me or true of me

I am comfortable at openly expressing my feelings to others.				
1	2	3	4	5

I tend to bottle up my feelings.				
1	2	3	4	5

Others tend to misread my feelings.				
1	2	3	4	5

I throw my toys out of the cot at times.				
1	2	3	4	5

I regularly feign emotions such as pleasure/friendliness?				
1	2	3	4	5

Multiply your score by 4 to arrive at a total out of 100.

Emotional expression scale									
10	20	30	40	50	60	70	80	90	100

Activity 2

Imagine a private psychology practice. Dr Jones does exceedingly well and the patients roll in. Dr Green, on the other hand, initially did equally well, but as time went on his numbers declined until, at last, his office closed. What might the factors involved be if we consider that both were excellent academics?

Activity 3

In dyads, take turns to role play the emotions below and try to identify what your partner is trying to express. Provide feedback.

Adoration Affection Agitation Agony Amusement Anger Anguish Annoyance Anxiety Apathy Arousal Attraction Awe Boredom Calmness Compassion Contempt Contentment Defeat Depression Desire Disappointment Disgust Ecstasy Embarrassment Empathy Enthrallment Enthusiasm Envy Euphoria Excitement Fear Frustration Gratitude Grief Guilt Happiness Hatred Homesickness Hope Horror Hostility Humiliation Hysteria Infatuation Insecurity Insult Interest Irritation Isolation Jealousy Joy Loneliness Longing Love Lust Melancholy Neglect Nostalgia Panic Passion Pity Pleasure Pride Hubris Rage Regret Rejection Remorse Resentment Sadness Sentimentality Shame Shock Shyness Sorrow Spite Stress[20]

 Activity 4

Look in the mirror and try to convey the emotions above. Do your facial expressions resemble them?

 Activity 5

Think of an incident where you and a co-worker were in conflict. When you voiced your opinion and displayed your feelings, what reaction did you elicit? What did your body language convey? Your tone of voice and facial expression?

Group activity

 Activity 6

There is a fight among kids in a family restaurant in South Africa. A man shouts at the mother of the child bothering his child. She lets him, in no uncertain manner, have a piece of her mind. Things turn sour and racial. You are the manager. What will you do and say?

 Activity 7

An air hostess serves a woman on a flight to the Middle East. The passenger throws the food parcel right back in the face of the hostess. How should the hostess and crew react?

 **Activity 8**

An elderly lady is admitted to a psychiatric unit. She was requested to bring her own wheelchair since there is only one available in the unit. She comes without. The overworked senior sister is furious and untactful when she notices her occupying the only available wheelchair. The next moment another patient falls and urgently needs the wheelchair. The senior sister loses control over her emotions. The next day a complaint is leveraged at the sister. What do you imagine the sister said to the patient? How would you advise?

 **Activity 9**

Role play a strong difference in opinion between a CA and his line manager on whether to assist a difficult client. Do this non-verbally. What do the other participants notice regarding non-verbal behaviour, experienced emotions etc.?

REFERENCES

Bar-On, R. (2010). Emotional intelligence: an integral part of positive psychology. *South African Journal of Psychology*, 40(1), 54-62

Bodie, G.D. & Burleson, B.R. (2008). Explaining variations in the effects of supportive messages: A dual-process framework. *Communication Yearbook*, 32, 355–398.

Butler, E.A., Lee, T.L. & Gross, J.J. (2007). Emotion regulation and culture: Are the social consequences of emotion suppression culture-specific? *Emotion*, 7, 30–48. doi:10.1037/1528-3542.7.1.30.

Chen, W., Lander, K. & Liu, C.H. (2011). Matching faces with emotional expressions. *Frontiers in psychology*, 2, 206.

Darwin, C. (1872). *The Expression of the Emotions in Man and Animals*. London: John Murray.

Dorset Research & Development Support Unit. (2003). *Emotional Expression* [Online]. Available at: http//:www.emotionalprocessing.org.uk/Emotion Concepts/Emotionalexpression.html [Accessed July 23, 2007].

Ekman, P. & Friesen, W.V. (1975). *Unmasking the face: A guide to recognizing emotions from facial cues*. Englewood Cliffs, NJ: Prentice Hall

Ekman, P., Davidson, R.J. & Friesen, W.V. (1990). The Duchenne Smile: Emotional Expression and Brain Physiology. *Journal of Personality and Social Psychology*, 58, 342-353.

Fredrickson, B.L. (1998). What good are positive emotions? *Review of General Psychology*, 2(3), 300–319. doi:10.1037/1089-2680.2.3.300.

Galor, S. (2011). *The benefits of Emotional Expression* [Online]. Available at: https://drsharongalor.wordpress.com. [Accessed March 29, 2017].

Goleman, D. (2013). *Focus: The hidden driver of excellence*. New York: A&C Black.

Gunderman, R.B. (2011). Emotional Intelligence. *Journal of the American College of Radiology, 8*(5), 298–299. doi:10.1016/j.jacr.2011.02.007.

Hughes, M. & Terrel, B.J. (2012). *Emotional intelligence in action: training and coaching activities for leaders, manager, and teams* (2nd ed.). San Francisco: Pfeiffer.

Lanciano, T. & Curci, A. (2015). Does emotions communication ability affect psychological well-being? A study with the Mayer–Salovey–Caruso Emotional Intelligence Test (MSCEIT) v2. 0. *Health communication, 30*(11), 1112-1121. Doi: 10.1080/10410236.2014.921753.

Lane, R.D. (2000). Levels of emotional awareness: Neurological, psychological, and social perspectives. In R. Bar-On & J.D.A. Parker (eds.). *The handbook of emotional intelligence: Theory, development, assessment, and application at home, school, and in the workplace.* San Francisco: Jossey-Bass, p. 186.

Markus, H. & Kitayama, S. (1991). Culture and the self: Implications for cognition, emotion, and motivation. *Psychological Review, 98,* 224–253. doi:10.1037/0033-295x.98.2.224.

Markus, H.R. & Kityama, S. (2007). Culture and the self: Implications for cognition, emotion, and motivation. *Psychological Review, 98*(2), 224–253. doi:10.1037/0033-295X.98.2.224

Marshall, T.C. (2005). *Emotional intimacy in romantic relationships: A comparison of European and Chinese Canadian students.* London: University of Western Ontario

Matsumoto, D. (2008). Facial Expressions of Emotions. In L. Feldman-Barrett. *Handbook of Emotion.* New York: Guilford Press, p. 211–234.

Miyahara, A. (n.d.). Toward Theorizing Japanese Communication Competence from a Non-Western Perspective. *American Communication Journal, 3*(3), 279-283.

Multi-Health Systems Inc. (2011). *The complete EQ-i 2.0 experience.* Toronto: Multi-Health Systems Inc.

Multi-Health Systems Inc & Jopie van Rooyen Psychometrics. (2011). *The complete EQ-i 2.0 experience.* Toronto: Multi-Health Systems Inc.

Niedenthal, P.M., Krauth-Gruber, S. & Ric, F. (2006). *Psychology of Emotion Interpersonal, Experiential, and Cognitive Approaches.* New York: Psychology Press, p. 5, 305–342.

Pennebaker, J.W. (1997). *The healing power of expressing emotions.* New York: Guilford Press.

Shariff, A.F. & Tracy, J.L. (2011). What Are Emotion Expressions For? *Current Directions in Psychological Science, 20*(6), 395–399.

Stein, S.J. & Book, H.E. (2011). *The EQ Edge: Emotional Intelligence and your success* (3rd ed.). Ontario: John Wiley & Sons.

Takahashi, K.N.O., Toni, C. & Antonucci, H.A. (2002). Commonalities and differences in close relationships among the Americans and Japanese: A comparison by the individualism/collectivism concept. *International Journal of Behavioral Development, 26*(5), 453–465. doi:10.1080/01650250143000418.

Uchida, Y., Townsend, S.S.M., Markus, H.R. & Bergseiker, H.B. (2009). Emotions as within or between people? Cultural variations in lay theories of emotion expression and inference. *Personality and Social Psychology Bulletin, 35*(11), 1427–1438. doi:10.1177/0146167209347322. PMID 19745200.

Wikipedia. (2011). *Emotional Expression* [Online]. Available at: https://en.wikipedia.org/wiki/Emotional_expression. [Accessed March 28, 2017].

Wikipedia. (2013). *Non-Verbal Communication* [Online]. Available at: https://en.wikipedia.org/wiki/Nonverbal_communication. [Accessed March 28, 2017].

ENDNOTES

1. Bar-On, 2010.
2. Hughes & Terrell, 2012.
3. Niedenthal, Krauth-Gruber & Ric, 2006.
4. MHS, 2011:9.
5. Stein & Book, 2011.
6. Niedenthal et al., 2006.
7. MHS & JvR, 2011:7.
8. MHS & JvR, 2011:7.
9. Galor, 2011.
10. Lane, 2000.
11. Selman in Lane, 2000.
12. Fredrickson, 1998.
13. Dorset Research and Development Support Unit, 2003.
14. MHS & JvR, 2011:7.
15. Galor, 2011.
16. Wikipedia, 2013
17. Wikipedia, 2011.
18. Ekman, Davidson & Friese, 1990.
19. Chen et al., 2011.
20. Wikipedia, 2011.
21. Darwin, 1872.
22. Ekman & Friesen, 1975.
23. Niedenthal et al., 2006.
24. Markus & Kitayama, 2007.
25. Uchida et al., 2009.
26. Markus & Kitayama, 1991.
27. Niedenthal, 2006; Miyahara, n.d.
28. Niedenthal, 2006.
29. Takahashi et al., 2002.
30. Butler et al., 2007.
31. Gunderman, 2011.
32. Galor, 2011.
33. Pennebaker, 1997.
34. Bodie & Burleson, in Lanciano & Curci, 2015:1119.
35. Bodie & Burleson, 2008.
36. Hughes & Terrel, 2012.
37. Goleman, 2013.
38. Hughes & Terrell, 2012.
39. Hughes & Terrell, 2012.
40. Wikipedia, 2011.

Chapter 7

ASSERTIVENESS: A FINE ART IN EMPOWERMENT

Annette Prins

The more arguments you win, the fewer friends you'll have.
– Anonymous

SECTION 1: OVERVIEW

Assertive behaviour "enables a person to act in his or her own best interest, to stand up for herself or himself without undue anxiety, to express honest feelings comfortably and to exercise personal rights without denying the rights of others".[1] Assertive behaviour is furthermore about making reasonable demands on people, being persuasive and managing conflict.[2] Conflicts and differences in opinion are ever-present. Assertiveness requires an individual to be direct, show finesse and be considerate of others.[3] Assertiveness is not aggressiveness since it is not about militancy, obtrusiveness or combativeness.

Assertiveness is a frequently misunderstood concept. It involves the ability to "... communicate clearly, specifically and unambiguously, while at the same time being sensitive to the needs of others and their responses in a particular encounter". There is no single way of being assertive; people have their own style. "You can be humorous or serious, concise or eloquent."[4]

After completing this chapter, you should be able to:

- define assertiveness;
- understand the theory informing thinking on assertiveness;
- understand how the alternative behavioural styles may shape your life;
- recognise and understand both the causes and consequences of:
  ○ passive/unassertive behaviour; and
  ○ aggressive behaviour.
- understand why some find it so difficult to act assertively;
- argue in favour of the benefits that derive from being assertive;
- understand pathways to becoming more assertive;
- effectively set boundaries and create an aura of authority through assertiveness;
- identify assertive individuals;
- assess your own level of assertiveness; and
- implement individual and group activities to enhance assertiveness.

DEFINITION OF ASSERTIVENESS

"Assertiveness is a way of acting that strikes a balance between two extremes: aggressiveness and submissiveness."[5]

Stein and Book[6] contend that assertiveness includes three aspects:

- "the ability to express feelings (for example, to accept and express anger, warmth, and sexual feelings);
- the ability to express beliefs and thoughts openly (being able to voice opinions, to disagree, and to take a definite stand, even if it is emotionally difficult to do so and even if you have something to lose by doing so); and
- the ability to stand up for your personal rights (not allowing others to bother you or take advantage of you)."

In order to act assertively one firstly requires sufficient self-awareness to distinguish between different emotions before expressing them. Secondly, one should exercise impulse control so as to express negative emotions, including anger, in an appropriate way and with an adequate amount of intensity. Third and lastly, an individual should stand up for his or her own rights and beliefs whilst being sensitive to the needs of others, therefore one should preferably pursue a constructive win-win outcome.[7]

THEORY INFORMING THINKING ON ASSERTIVENESS

Alternative behavioural styles that may shape your life

Assertiveness strikes a balance between behaviour that is:

| Humble [non-assertive] | Assertive | Aggressive |

Assertiveness both empowers us and help us define ourselves to others.

Non-assertive, submissive, or passive behaviour

Being unassertive, may, in the short term, bring temporary relief from anxiety as potential conflict is avoided. One may also escape guilt by avoiding a particular situation. This may, in turn, reinforce non-assertive behaviour.[8] However, in the long run, unassertiveness can contribute to a further eroding of an existing fragile and low self-esteem. Supportive skills include interpersonal relations, emotional self-awareness and empathy.[9]

Do you:

- Experience difficulty in expressing your opinion in a group especially in the face of opposition?
- Relinquish responsibility and tend to assume the role of victim in social interactions with others?
- Struggle to correct someone who is doing a poor job?
- Feel self-conscious when accepting a sincere compliment?
- At times use sarcasm or intimidation to get what you want?
- Reluctantly ask others to alter their behaviour when it affects you adversely?
- Often put the needs of others before your own?
- Tend to feel guilty when turning down requests?
- Give in to unreasonable requests?
- On the surface seem satisfied but inside hide a deep simmering resentment?
- Complain behind people's back about your treatment rather than to their face?

If you answered "yes" to any of the above questions, you may need to enhance your level of assertiveness.

> *The trouble with being too submissive or passive is that your special way of being yourself and thinking will remain unexpressed and the world will be a poorer place.*

Causes of non-assertive behaviour

These include a fear and anxiety of:

- being rejected;
- conflict;
- making mistakes;
- upsetting or hurting others; or
- disagreement which may be misinterpreted as a dislike of the other person.

Passive individuals find it difficult to express themselves and therefore bottle things up rather than dealing with uncomfortable situations. Such individuals therefore frequently don't have their needs met and often miss out on opportunities whilst others take advantage of them.[10]

The individual may also lack confidence, be overly sensitive to others' feelings, hold false self-beliefs such as feeling that he or she is unworthy of personal rights, and believe that others' opinions are more valid than his or her own. In the work context they may fear losing their job if they do not comply, especially with those in positions of authority.[11] They may thereby avoid taking responsibility and being blamed if something goes wrong. It may also help them gain the protection of someone seen as stronger than they are.

Some non-assertive individuals may believe assertiveness indicates self-centredness and that non-assertion equals politeness. Others may simply never have learnt the skill of assertiveness. See Figure 7.1 below for other influential factors.

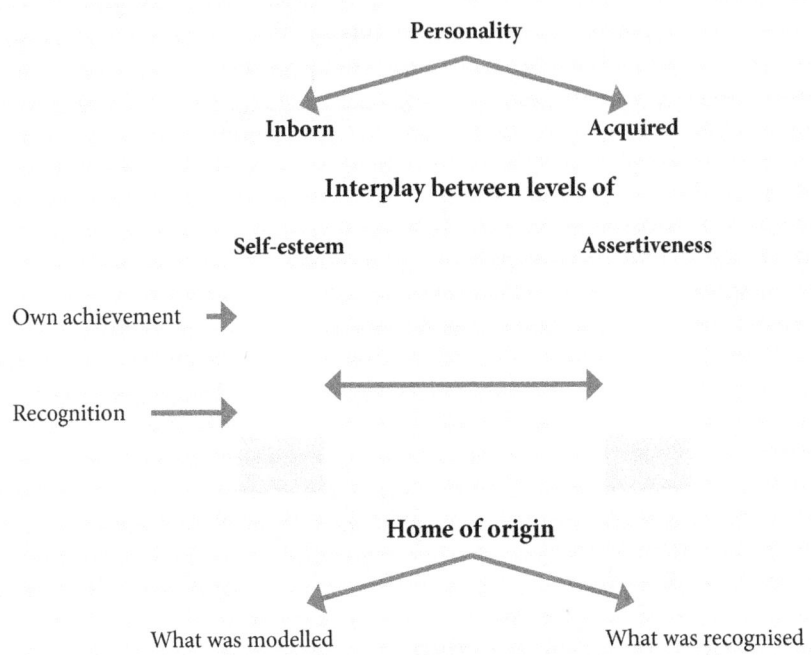

Figure 7.1: Other influential factors[12]

As indicated in Figure 7.1, genetics and the resultant inborn personality influence one's predisposition to being more humble and submissive or more aggressive. Another influential factor is the individual's level of self-esteem. The higher the level of self-esteem, the easier he/she finds it to act assertively. The level of self-esteem and the level of assertiveness therefore tend to co-vary. When the level of self-esteem rises, for example via own achievement or through the positive feedback of others, the person's level of assertiveness may accordingly rise. Also, behaviour that was rewarded in the home environment may influence current-day assertiveness.[13] If being humble was role-modelled and rewarded, the individual may find it more difficult to act assertively.

Consequences of non-assertive or passive behaviour

Non-assertive individuals typically tend to yield to other's preference(s); consent to things they don't want to do; feel resentment or a churning feeling inside; and consequently experience heightened tension. Feelings include irritability, anger, guilt, frustration, self-pity and resentment.[14] These feelings may give rise to physical symptoms associated with chronic stress including pain in muscles, neck and back aches, as well as headaches. People may initially feel pity for them but will ultimately lose respect for them, doubting the person's integrity. They may become involved in conflict and explosive relationships, and others may speak behind their backs about their lack of self-control. ("Have you seen, Jeanine threw her toys out of the cot again?") They feel guilty when expressing their own needs, and thus discount such needs and don't let others know what they want. Others therefore remain ignorant of their feelings and wants and typically do not respond as expected.

Angry and aggressive feelings are expressed in a covert way rather than openly, and they frequently use passive resistance to express their resentment, such as turning up late for an engagement they did not actually want to keep. They may 'forget' to do important work, thereby throwing a bad light on the line manager, and often complain or moan about things rather than express their needs openly. They may avoid making difficult decisions thereby contributing to things getting worse.

The result is that they seldom have what they want because they don't get their needs across. They are frequently stuck with the unpleasant jobs because of their inability to say "no", are frequently not paid what they deserve, and remain trapped with second-rate service and goods.

Extremely submissive individuals tend to avoid eye-contact; demonstrate nervous, hesitant behaviour; and may even adopt a hunched posture and false smile. They tend[15] to "speak in a quiet, uncertain, shaking monotonous voice filled with hesitance, pauses and throat clearing". Content may reflect long rambling statements, taking ages to get to the point. They apologise excessively and repeatedly ask permission.

Because of the accumulation of bad experiences, non-assertive individuals may begin to avoid social situations owing to anxiety that builds up in them, as a result of their negative experiences.

Success frequently eludes passive people since they are "not clear in their own minds about what they want".[16] They furthermore have difficulty in clearly expressing wishes and needs, which leads to them blocking their own path to success.

Manipulation

Some unassertive individuals attempt to get what they want by making the other person feel guilty, while others play the role of victim to get people to take care of them. If it doesn't work, they become openly angry or feign indifference. Manipulators are good at persuading others that they are truthful when they are not straight and honest with them.[17] The person being manipulated feels confused and later on becomes angry and resents the manipulation.

Aggressive behaviour

Assertiveness is often confused with aggression,[18] therefore some people are cautious of assertiveness since they wrongly believe that it equals aggression and do not wish to hurt others. Assertiveness provides for a clear statement of beliefs/feelings whilst being considerate of others' thoughts and feelings. This point distinguishes assertiveness from aggression; "aggression leaves no room for compromise". In time, people react with mistrust and anger to aggression; they may seek to get even by undermining the aggressor, or they simply avoid or ignore further interactions with the aggressor. The aggressor frequently ends up being isolated and alienated without meaningful support, which may fuel the aggression and drive further deviant behaviour.

Aggressive individuals tend to get what they want at the expense of others by putting others in an inferior position by attacking, blaming, humiliating, being intimidating and punishing.[19] They attempt to force people into complying with their requests by communicating in demanding, superior, disrespectful, abrasive, and hostile ways. At a non-verbal level they make use of facial expressions such as raised eyebrows, firmly set jaws, a fixed or scowling gaze, fist thumping and finger pointing. They may also invade your personal space and stand upright to seem taller. Their voice may be raised with a hard and sharp tone. They tend to also be boastful and sarcastic, and put their own needs, wants, and desires above those of others. They inclined to be insensitive and dismissive of others' needs, rights and feelings. They succeed in getting their way through sheer force, thereby creating enemies and conflict by putting others on the defensive, leading them to withdraw or fight back rather than co-operate.[20]

Aggressive supervisors

Aggressive supervisors exhibit a style characterised by accusations, angry tones, belligerence, and intolerance of others. Thinking primarily of themselves, they fail to take account of others' rights and feelings. They tend to be bullies, except toward those who do not allow themselves to be dominated.

Causes of aggressive behaviour

Many aggressive individuals tend to experience feelings of insecurity that need to remain 'under cover'. In order to cover such feelings of powerlessness so that their helplessness does not become public, they may employ threats and react strongly to protect themselves. This reflects an inability to express their own needs and feelings appropriately. They are typically hypersensitive to critique, perceived injustices and unfairness, and tend to mistrust others, believing they are out to humiliate them.[21]

Consequences of aggressive behaviour

Aggressive behaviour may contain both positive and negative effects. Positive effects may include, in the short run, the desired effect. Some people are intimidated and may, grudgingly, provide what the aggressive person wants.

Negative effects may include, in the long run, that the individual gains only resentment, disapproval and condemnation rather than respect.[22] He or she may alienate friends and family, since the aggressive person always wants his or her own way.[23] Others may increasingly avoid the aggressive person, *inter alia*, to reduced self-esteem. The result is that this may contribute to stress symptoms, including emotional reactions such as guilt, anger, self-doubt, and anxiety, and physical symptoms such as headaches, rashes, stomach aches, and general fatigue.

Aggressive people frequently struggle to achieve their goals since they belittle others and are inconsiderate and disrespectful. As a result, others perceive them to be self-serving, destructive and self-centred, and therefore avoid going along with them.[24]

Passive-aggressiveness

Some individuals tend toward passive-aggressiveness. On the surface, they seem to oblige whilst inside they seethe with bitterness and suspicion since they are frequently exploited by others. They repress their anger only to lash out inappropriately.[25]

Assertiveness

Assertive people, knowing their rights, will ask for what they want clearly and firmly, but gently. They are able to express their feelings, opinions, beliefs and needs openly, directly and honestly while not violating others' personal rights, and are able to say no to something they don't want to do. Assertiveness involves self-awareness and requires knowledge of your needs and wants; a belief in your basic rights; and a certain level of self-esteem. It also enhances self-respect and dignity while gaining others' respect.[26]

Relationships tend to be governed by power relations. Everyone involved wishes to maintain enough power to 'master' the other person or the situation. A large amount of groundwork is done to manipulate the situation successfully. See Figure 7.2, where the role of power is demonstrated against the background of Eric Burns' transactional analysis. If, for example, a supervisor needs to have firm control over his or her employees, he or she may manipulate them into feeling guilty, unworthy and childlike, very much in the same way as in 'Big Brother'. He or she may, at times, provide positive feedback, forcing the subordinate to forgive what has happened, and thereby setting up a new cycle of manipulation. Ambiguity is created in the subordinate, diminishing whatever power he or she had. Assertiveness helps to equalise such power relations.

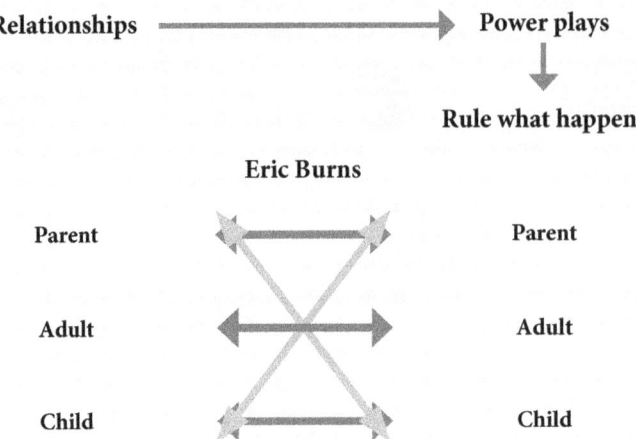

*To control the umwelt – Maintain your position despite opponent.
Develop an aura of authority.*

Figure 7.2: Depiction of the role of power in relationships[27]

Assertive behaviour reflects a positive, confident, direct and honest approach, while communicating respect for self and others. The assertive person influences, listens and fairly negotiates win-win results for all.

Assertive behaviour marks a way of living where you think for yourself and don't simply follow others; you make your own decisions and choices without feeling guilty. You say "no" without guilt, get help when you need it, speak your mind clearly and effectively, and learn to disagree without seeming hostile.

Therefore, be aware of your own self-worth; express your own ideas, opinions and talents so that you may serve the world in your own special way. Do not simply react in accordance with others' wishes or do and think what others tell you to. Rather take time to figure out what you want, need or think.

WHY SOME FIND IT DIFFICULT TO ACT ASSERTIVELY

Those who struggle with assertiveness believe that others may reject them or not like them when they act assertively. They are afraid that they may hurt or disappoint someone when saying "no", and frequently believe that others should come first, believing that their rights and opinions are of lesser importance. Furthermore, some who struggle with assertiveness do not know what they want but simply go along with others who hold stronger opinions than they do. Many suffer from high levels of fear and lack the skills for appropriate self-expression.

BENEFITS DERIVED FROM ENHANCED ASSERTIVENESS

Personal benefits

Assertiveness is full of benefits and liberates the formally passive person. It helps one move into close and more honest relationships. When being assertive, the other person feels respected and not put down.[28] Enhanced assertiveness can "exponentially increase our value, impact and well-being".[29] "When we employ these skills elegantly, we behave neither as victims nor as instruments of mass destruction"; we don't bottle up negative feelings or stress others out by exploding all over them. Acting assertively promotes self-confidence as you learn to make better decisions for yourself and increase the chances of getting what you want from life. You may maximise your sense of control over your life and emotions while you appropriately express your concerns, rather than bottling them up. You and not those around you are therefore in control. You may command others' respect owing to a rise in your self-esteem resulting from achieving your personal and professional goals. Others may start noticing and responding positively to you.

How others benefit

Assertive behaviour has a direct and positive effect on relationships by helping to equalise the balance of power in relationships, ruling the giving and receiving of respect while leaving room for compromise in conflict. Others feel comfortable around you because when you establish your boundaries, it provides certainty on what others may expect. It is appreciated when someone is honest and forthright, since it reduces the levels of ambiguity that the non-assertive person usually projects, thereby minimising possible conflict and misunderstanding.

DRAWBACKS TO ASSERTIVENESS

Being assertive does not promise a perfect, problem-free existence. It does, however, increase the chances (but does not guarantee) that you will be happy and fairly treated by others. Nor does it promise you that all problems will be solved or that you will always get what you want. Others may in fact initially resist your style and try to have you undo it.[30] They may even become hostile when you disagree with them, especially if, in the past, you mainly agreed with them. Some may even interpret the new style as your acting in a superior fashion.

Countering drawbacks

Once you have chosen a different behaviour path, staying with it can be challenging. However, sticking to assertion as consistently as possible is a prerequisite if you wish to establish a new way of living. In the process, you may have to ignore childish or opposing behaviour. In the event of others being upset with the new style of behaviour, you could express regret at others being taken aback with the new behaviour (but stick to the assertion). You need to be consistently assertive so as not to confuse others and create a new cycle of ambiguity. Trust that those who care about you will accept the new behaviour; request their support and be careful of those wanting to sabotage the transformation. Try to respond immediately to something which is bothering you – do not let a problem build up, luring you into explosive behaviour.

DEVELOPING ASSERTIVE BEHAVIOUR

Assertive skills can be learnt via education about the different styles, by getting to know your rights both at a personal and a work level, and by developing assertive attitudes and behaviours.[31] Changing how we think is influential; if we believe ourselves to be inferior to others, or that others aim to disadvantage us, we may act defensively and even elicit what we do not want. It is therefore frequently the meaning we attach to events rather than the actual events that elicit unassertive behaviour. We need to replace dysfunctional thoughts with more functional thoughts. Such thoughts get established in childhood due to our respective life experiences and tend to consolidate in adulthood.[32] This becomes the spectacles through which we observe and interpret life events. In developing assertive behaviour you need to ask a few important questions, such as: When should I act assertively? Is it worth the effort in this particular situation? For example, if this is a once-off situation, is it worthwhile putting a lot of energy into acting assertively with a difficult person you may never encounter again? You may choose to let the situation be.

Being effective at asserting oneself involves, *inter alia*, knowing how to read the situation well and to keep one's cool. It requires a level of flexibility and the use of so-called 'I-messages', which will be explained further on. A change in one's typical non-verbal behaviour is also required to support the new style.

As stated earlier, the unassertive individual first has to establish his or her own needs and wants. For the non-assertive person this can be very difficult, since they have put their own needs on hold for such a long time that they may have great difficulty uncovering them. Without knowing what these are it is difficult to act assertively, therefore this is really a starting point.

Setting boundaries to create an aura of authority through assertiveness

Along with establishing personal needs and wants, the individual has to establish and assert his or her boundaries when interacting with others.[33] See Figure 7.3 in this regard.

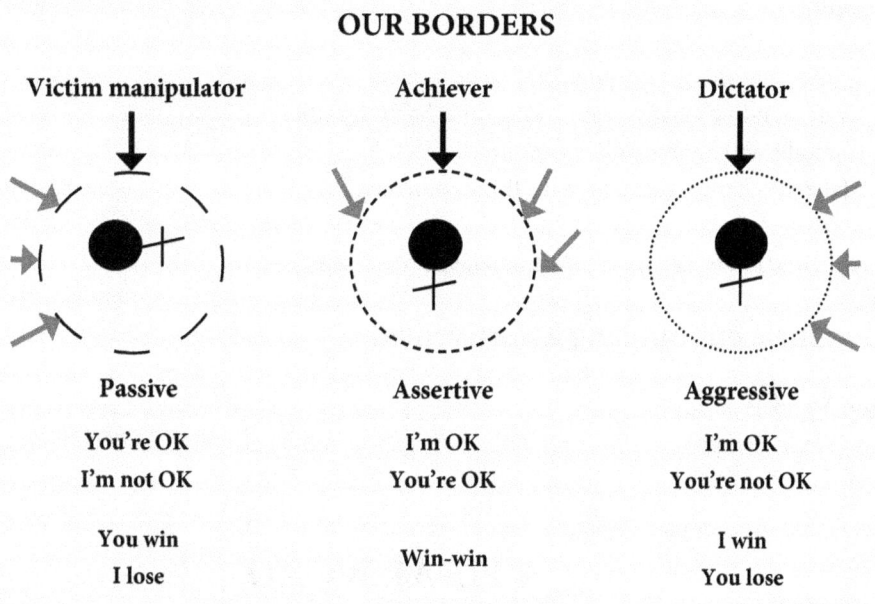

Figure 7.3: The role of boundaries in assertiveness[34]

Borders aim to protect us and provide a safe personal space. In much the same way as the borders of a house, our personal borders should be ours to allow people in or keep them out, according to our preference.

In viewing the above figure, it is clear that the non-assertive individual's borders are wide open, allowing too much influence from the outside to "intrude" and influence what happens "inside". Individuals feel victimised by what they frequently view as their "fate". They passively allow others to intrude into their personal space and feel they have little ability to defend. They experience the other as "OK" (acceptable) and themselves as "not-OK" (unacceptable). They expect to lose rather than win, and the non-decisive steering of their own lives invites and allows others to manage and manipulate them. They are therefore too flexible and act in this way to their own detriment, losing own and others' respect.

The aggressive person, on the other hand, inflexibly dictates his or her environment, keeping a tight rein on his or her borders, allowing in only those who are in awe of his or her power, shutting out critique that may require change. The aggressor takes on an approach of "I am OK, you are not OK; I win, you lose. There is only one way, and that is **my** way".

When viewing the borders of the assertive individual, it is clear that these are protective but open enough to allow for information flow from the outside world in order to adapt effectively. The assertive person, is, however, not unduly influenced by the outside world. He or she holds the view that both he or she and the other individuals are OK, and that both stand to win from their interactions or encounters. Effective borders allow the individual to maintain his or her position despite the opponent, and thereby to create an "aura of authority".

Remember:

- People treat you the way you "ask" to be treated.
- Understanding what you are asking for is half the battle.
- Carefully and honestly observe yourself.
- Make the changes that will make things different.

The real question is, are you ready to make the decision?

Individuals epitomising assertiveness

Nelson Mandela ... why?
FW de Klerk ... why?
Desmond Tutu ... why?

A FINAL WORD

People who are unable to assert themselves frequently find life a long haul. They yearn for others' respect and appreciation, but by allowing themselves to be taken advantage of, they lose the very respect they long for; they struggle to find their own rightful place and to display their own talents. However, when individuals learn to express their thoughts, feelings, and beliefs, defending their rights without denying the rights of others, assertiveness helps them to equalise power relations.

SECTION 2: ACTIVITIES FOR SKILLS DEVELOPMENT

Self-assessment

Individual activities

 Activity 1: Benchmark the level of your self-assertiveness

Spend a few moments assessing your level of assertiveness. Respond to the statements below honestly. Assign a number to each item using this scale:

1 = Very seldom or not true of me
2 = Seldom true of me
3 = Sometimes true of me
4 = Often true of me
5 = Very often true of me or always true of me

I have no difficulty expressing my honest opinions to a figure of authority, such as my boss.

1	2	3	4	5

I can ask a colleague to do something for me without feeling guilty or anxious.

1	2	3	4	5

I am comfortable when speaking to a large group of people.

1	2	3	4	5

I am able to stand up for my rights.

1	2	3	4	5

I am able to disagree with others without feeling anxious or guilty.

1	2	3	4	5

I believe that my ideas are as important as the next person's.

1	2	3	4	5

I can express my feeling of displeasure with a colleague.

1	2	3	4	5

I feel comfortable meeting strangers in a social situation.

1	2	3	4	5

I have clear opinions on a variety of topics.

1	2	3	4	5

When I make a mistake, I am the first to acknowledge it.

1	2	3	4	5

Total (x 2) = ...

Assertiveness scale

10	20	30	40	50	60	70	80	90	100

 **Activity 2: Becoming assertive**

In what type of situation do you struggle to act assertively?

....

....

With what type of person?

....

....

Are there people or colleagues who may experience you as overbearing?

....

....

Group activity

Activity 3

Role play 1

Dr Jones is a very good man at heart. He works very hard and is dedicated to what he does. He earns the respect of many. However, he struggles to contain his easily-aroused anger. He then becomes cold and extremely critical of both his superiors and subordinates, who can then do nothing right. He belittles them, so that subordinates often leave meetings in tears. He apologises later on and is frequently forgiven, while his colleagues hope that this was the last time. The atmosphere is tense, and everyone is on edge.

You are requested to manage the situation. Allocate people in the group to take up different roles.

....

....

Role play 2

Cia, a secretary to an HOD, is trustworthy, loyal, and excellent at what she does. Of late she has been very unhappy and considers leaving after 18 years. Since the current HOD was appointed, Cia's workload has increased exponentially. She is expected to take over duties of her seniors and has to constantly battle to get her work done, working until late at night, over weekends and even when the campus is closed due to unrest. The HOD is disrespectful about her personal matters and manipulates her to feel guilty and unworthy. The HOD targets people and successfully "works them away", threatening them with verbal and written warnings. Cia, being humble, has never had to fight for her position and finds it very challenging to stand up for herself.

You are required to assist Cia. Create a role play in which you help her sharpen her assertiveness skills. Read the information provided under point 4 below to assist you in this task.

Own work for personal growth: a to-do list for the next fortnight

 Activity 4

1 **Develop your non-verbal assertive behaviour:**

- Maintain good eye contact but do not stare.
- Practice an open, relaxed posture versus a closed one.
- Stand your ground and don't move away whilst respecting the personal space of the other.
- Stay calm and avoid, at all costs, angry outbursts or an aggressive stance, for example hands on hips.
- Display a sincere and non-threatening facial expression.
- Maintain a firm and steady tone of voice.[35]
- Practice in front of a mirror until you are comfortable with your posture.

2 **Recognise and be willing to exercise your basic rights**

- The right to choose
- The right to "be"
- The right to be respected
- The right to make mistakes
- The right to say "no"
- The right to ask for what you want
- What, for the first time, would you like to claim as a right?
- The right not to be bullied
- The right to be treated as an equal
- The right to express an opinion/preference
- The right to disagree/change your mind
- The right to fair treatment in the workplace

You and others have these rights!

3. **Become aware of your own unique feelings, needs and wants.**

   - Being in touch with your own feelings is essential for assertiveness. Practice daily by stopping yourself and trying to identify what you are feeling at that precise moment. Start right now.

   - It is difficult to be assertive if you don't know what you feel, want, or don't want. Spend a few minutes identifying your unmet needs and wants.

   - *I want...* ....
   ....

   - *I need...* ....
   ....

Observe yourself and repeat this after any unsatisfying interpersonal encounter, asking yourself what you wanted or needed so that you might have handled the situation better.

Next time, decide in advance how you wish the encounter to go and prepare yourself by knowing what you want and need. This will assist you to communicate clearly and unambiguously. Remember that you also serve the other person when you are clear about your needs and wants.

4. **Know what you feel and say what changes you want.**
   - For example, start by saying, "I feel upset and I want you to listen to me".
   - Do not assume others know your needs; you have to make your needs known!
   - Use a recent example where you felt upset or where your needs were not met. Decide how you felt and what changes you want to make.

5. **Practice assertive responses, first through role play, then try it in real life.**
   - **Specify your problem situation**
     - Who, when, what, how, goal.
   - **Developing an assertive response**
     - Evaluate your rights in this situation.
     - What do you have the right to ask?
     - Designate a time for discussing what you want.
   - **State the problem and its consequences for you**
     - "I need your feedback to know whether I am on the right track."
   - Express your feelings about particular situations
     - **Own** your reaction, don't **blame** others.
     - You don't care about me ... x
     - I feel unloved because ...√

- Make your request for changing the situation
  - Use assertive non-verbal behaviour.
  - Keep your request simple: "I would like…".
  - Avoid asking for more than one thing at a time.
  - Be **specific**: "I would like you to be home by 14:00."
  - Use I-statements: "I would like, I want to, I would appreciate it if…".
  - Object to behaviours, not personalities: "My problem is that you don't let me know" versus "You inconsiderate slob!", thereby preserving others' dignity.
  - Don't apologise for your request, and decline a request politely but firmly.
  - Make requests, not demands.
- Tell the person the consequences of gaining/not gaining his or her co-operation
  - "If you walk the dog, I'll rub your back."
- Describe natural consequences
  - "If you are late, I will leave without you."

6 **Learn to say "no".**
- Say no to requests you do not want to meet.
- Set limits on other people's demands for your time and energy when such demands conflict with your own needs and desires, without feeling guilty.
- *Example*:
  - Acknowledge another person's request by repeating it.
  - Explain your reason for declining.
  - Say no! If appropriate, propose an alternative where both individuals' needs will be met:
- "I understand you would like us to go to the show tonight. I have had a tough day and am exhausted. Could we make it…?"

7 **Learn to avoid manipulation.**
- Don't play the victim:
  - "I'm stupid and I cannot do this, but you are clever. Can you help me?"
- Stop feeling guilty and subordinate.
- Develop healthy communication – let others know about your needs, concerns and feelings.
- Develop your self-respect – the true key in developing and maintaining healthy relationships.
- Self-respect develops when we consistently strive to make healthy, fair and ethical choices.
- Self-respect is where assertiveness begins and manipulation ends.?
- Evaluate your rights.
- Make your requests:
  - "I would like"; "I want".

- Your statement needs to be:
    - firm;
    - simple and to the point;
    - without apology;
    - non-judgemental and non-blaming; and
    - always a request and not a demand.

Remember: assertive behaviour helps to develop:

- self-respect;
- self-worth.
- The pleaser wants to be perfect – to do things for others that he or she does not **really** want to do.
- This produces tension and conflict among:
    - family;
    - friends; and
    - work.

Assertive behaviour gains others' respect.

REFERENCES

Bamber, M.R. (2011). *Overcoming your workplace stress: a CBT-based self-help guide.* Hove, East Sussex: Routledge.

Bourne, E.J. (2000). *The anxiety and phobia workbook* (3rd ed.). Oakland, CA: New Harbinger Publications Inc.

Chandler, R. & Grzyb, E. (2000). *Is assertiveness the only way?* London: Impact Factory Copyright.

Hughes, M. & Terrel, B.J. (2012). *Emotional intelligence in action: training and coaching activities for leaders, manager, and teams* (2nd ed.). San Francisco: Pfeiffer.

Multi-Health Systems Inc. (2011). *The complete EQ-i 2.0 experience.* Toronto: Multi-Health Systems Inc.

Multi-Health Systems Inc & Jopie van Rooyen Psychometrics. (2011). *The complete EQ-i 2.0 experience.* Toronto: Multi-Health Systems Inc.

Podesta, C. (2012). *Get What You Want...The Right Way™ Coaching.* [Online] Available: http://conniepodesta.com/wp-content/uploads/arbonne/Connie-Podesta-Life-Would-Be-Easy-Part-3.pdf [Accessed 8 February 2018].

Prins, A. (2009). *Assertiveness: A fine art in empowerment.* (Unpublished workshop presentation). Bloemfontein: University of the Free State.

Prins, A. (2010a). *Emotional intelligence and leadership: A work wellness perspective.* Saarbrücken: VDM Verlag Dr Müller.

Prins, A. (2010b). *Wellness in the workplace.* (Unpublished presentation). Bloemfontein: University of the Free State.

Sadock, B.J., Sadock, V.A. & Ruiz, P. (2015). *Kaplan & Sadock's synopsis of psychiatry: behavioral sciences/ clinical psychiatry* (11th ed.). Philadelphia: Wolters Kluwer.

Stein, J.S. & Book, H. (2011). *The EQ Edge: Emotional intelligence and your success* (3rd ed.). Ontario: John Wiley & Sons.

Wall, B.L. (2007). *Coaching for emotional intelligence: the secret to developing the star potential in your employees.* New York: Amacom.

Williams, C. (2000). *Being assertive.* Leeds: University of Leeds Innovations Ltd (ULIS).

ENDNOTES

1. Saddock et al., 2015:879.
2. Wall, 2007.
3. Hughes & Terrell, 2011.
4. Stein & Book, 2011:107.
5. Bourne, 2000:277.
6. Stein & Book, 2011:105.
7. Stein & Book, 2011:108.
8. Bamber, 2011.
9. MHS & JvR, 2011.
10. Stein & Book, 2011:114.
11. Bamber, 2011.
12. Prins, 2009; 2010.
13. Williams, 2000.
14. Bamber, 2011.
15. Bamber, 2011:107.
16. Stein & Book, 2011:118.
17. Bamber, 2011.
18. Stein & Book, 2011:108.
19. Bamber, 2011.
20. Bourne, 2000.
21. Bamber, 2011.
22. Bamber, 2011.
23. Williams, 2000.
24. Stein & Book, 2011:118.
25. Stein & Book, 2011:114.
26. Bourne, 2000.
27. Prins, 2010a; 2010b.
28. Stein & Book, 2011:117.
29. Hughes & Terrell, 2011:60.
30. Chandler & Grzyb, 2000.
31. Bamber, 2011.
32. Bamber, 2011.
33. Chandler & Grzyb, 2000.
34. Prins, 2010a; 2010b.
35. Bamber, 2011.
36. Podesta, 2012.

Chapter 8

INDEPENDENCE

Annette Weyers

The mark of an educated mind is to be able to entertain a thought without accepting it.
—Aristotle

SECTION 1: OVERVIEW

The capacity for independence implies the ability to be self-directed and to withstand the appeal to conform. Guided by your own inner standards, you can construct your life in a way that is best suited to pursue your interests and realise your personal aspirations. It seems the capacity for independence is central to health and happiness – a compelling reason to broaden your ability to think and act in an independent manner.

After completing this chapter, you should be able to:

- define independence;
- understand the theory informing independence;
- differentiate between independent and dependent behaviours;
- understand individualist and collectivist societies/cultures;
- understand the value of independent behaviour;
- reflect on ways to improve own levels of independence;
- identify individuals who epitomise independence;
- assess your own level of independence; and
- implement individual and group activities to enhance independence.

INDEPENDENCE DEFINED

Independence can be defined in more than one way, for example:

- Independence is the ability to be self-directed and self-controlled in one's thinking and actions and to be free of emotional dependency.[1]
- Independence is the ability to think for oneself and not be unduly influenced by the thoughts, desires and emotions of others.[2]

- Independent behaviour refers to one's ability to act independently of environmental pressures and the strength to resist unnecessary conformity or obedience to authority.[3]
- Independence is the ability to care for oneself and be free from the control or power of another.[4]

THEORY INFORMING INDEPENDENCE

Individualism and collectivism

Most cultures can be defined according to the relative value they place on either individualism or collectivism. These two contrasting orientations represent two divergent models of self.[5] Simply put, whether the self is identified as independent or interdependent is influenced by either the individualistic or the collectivistic cultural system. The eventual identity individuals adopt (individualistic or collectivistic) will influence their thoughts, emotions, the goals they consider meaningful, the values they endorse, and how they interact with their environment.

Individualistic cultures are mostly associated with Western societies: Europe, North America, Great Britain, Australia and New Zealand. These cultures define identity in terms of a unique combination of personal attributes and abilities rather than group membership, and assign greater importance to individual goals, values, individual freedom and personal responsibility. Self-reliance, individual choice and assertiveness are highly valued. The collectivist cultures, which are mostly associated with Eastern and African cultures, emphasise an interdependent identity construct (defined as part of a social network). Individuals give priority to the group's goals, treasure the welfare of the group, have a great sense of social responsibility, and their first choice would be to cooperate with others.[6]

Ideal typical identities of individualistic and collectivistic cultures[7]

Individualism	Collectivism
• Independent view of self	• Interdependent view of self
• Emphasise individual rights	• Put the interests of the group first
• Self-directed	• Emphasise cooperation with others
• Individual choice	• Fulfil social roles
• Self-reliant	• Value connectedness to family, peers, religion
• Assertiveness	• Accept subordination
• Individual rights and freedom	• Collective rights and freedom
• Individual responsibility	• Social responsibility

It would be a misconception to assume that every person in either an individualistic or a collectivistic culture displays all the typical traits engendered by that culture.

Autonomy as a basic human need

All humans share the need for autonomy, and as with other basic needs, the fulfilment of the need for autonomy is considered essential for growth. Although one of the key developmental tasks in adolescence is to achieve a sense of autonomy, expanding and maintaining a sense of autonomy is a process that continues through all stages of life.[8]

A sense of autonomy entails feeling free to be who you are, i.e. having well-defined internal standards, being confident in your own opinions, being comfortable with self-direction, and being generally free of coercion from others. The need for autonomy is met when you pursue self-selected goals and interests that have personal relevance - your choices cohere with your needs and values and activities are inner directed. A well-developed sense of autonomy fortifies the ability to act in an independent manner.[9]

Independent and dependent personalities

The maxim, "to stand on your own feet", aptly describes the **independent personality**. This is the person who resists social pressure to conform to predictable life patterns. Instead, he or she makes life choices that cohere with his or her interests, values and self-selected goals. The independent person has the courage to persist with a chosen course of action, regardless of disapproval and opposition. Independence should not be confused with a self-centred preoccupation with own interests at the expense of other people. Nor does independence infer a detachment from others; you can be independent but still have supportive relationships and be part of an extensive social network. Rather, independence assumes flexibility and the wisdom to know when to ask for input from others and then make a decision that is personally acceptable to you.[10]

Note: Remind yourself that others also have a need for independence and extend them the courtesy of expressing their independence.

The traits of the **dependent personality** are anti-ethical to those of the independent personality. Dependent people lack a healthy self-esteem and self-confidence, so they constantly refer to others for reassurance. They need copious amounts of advice before making even insignificant decisions, and they submit their own needs to those on whom they are dependent. Their unassertive behaviour and failure to determine their own aspirations and needs defeat any attempt to set goals that will enable them to develop their full potential and to achieve success at both a personal and organisational level. Their clingy nature eventually irritates others and they do not gain the respect they so desperately seek, leading them to become even more submissive. In instances where functioning is severely affected, **dependent personality disorder** may be diagnosed. According to the DSM-V

(2013), dependent personality disorder refers to "a pervasive and excessive need to be taken care of that leads to submissive and clinging behaviour and fears of separation. It begins in early adulthood and is present in a variety of contexts". (For more information on dependent personality disorder, consult the DSM-V.)

The table below highlights the differences between independent and dependent personalities:[11]

Independent personality	Dependent personality
• High levels of self confidence	• Lacks confidence in own abilities
• Prepared to take calculated risks	• Pervasive feelings of helplessness
• Trusts own judgement	• Limited capacity to make decisions
• Takes initiative	• Lacks self-motivation
• Takes responsibility for decisions	• Driven by fear of displeasing others
• Demonstrates effective behaviour	• Fearful of taking care of themselves
• Pursues own ideas and course of action	• Does not cope well with life demands
• Not dominated by others	• Overly reliant on others – seek external approval
• Creative and interested to pursue novel ideas	• Fear of making mistakes

How would you rate yourself regarding the personality traits in the table above?

....

....

THE BENEFITS OF INDEPENDENCE

When the skill of independence is well developed it yields generous rewards in your personal and work life.

Personal functioning

Independence is an important skill that contributes to emotional, psychological and spiritual well-being. It helps you to set parameters for a way of life that is personally meaningful. As a consequence, one may experience positive emotions such as satisfaction, contentment and a sense of achievement. Psychological well-being is promoted when independence engenders the experiences of being in control, effective, self-motivated, self-confident and competent.[12] Independence creates the conditions that allow for the expression of one's true self, to live according to one's own values, and to fulfil one's life purpose. In this manner, independence enhances one's spiritual well-being.[13]

At work

Companies are increasingly encouraging "...less centralized control and the empowerment of employees to be self-efficient and to self-manage...".[14] The demand for greater self-management and self-efficiency underscores the importance of independence as a core competency for optimal functioning at work. Independent employees are more likely to experience career success because they:

- can work without constant supervision or reassurance;
- are prepared to take calculated risks;
- show initiative;
- engage in challenging tasks with confidence;
- set career goals aligned with their personal aspirations;
- seek out novel ways to hone their skills;
- are self-motivated to achieve career goals;
- are able to pursue their own ideas;
- readily accept responsibility for their own decisions and actions;
- when called for, analyse situations on their own; and
- formulate solutions without constantly second guessing themselves.[15]

Self-directed employees are competent in managing their career paths; they are more likely to increase their personal effectiveness and to achieve their career goals.

Note: Independence is not to be confused with high-handed behaviour that forces its own agenda on co-workers. Although highly independent, one needs to remain sensitive to colleagues' emotions and opinions. Be prepared to listen to other views, be open to coalitions, and aim to build collaborative relationships.

STRATEGIES TO DEVELOP INDEPENDENCE

One's level of independence can be expanded by strengthening your relevant EI capacities, employing mental rehearsal and improving your internal dialogue.

Emotional intelligent capacities

The ability to act independently can be improved, particularly when it is done in tandem with related EI competencies such as self-regard, assertiveness and problem-solving. For example, positive self-regard gives you the confidence to uphold and live according to your inner standards; assertiveness is a vital skill when you are pressured to conform to norms you cannot support; and problem-solving is an extremely useful skill when obstacles interfere with the pursuit of your goals.

Mental rehearsal

Mental rehearsal is a psychological technique in which you mentally perform rather than behaviourally act out a scenario, i.e. you imagine performing the scenario in your mind's eye without actually doing it.

Steps in mental rehearsal

Mental rehearsal can help you convey decisions in such a way that you do not hurt collaborative relationships. Rather than simply marching off in your own direction, consider how your decisions would affect those who work with you. With the help of mental rehearsal, you can practice how to gain the support of key role players and involve others in the decision-making process.

Mental rehearsal involves the following steps:

1. Close your eyes, breathe deeply and relax.
2. Mentally tell yourself that you can gain support for your decisions without hurting working relationships.
3. Mentally picture yourself approaching the relevant role players.
4. Make sure you stay relaxed and focused.
5. Mentally rehearse what you will say and how you will involve and motivate co-workers. Carefully consider and rehearse the words you will use and your tone of voice, and picture how your body language can support your message.
6. Repeat step five several times.
7. Praise yourself for successfully having performed this task – praising yourself is helpful because self-reinforcement is a key to self-motivation.

Internal dialogue

The brain is always active; it is estimated that a person has about 60 000 thoughts a day. Regrettably, not all of these thoughts are productive, therefore the contents of your internal dialogue need to be scrutinised. Most of us are oblivious of our self-talk, for example, you may constantly berate yourself with self-criticism. "I will never be able to express my view", or "I do not have the guts to tell the rest of the group that I do not agree with them". The good news is that inner dialogue can be improved.

Steps to improve self-talk

Here are a few guidelines in respect of self-talk:

1. Tune in to your self-talk.
2. Replace self-defeating messages with positive affirmations.
3. Practice your positive affirmations often.
4. Refer to past successes.

Here are some examples of positive self-affirmations:

- "I can trust that things will work out."
- "I meet problems with confidence and poise."
- "I have the courage to express my views."

Individuals epitomising independence

Winston Churchill
Albert Einstein
Martin Luther King
Emily Hobhouse
Others?

A FINAL WORD

The absence of reflective reasoning increases the risk of creating a culture of mindless conformity. Being part of the "in group" or being on the right side of the popular view has an almost irresistible appeal. At the peril of their independent point of view, people often witlessly repeat whatever ideology is most popular, rather than taking a contradictory stance or arguing for their beliefs.

It is hard work to formulate your own convictions; you will have to revisit old assumptions, question unedited information, abandon "groupthink" and consider all the relevant facts. Without the capacity for independence, you become a parrot of others' ideas, denying your own creativity and living a life that imitates what is considered the most in vogue at the time.

SECTION 2: ACTIVITIES FOR SKILLS DEVELOPMENT

Self-assessment

Individual activities

 Activity 1

Spend a few moments assessing your level of independence. Answer the questions honestly.

1 = Very seldom or not true of me
2 = Seldom true of me
3 = Sometimes true of me
4 = Often true of me
5 = Very often true of me or true of me

While I respect other people's opinions, I rely on my own judgement when making a decision.

1	2	3	4	5

I'm more a leader than a follower.

1	2	3	4	5

People tell me that I have a mind of my own.

1	2	3	4	5

People often come to me for advice.

1	2	3	4	5

I'm not afraid to disagree with people.

1	2	3	4	5

Multiply the total by 4 to arrive at a total out of 100.

My level of independence

10	20	30	40	50	60	70	80	90	100

 Activity 2

Consider the following:

You are out socialising with your manager and colleagues. You are all enjoying yourselves when the conversation turns to matters that are more serious, among them, affirmative action. You learn that your manager and your colleagues differ from your personal views in this regard.

How will you manage the situation?

....

....

 Activity 3

Group activity

Read the following case study, and then answer the questions:

> Janet is a 34-year-old librarian who lives with her mother. She is attracted to men with strong personalities. Invariably her relationships begin well, but with time they become abusive. Janet usually builds her life around a particular male partner. She has great difficulty making decisions without an excessive amount of advice and reassurance from others. Janet does not know what she wants in life; when she is abused or misused in a relationship, she is submissive and has difficulty expressing her disagreement. She is unwilling to make even reasonable demands from her friends or colleagues for fear of losing their approval. Unfortunately, what Janet does not realise is that, for the most part, her male partners are irritated by her clinging behaviour. They begin to lose respect for her and then end the relationship.

You are Janet's colleague/friend/counsellor. How would you go about helping Janet to achieve a greater level of independence?

....

....

 **Activity 4**

In your groups, discuss the potential downside of too much emphasis on individualism as exemplified in Western culture. Comment on the notion of 'individualism'.

....

....

What are the boundaries of independence in leadership?

....

....

Does your company encourage independent thinking?

....

....

What would the consequences be for your company if there was an absence of independent thinking?

....

....

Own work for personal growth: a to-do list for the next fortnight

Activity 5: Independence of mind

How independent of mind are you?

....

....

Consider the last four weeks (in your place of work, family, at leisure) and identify occasions where you acted independently.

....

....

Identify the obstacles that prevent you from acting independently.

....

....

How would you go about improving your level of independence?

....

....

REFERENCES

American Psychiatric Association. (2013). *Diagnostic and Statistical Manual of Mental Disorders* (5th ed.). Washington: American Psychiatric Association.

Bar-on, R. & Parker, D.A. (2000). *The Handbook of Emotional Intelligence: Theory, Development, Assessment and Application at Home, School, and in the Workplace.* San Francisco: Jossey-Bass.

Baumgardner, S. & Crothers, M. (2014). *Positive Psychology* (1st ed.). New Delhi, India: Pearson.

Bergh, Z. (2007). Work Adjustment and Maladjustment. In Z. Bergh and A. Theron (eds.). *Psychology in the Work Context.* Cape Town: Oxford University Press.

Bergh, Z. & Theron, A. (2007). *Psychology in the Work Context.* Cape Town: Oxford University Press.

Carkuff, R.R. (1981). *Toward Actualising Human Potential.* Amhurst: Human Resource Development Press.

Compton, W.C. (2005). *An Introduction to Positive Psychology.* London: Thompson Wadsworth.

Hughes, M. & Terrel, J.B. (2012). *Emotional Intelligence in Action* (2nd ed.). San Francisco: Pfeiffer.

Merriam-Webster Online Dictionary. (2010). *Independence* [Online]. Available: http://www.merriam-webster.com/dictionary/independence [Accessed 4 May, 2010].

O'Connor, R. (2005). *Undoing Perpetual Stress: The Missing Connection Between Depression, Anxiety, and 21st Century Illness.* New York: Berkley Books.

Sigelman, C.K. & Rider, E.A.)2009). *Life Span Human Development* (6th ed.). Belmont: Wadsworth.

Stein, S. & Book, H. (2011). *The EQ edge: Emotional Intelligence and your Success* (3rd ed.). San Francisco: Jossey-Bass.

Weiten, W. (2002). *Psychology Themes and Variations* (5th ed.). Belmont: Wadsworth.

ENDNOTES

1. Stein & Book, 2011:76.
2. Hughes & Terrel, 2012:63.
3. Compton, 2005:178.
4. Merriam-Webster's Online Thesaurus, 2010.
5. Baumgardner & Crothers, 2014.
6. Weiten, 2002; Hughes & Terrel, 2012; Baumgardner & Crothers, 2014.
7. Sigelman & Rider, 2009; Baumgardner & Crothers, 2014.
8. Sigelman & Rider, 2009; Baumgardner & Crothers, 2014.
9. Baumgardner & Crothers, 2014.
10. Stein & Book, 2011; Hughes & Terrel, 2012.
11. Carkuff, 1981; Stein & Book, 2011; Hughes & Terrel, 2012; O'Connor, 2005; Bergh & Theron, 2007; Sigelman & Rider, 2009; Baumgardner & Crothers, 2014.
12. Stein & Book, 2011; Hughes & Terrel, 2012; Baumgardner & Crothers, 2014.
13. Baumgardner & Crothers, 2014.
14. Berg, 2007:435.
15. Bar-On & Parker, 2000; Berg, 2007; Stein & Book, 2011; Hughes & Terrel, 2012.

SECTION C: INTERPERSONAL

Interpersonal represents the ability to build relationships based on trust and caring; to express an understanding of a different perspective; and to act responsibly while caring for others, your team, and the larger organisation/society of which you form part.

The following skills are discussed:

Chapter 9: Interpersonal relationships
Chapter 10: Empathy
Chapter 11: Social responsibility

Chapter 9

INTERPERSONAL RELATIONSHIPS

Annette Weyers

Personal relationships are the fertile soil from which all advancement, all success, all achievement in real life grows.
—Ben Stein

SECTION 1: OVERVIEW

Humans are fundamentally social animals with an innate propensity to share their lives with others. Unless you live on a deserted island, you cannot avoid being in a variety of relationships throughout the course of your life. The quality of these relationships has a profound influence on your life; indeed, high-quality relationships are deemed essential for your emotional and psychological well-being.[1] Fulfilling and meaningful relationships do not come about by accident; rather, they are the product of hard work, commitment, a willingness to master the skills necessary to build relationships, and at times personal sacrifice.

After completing this chapter, you should be able to:

- define interpersonal relationships;
- understand the theory informing interpersonal relationships;
- describe the benefits of sound interpersonal relationships;
- identify individuals who epitomise competency in interpersonal relationships;
- reflect on ways to improve your own competency in interpersonal relationships; and
- implement individual and group activities to enhance the quality of interpersonal relationships.

INTERPERSONAL RELATIONSHIPS DEFINED

Interpersonal relationships are defined as:

- social phenomena formed through the interaction between participants. These relationships cannot exist outside the participants involved.[2]
- the ability to establish and maintain mutually satisfying relationships that are characterised by the ability to both "give" and 'take" in relationships, where trust and compassion are openly expressed in word or by behaviour.[3]
- emotional closeness, intimacy and giving and receiving affection.[4]

THEORY INFORMING INTERPERSONAL RELATIONSHIPS

Social sciences, which are interested in the social nature of human behaviour, have affirmed by means of a plethora of studies that relationships play a key role in the health and happiness of humans. For example, it was reported that "of the many factors that contribute to well-being, only social relationships consistently predict happiness across widely differing cultures".[5] Because of the overwhelming evidence that connects well-being to relationships, it is an area of keen interest in the broader field of positive psychology. Consequently, emotional intelligence as an integral part of positive psychology also endorses the development of interpersonal skills, in order to enhance optimal functioning and overall well-being.

The need for interpersonal relationships

The urge to create collaborative bonds with others could be described as a built-in biological motive, which has been imperative from the beginning of time for the survival of humans. Therefore, this sense of belonging is considered a fundamental human need, compelling the formation of "at least a minimum quantity of lasting and significant interpersonal relationships".[6] It could be said that to survive the jungle that is the modern world, the establishment of cooperative alliances is as imperative as it ever was.

Living and working in a social context necessitates interactions within a diversity of relationships on a daily basis - from casual associations to close and intimate connections. Furthermore, interpersonal relationships are important in all spheres of life: family, friendship, work, romantic affiliations, leadership, teams and community. The importance of high-quality relationships is emphasised by Hughes and Terrel[7], who observed that "the quality of our interpersonal relationships establishes the social and emotional climate in our families, neighbourhoods, and workplaces. When our relationships are working well, they provide the common ground where we get to enjoy our own experience of humanness through sharing it with others".

We need high-quality interpersonal relationships to thrive. This is evidenced in the crucial role that relationships play in providing a medium that is conducive to:

- optimal development;
- shaping of a sense of self;
- personal growth;
- fulfilling the need for belonging;
- social support;
- nurturing; and
- intimacy.[8]

> *Interpersonal relationships offer the opportunity to practice being the best person we can be: to be patient, kind, tolerant, forgiving, unselfish, remorseful, affectionate, to seek forgiveness, to live up to our promises.*[9]

The nature of positive interpersonal relationships

An understanding of the nature of positive relationships can be helpful when we strive to establish meaningful connections with others.

Close interpersonal relationships

In close relationships, people spend time together in different life spheres, more so than in casual relationships. The depth of connection in these relationships is characterised by:

- an interdependence in day-to-day interactions;
- unconditional support, compassion, and affirmation;
- assured fairness and equity in interactions;
- participation in various joint activities over an extended period of time; and
- an ongoing and intense impact on one another in various settings.[10]

Intimacy is the key element that is most central to the distinction between casual and close relationships. It refers to mutual understanding, depth of connection and degree of involvement.[11] The person in an intimate relationship has the experience of being understood, affirmed and cared for. Intimacy is established through:

- *knowledge* – intimate knowledge about the 'true self' of the other person, including extensive knowledge about their personal history, deepest feelings, strengths and faults;
- *trust* – mutual trust that confidences will not be broken;

- *caring* – genuine concern for the other, paying attention to the other person's feelings, monitoring and maintaining the quality of the relationship, being understanding and offering understanding;
- *interdependence* – intertwined lives and mutual influence on one another's feelings, actions and thinking;
- *mutuality* – the sense of 'we-ness'; and
- *commitment* - the intention to stay in the relationship through the good and the bad.[12]

None of these characteristics in and of themselves guarantee an intimate relationship; all relationships require hard work, giving your best effort, keeping your word, loyalty, and at times, personal sacrifice.[13]

Transforming relationships

Relationships can be transformed and strengthened by:
- integrity;
- warmth;
- kindness;
- tolerance;
- dependability;
- support;
- honesty;
- accountability;
- a sense of humour;
- loyalty;
- trust; and
- sincerity.[14]

What would you add to the list?

Note: It is important to be able to discern between relationships you can invest in and those from which you have to walk away, for example abusive relationships.[15]

Relationships at work

A significant part of our day is spent at work, making it practically impossible to avoid interactions with co-workers. On a personal level, these relationships play a critical role in job satisfaction, effective performance and career progress. Interpersonal relationships also have a significant impact on organisational functioning through their effect on the organisational climate, productivity, collaboration and work processes. Therefore, workplace relationships are of vital importance to the employee and the organisation. As a business strategy, relationships are a valuable asset that may give companies an edge over their rivals.[16] However, developing and managing relationships as a business resource pose an immense challenge.

The relationship networks of a company not only include employees and customers, but also every individual or group with whom the company interacts. All relationships within the company, as well as the relationships with every person the company has contact with, have the potential to affect success. Far-sighted organisations appreciate the importance of their relationship networks, and prudently and intentionally strive to build solid personal relationships with business partners and co-workers.[17]

Four categories of work relationships are discussed below.[18] How would you rate these four types of relationships in terms of their ability to promote organisational functioning?

- **Traditional transactional relationships:** when employees are treated as commodities that only have value in terms of the work they perform.
- **The paternalistic relationship:** the relationship between managers and employees is similar to that of parents and their children. Management provides security and benefits, but members of staff are not encouraged to exercise independent judgement. The aim is to control employees.
- **Adversarial relationships**: generate negativity, tension and low motivation. Relationships are characterised by disagreements, antagonism, mistrust and conflict. When conflict is not externalised, it may be expressed through passive-aggressive behaviour.
- **Partnerships:** encourage a "...collaborative approach and a willingness to distribute power so that everyone can contribute and win – a 'win-win' situation".[19]

Almost all organisations require their employees to work in teams. In high-performing teams, trust is a key aspect of the relationship between members. Team members are more willing to collaborate and share information when they trust one another. The following dimensions help to build trust:

- *Integrity* – honesty and sincerity.
- *Competence* – interpersonal skills and knowledge.
- *Consistency* – reliability, stability and predictability.
- *Loyalty* – a willingness to protect and save face for someone.
- *Openness* – a willingness to share ideas and information.[20]

What would you add to this list?

Note: There are no overall differences in emotional intelligence between male and female leaders, however female leaders do score higher on relationship skills, suggesting that they are better at initiating, developing and maintaining relationships.[21]

THE BENEFITS OF POSITIVE INTERPERSONAL RELATIONSHIPS

The value of high-quality, positive interpersonal relationships can be observed in both one's personal and work lives.

Personal functioning

To be involved in nurturing relationships is one of life's great rewards. These relationships offer succour, validation, stability, intimacy and connectedness. Predictably, positive relationships greatly contribute to various positive outcomes in the physical, emotional, psychological and social life domains, for example:

Physical well-being – The findings of extensive research report that being part of satisfying relationships is associated with greater resistance to disease, lower rates of coronary disease, faster recovery from heart surgery, lower mortality, and being less likely to die prematurely.[22] The bottom line - sound relationships are good for your health!

Emotional well-being – Positive relationships are an ongoing source of positive affect such as joy, optimism, contentment, and the experience of being valued and loved.

Psychological well-being – rewarding relationships significantly contribute to psychological adjustment, increased resilience, positive self-esteem, and greater confidence. It fulfils the need for intimacy and provides powerful affirmation and acceptance of the true self.

Social well-being – the positive relationships of a social network (family, friends, colleagues, members of a community) provide the context in which to cultivate social well-being. For example, they offer the opportunity for *social engagement,* referring to the sense of being actively involved with others and fully engaged in life; *social contribution,* or the gratifying experience of making a valuable contribution to society; and *social integration,* meaning the sense of belonging to a community, as well as the experience of being comforted and supported by the community. The support from a social network acts as a buffer against adversity and stress.

> ## Social support
>
> The following are examples of various types of social support:
>
> - **Emotional support** – when empathy, understanding and love are offered.
> - **Material or instrumental assistance** - this include tangible forms of help, for example providing goods, finances or transport.
> - **Information** – providing helpful information, giving advice and offering suggestions.
> - **Esteem support** - provides positive feedback in the form of encouragement and praise.[23]

The diverse and significant benefits generated by relationships serve to further support the notion that healthy interpersonal relationships are essential to well-being.

Success at work

The work environment comprises a complex system of relationships. How these relationships are managed has a profound effect not only on the individual employee's career success, but also on the prosperity of the organisation.

An organisational system that is directly influenced by relationships is the organisational climate; a positive ambiance substantially increases the probability that an employee and his/her organisation will succeed.

The benefits for the employee could include:

- higher levels of job satisfaction;
- lower stress level;
- more positive affect;
- greater expectation of career progress; and
- an increased sense of well-being.[24]

The benefits for the organisation could include:

- employee loyalty and commitment;
- a motivated workforce;
- lower absenteeism;
- enhanced work engagement;
- greater productivity;
- better teamwork and co-operation;
- more likely to generate solutions;
- lower staff turnover; and
- better organisational functioning.

How would you rate the emotional climate in your organisation?

....

....

STRATEGIES FOR DEVELOPING INTERPERSONAL RELATIONSHIPS

Until we find a substitute for personal relationships, we will have to undertake the hard work required to build and maintain mutually satisfying relationships.

Emotional intelligence

The ability to build satisfying relationships is not the only component of this EI subscale; according to Stein and Book,[25] it also includes "the ability to feel at ease and comfortable in such relationships and to possess positive expectations concerning social intercourse". All the emotional intelligence competencies contribute to some extent to the competency to build relationships and to feel comfortable in them. Competencies such as assertiveness, flexibility, reality testing and impulse control are valuable assets that can assist you in the quest to create and sustain sound relationships. In particular, the ability to be *empathic* is invaluable when interacting with others as it helps you to connect to others in a more meaningful way. The communication skills highlighted in the module on empathy are essential for the development of meaningful relationships. Please refer to Part One: Competencies related to EI behaviour.

Developing social skills

Competency in social skills largely determines success or failure in relationships. Those who have mastered social skills tend to be more confident and more open in social interactions.[26] The good news is that social skills can be learned and improved!

There are many programmes to choose from should you decide to expand your social skills. One example of such a programme is that of Turner and Beidel (in Stein and Book[27]) called *Social Effectiveness Training*. It is beyond the scope of this book to discuss the whole programme, however the examples below serve as an illustration of how social skills may be improved.

The programme is divided into three parts:

1. **Becoming aware of your social environment**

    Develop sensitivity as to when, where and why to begin and end contact.

2. **Interpersonal skills enhancement**

    Learn the skills of verbal and non-verbal communication, for example, how to be a good listener and when to switch topics.

3. **Presentation skills**
    Learn to be comfortable talking to groups; this skill will help you to cultivate useful networks and to establish meaningful relationships.

Building successful relationships

How does a close relationship between people develop? What does it take to build healthy relationships? These are not easy questions to answer, because there is not a fool proof, step-by-step instruction manual on how to undertake this task. However, an important step in creating meaningful relationships is to make sure that the following core elements (characteristic of high-quality relationships) are well developed:

- **Knowledge through self-disclosure:** In close relationships, people have extensive knowledge about one another. They share knowledge about their deepest feelings, beliefs, values and personal history through reciprocal self-disclosure. This facilitates the establishment of mutual understanding and forms the basis for the acceptance and affirmation of the other person's authentic self.

- **Attributions:** We attribute reasons to the way people behave; in other words, we try to explain to ourselves why people behave in a particular way. For example, when a colleague is late with a report you can attribute positively (he is swamped with work) or negatively (he did not plan well and now I have to wait). Relationship-enhancing attributions are more conducive to positive relationships. In contrast, persistence in distress-maintaining attributions will erode relationships over time. Positive attributions concerning minor events are not to be confused with making excuses for gross negligence or abusive behaviour.

- **Caring:** This is demonstrated through concern for the other person and by paying attention to their feelings; it conveys the message that the relationship is a high priority in our life. We express our appreciation of the relationship by caring about little things such as remembering anniversaries, birthdays and keeping in contact.

- **Trust:** Trust refers to the belief that the other person will not harm you and will not break confidences or share sensitive information about you with others. Trust is vital in relationships and a precondition for self-disclosure.

- **Reciprocity:** This involves the ability to give and take in a relationship; it implies not taking advantage of one other.

- **Commitment:** Commitment is associated with loyalty, keeping your word, giving your best effort, and being dedicated to working hard to make a relationship work. This is the opposite of the fair-weather friend who quickly departs at the first sign of difficulties.[28]

What would you add to the list above?

....

....

Self-knowledge

Whether we like it or not, we all have blind spots regarding our behaviour and how it affects people. This is a dilemma, because you cannot change what you are unaware of. However, there are techniques that can be used to increase self-awareness and uncover hidden behaviour patterns. One such technique was developed by Joseph Luft and Harry Ingram. The model they designed to facilitate the process is called the Johari Window.[29] This model is particularly useful for teams, but can be adapted for use in families and close relationships. The Johari Window generates information about feelings, behaviour patterns, attitudes and motivations, which can help you to improve communication and interpersonal relationships.

The model has two dimensions; the first involves feedback to yourself and what you know about yourself, while the second is about what other people know about you, including your blind areas. Within the feedback dimension are four elements - open, blind, hidden and unknown (see the model below), i.e. there are elements that are known and unknown to the self. The same applies to exposure to others - there are elements known to others and elements unknown to them.[30]

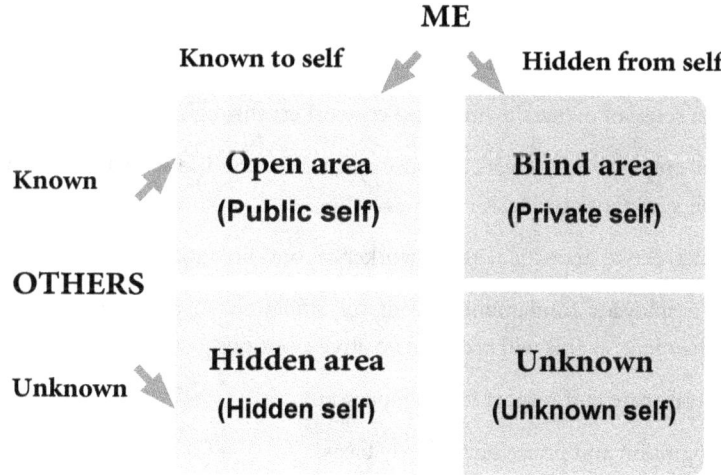

Figure 9.1: Johari window

- **Open area:** What everyone knows about you and you know about yourself. For example, everyone may know about your struggle with social skills, shyness or, on a more positive note, that you are optimistic or have a good sense of humour.

- **Blind area:** Things others know about you that you are unaware of. For example, people may experience you as warm and friendly, qualities you did not know you possess. On the negative side, people can experience you as abrasive or arrogant and unapproachable.

- **Hidden areas:** Those things only you know about yourself and which you keep from others. As you get to know and trust other people, you may decide to share personal information that can promote intimacy in a relationship, for example that you have a fear of rejection or failure.

- **Unknown areas:** Things you have never recognised about yourself and that no-one else is aware of.

The feedback will include positive and negative factors that have an impact on your relationships. Use this new knowledge about yourself to advance the positive factors that enrich relationships further, and change and improve those aspects of your communication and behaviour patterns that harm relationships.

Building effective relationships at work

Relationships in the workplace are more likely to be successful if they follow the principles of a partnership; the following strategies support this aim:[31]

- Affirm your belief that your co-workers are your equal. Interact with them on equal terms.

- Treat colleagues as partners and create rewarding wins for them.

- Develop a sense of ownership amongst co-workers through high-quality connections.

- Empower employees by creating opportunities for the individual or group to define and shape a response to a task.

- Build constructive dialogue with co-workers about direction and decisions.

- Address employees' fundamental needs for affiliation, involvement, recognition and accomplishment, as this will promote positive emotions.

- Demonstrate care and respect for each person.

- Give recognition and praise on a weekly basis.

- Regularly encourage personal and professional development.

Note: The best way to improve a relationship is usually to start with yourself, for example, ask yourself how committed you really are to make the relationship work. Be sincere when examining which of your actions and responses are hurtful or undermine the relationship. Do not wait for the other person to take the first step.

20 Robbins in Bergh & Theron, 2007.
21 Newman, 2008:131.
22 Compton, 2005; Bergh & Theron, 2007:204; Sigelman & Rider, 2009.
23 Bergh, 2007:204.
24 Bar-On & Parker, 2000; Bergh & Theron, 2007.
25 Stein & Book, 2011:125.
26 Bergh, 2007.
27 Stein & Book, 2011.
28 Breckler et al., 2006; Leimon & McMahon, 2009; Baumgardner & Crothers, 2014.
29 Albertyn & Koortzen, 2007.
30 Albertyn & Koortzen, 2007; Leimon & McMahon, 2009.
31 Newman, 2008:146.

Chapter 10

EMPATHY

Eugene van Niekerk

Sharing the other's innermost world – their setbacks, triumphs, sadness, grief and joy – is probably the greatest privilege known to man, second only to knowing the true nature of God.

– Eugene van Niekerk[1]

SECTION 1: OVERVIEW

When we honestly ask ourselves which person in our lives means the most to us, we often find that it is those who, of giving advice and solution or cures, have chosen to share our pain and touch our wounds with a warm and tender hand. The friend who can be silent with us in a moment of despair or confusion, who can stay with us in an hour of grief and bereavement, who can tolerate not knowing, not curing, not healing, and face with us the reality of our powerlessness; that is a friend who cares.[2]

Stephan Covey,[3] in a modern classic, *The Seven Habits of Highly Effective People*, considers empathy to be one of the most powerful of social tools. He has become famous for the saying "…seek first to understand, then to be understood". What many people do not realise is that Covey did not invent the word 'empathy'. It was Theodore Lipps[4] who first coined the German word *einfuhlung*, which literally means 'feeling into'. After that, the word 'empathy' made its way into the English language.

It was, however, Dr Carl Rogers,[5] the noted American humanist psychologist, who reconceptualised the term. Firstly it was applied as a technique for therapists and counsellors to create a remedial climate in which to facilitate the therapeutic process. Later, Rogers proposed empathy not only as an important therapeutic tool, but also as a vehicle to better communication and interpersonal relationships in all areas of life including work, family, and leisure. Shortly before his death, Rogers further extended the application of empathy to the socio-political domain. Of local significance is Carl Rogers's association with South Africa. He made two visits, one in 1979 and another in 1986, and was planning a third at the time of his death. During these visits he worked with groups (teaching empathy skills) including black, white and coloured people in an endeavour to solve the problems created in large measure by the ideology of apartheid.[6]

After completing this chapter, you should be able to:

- define empathy;
- have some understanding of the theory that informs empathy;
- know why empathy is important;
- be aware of the barriers to empathy;
- assess the level of your empathy;
- know how to develop your empathy skills; and
- understand and implement individual and group activities to enhance empathy.

> *Which famous/well-known people would you consider empathic?*

DEFINITION OF EMPATHY

Empathy is one of the most important qualities any person can possess.[7] While it is not a quality that is evenly distributed among people, each individual, for the most part, can teach himself or herself to be more empathic. In the words of Carl Rogers,[8] empathy is one's ability "to perceive the internal frame of reference of another with accuracy and with emotional components and meanings which pertain thereto as if one were the person, but without ever losing the 'as if' condition. Thus, it means to sense the hurt or the pleasure of another as he senses it and to perceive the causes thereof as he perceives them, but without ever losing the recognition that it is 'as if' I was hurt, or pleased, and so forth".[9] If we shrink our analysis to the physiological level, what do we find? Neuro-psychologists inform us that the so-called 'love hormone', oxytocin, plays a role in empathy. The body's inability to secrete oxytocin is associated with the inclination to manipulate, narcissism, psychopathy, and the inability to express empathy.

> ## *Further perspectives on empathy*
>
> *Empathy is the capacity to think and feel oneself into the inner life of another person* – Heinz Kohut.
>
> *[Empathy is] the ability to put oneself into the mental shoes of another person, to understand her emotions and feelings* – Alvin Goldman.
>
> *To empathise means to share, to experience the feelings of another person, to understand her emotions and feelings* – R.R. Greenson.
>
> *[Empathy is] the capacity to know emotionally what another is experiencing from within the frame of reference of that other person; the capacity to sample the feelings of another or to put oneself in another's shoes* – D.M. Berger.

> *[Empathy] is what happens to us when we leave our own bodies ... and find ourselves either momentarily or for a longer period of time in the mind of the other. We observe reality through her eyes, feel her emotions, share in her pain* – Khen Lampert.
>
> *[Empathy is] putting oneself into the psychological frame of reference of another, so that the other person's thinking, feeling and acting are understood and, to some extent, predictable. [Empathy is our ability] to accompany another to wherever the other person's feelings lead him, no matter how strong, deep, destructive or abnormal they may seem* – Robert Campbell.[10]

THEORY INFORMING EMPATHY

Daniel Goleman's number one bestseller, *Emotional Intelligence,* is arguably the best general overview on this subject.

We summarise here what he and other experts have to say.

Goleman views empathy as our ability to understand others' feelings, view matters from their perspective, and respect differences in how people feel about things. Relationships are a major focus, including learning to be a good listener and asker of questions; distinguishing between what someone says or does and your own reactions and judgements; being assertive rather than angry or passive; learning the arts of co-operation and conflict resolution; and negotiating compromise.[11]

Our ability to empathise is fundamental to all life theatres – work, love and play. Its absence is often reflected in the behaviour of psychopaths, child molesters and rapists. At the very root of emotional intelligence lies the self-awareness skill – the ability to "know thyself", to borrow a term from Socrates. As we have already learned, self-awareness is the mind's ability to monitor its own inner workings, including thoughts, moods, and emotions – in brief, to observe and scan its own experience. Other EI skills are built on these foundations, most notably empathy. As Goleman opines, "for one, there is self-awareness, which fosters self-management. Then there's empathy, the basis for skill in relationship. These are fundamental skills in emotional intelligence – weakness here can sabotage a life or career, while strengths increase fulfilment and success".[12]

When we empathise with another, we are in effect telling that person, "I hear what you are saying, you have my full attention and I am not judging you". In this process, the speaker is encouraged to express him- or herself fully, free of interruption and criticism. Being empathic does not necessarily mean that we agree with each person's perspective. Empathic individuals (those highly skilled in empathy) do not necessarily pity others – that would be sympathy. When we sympathise with someone we share their experiences without the "as if" qualification that Rogers makes clear in his definition at the beginning of this chapter.

More often than not, emotions are expressed non-verbally in various ways, including pitch and tone, pace of voice, facial expression, posture, eyes, and so on. Goleman goes so far as to assert that 90% or more of emotional messages are non-verbal. To this Tian Dayton,[13] author of *Emotional Sobriety*, adds: "Words are not our first form of communication. Long before language formally enters the picture, we humans learn a rich tapestry of gestures, actions, signs, and facial expressions to communicate our needs and desires, and each tiny physical gesture is double-coded with emotion and stored by the brain and body with emotional purpose and meaning attached to it."[14]

THE CASE FOR DEVELOPING EMPATHY

One very important outcome of empathy (and emotional intelligence) is our ability to interact successfully with significant others – be they our managers, colleagues, subordinates, family members, or friends. If we think about it carefully, what can be achieved without the active support and help of others? Very little! In that sense, empathy is considered a key (emotional intelligence) skill that provides us with the means to engage in the social world successfully.

Empathic individuals experience higher levels of emotional health and psychological well-being – they are overall more popular, sociable, open, warm, friendly, approachable, and outgoing. Empathic individuals tend to experience better relations with the opposite sex and experience a fulfilling romantic life.

What we just noted is no less true for learners. Pupils judged to be competent in empathy are found to be more emotionally stable, achieve better academically, and are more liked by their cohorts and teachers. In a similar vein, empathy is key to an effective functioning workplace. Empathic managers are sensitive in recognising the needs of clients, customers and subordinates. An empathic (resonant) manager is often author to a positive work climate, employee job engagement, and increased productivity. Similarly, empathy is a critical skill in getting along with the cultural other. As Goleman aptly reminds us "… cross-cultural dialogue can easily lead to miscues and misunderstandings. Empathy is an antidote that attunes people to subtleties in body language, or allows them to hear the emotional message beneath the words."[15]

Empathic individuals are also:

- less likely to be overlooked for promotion;
- superior communicators, especially at the intercultural level;
- excellent at managing conflict;
- better parents, lovers and spouses;
- able to experience a better overall quality of life; and
- able to enjoy a functioning immune system, health, and longevity.

COMMON BARRIERS TO EMPATHY

Our ability to empathise and read emotion – as with all other skills – lies on a continuum; some are better at it than others. Before we turn our attention to common barriers to empathy, we need to quickly refer back to alexithymia, which when literally translated means "no words for emotions", from the Greek *a* for "lack," *lexis* for "word" and *thymos* for "emotion". Such individuals are marked by an inability to describe their own feelings verbally and to understand the feelings of others. They also have trouble differentiating between feelings. Alexithymics often have difficulty experiencing close relationships and are commonly described by others – including spouses and colleagues – as detached and aloof. What puts these people at such a disadvantage is their inability to empathise with others. Nevertheless, their condition is not without hope, say the experts. Empathy can be learned, but it requires practice.[16]

One major barrier to empathy is context – the conditions under which people live and work. For example, it is easier to demonstrate empathy when we are happy and life is going according to plan. However, when we are faced with high levels of pressure and stress, empathic behaviour becomes more difficult to achieve. An example is tele-consultants at large call centres, whose empathic (listening) skills are often put to the test by the sheer volume of calls they need to handle, and at times ill-mannered client behaviour.

Listed below are some further barriers to empathy:

- Self-focus or being self-absorbed.
- Stereotyped notions concerning gender, race, and culture.
- Evaluating other people according to our own values and norms.
- Narcissism – characterised by self-importance, boastfulness, and an excessive need for admiration.
- Negative emotion or mood.
- Being too task-orientated.

DEVELOPING EMPATHY SKILLS

Communication is without question the most important skill in life, pens Stephen Covey,[17] author of *The 8th Habit*. Communication takes on four forms: reading, writing, speaking and listening. Most people spend much of their waking life engaged in these four activities. According to Covey, the art of listening is the most neglected form of communication. Most people, he says, believe that they are good at listening because they are doing it all the time. What they do not, however, realise is that they are listening from their own frame of reference. Covey proposes five levels of listening: ignoring, 'pretend' listening, selective listening, attentive listening, and empathic listening. Empathic listening is the only form of listening where the individual brackets his personal biography (values, needs, prejudices and stereotypes) and enters another's internal frame of reference.

> ## *On listening*
>
> *When I ask you to listen and you start giving advice, you have not done what I have asked. When I ask you to listen to me and you begin to tell me why I shouldn't feel that way, you are trampling on my feelings. When I ask you to listen and you feel you have to do something to solve my problem, you have failed me, strange as it may seem.*
>
> *Listen! All I ask is that you listen; not talk or do – just hear me ... I can do for myself. I'm not helpless. Maybe discouraged and faltering, but not helpless. When you do something for me that I can and need to do for myself, you contribute to my fear and feeling of inadequacy. But when you accept as fact that I do feel what I feel, no matter how irrational, then I can quit trying to convince you and can get about the business of understanding what's behind this irrational feeling. And when that's clear, the answers are obvious and I don't need advice.*[18]

Some people are naturally empathic individuals; projecting themselves into the private world of others comes naturally. For most, however, empathy is a learning process acquired through practice. Lack of empathy can sometimes have a genetic cause or be traced back to early childhood experiences. For example, some families discourage the expression of feelings or emotions. Take as an example Western culture, in which showing emotions – especially in men – is generally frowned upon.

Fortunately, empathy is a learned skill. One way to sharpen empathy skills is to imagine another's circumstances. It is, of course, true that we cannot understand another's hurt (experiences) entirely. For example, when parents lose their only child to illness, it is difficult to understand their grief fully, especially if we have never experienced such a loss ourselves. It is, however, possible to imagine their plight and convey some feelings of understanding to the grieving couple.

As our definitions above convey, empathy requires that we enter the other's personal frame of reference – less technically, we need to feel, understand or comprehend their pain. As we have learned in Chapter 5 (emotional self-awareness), a prerequisite for developing empathy is to be emotionally literate, that is, to understand and be aware of the emotions that we are experiencing. We need to be able to tag our emotions. Self-awareness also requires us to be aware of our values, prejudices, needs, and concerns. Empathy requires us to distance ourselves from our biography, for example, if our colleague were a divorcee, an alcoholic, a drug addict, or from a different cultural or religious background, it would be good to be aware of our own prejudices in order to reach out to them effectively. In other words, we do not have to approve of the other's behaviour in order to act empathically. We do not even have to like the other in order to show empathy.

Empathy also requires us to remain in the present - the here and now. If your mind wanders into the past and future, you may forfeit the quality of your empathic response. This means that we must learn to listen. Let the person know (through eye contact, posture and tone of voice) that you are focused and giving him or her extra attention. You are letting the other person know through verbal and non-verbal language - "I understand your pain, I hear what you are saying, and I will not judge or blame you".

LISTENING SKILLS

Key to developing empathy is our ability to listen attentively. We now draw on the work of Barger and Kirby,[19] who provide five areas to which we need to pay attention: listen, acknowledge, respect, appreciate, and follow through.

Listen

- Make the person the focal point of your attention – convey to the individual by means of body language and facial expression that this interaction is of great importance right now.
- Listen non-judgementally – open yourself up to what the person has to say.
- Strive to understand the essence of the person's view.
- Be sensitive to the other person's emotions regarding the issue. Note non-verbal cues and try to pinpoint meaning and the images behind the message.
- Ask specific questions to uncover the true meaning that the person attempts to convey, for example, "How do you feel when this happens?"; "Help me to understand better how this affects you".
- Provide both non-verbal and verbal support, for example, nod in empathic support.

Active listening conveys a message of empathic engagement. Relatively more time should be spent on listening to grasp the essence of what the person wishes to disclose.

Acknowledge

- Confirm your understanding of the individual's experience – both verbally and non-verbally.
- Validate the importance of the issue for the person.
- Acknowledge the impact this has on them: "You seem to be irritated by your husband's drinking."
- "I can understand that you must feel very upset by his behaviour."
- "I have had similar experiences, and know how upsetting it must be."
- Acknowledgement validates experience.

Respect

- Never invalidate another's experience – it is his or her reality.
- Be careful not to underplay the importance of an incident – for the person it may be very meaningful.

- Do not use ridicule or sarcasm.
- Acknowledge the person's perspective and do not try to persuade him or her to feel differently about it.

Appreciate

- "I understand how difficult it is for you to talk about these things: I appreciate the effort it must take to talk to someone about this."
- "Thank you for sharing this information, though painful. It is most revealing."
- "Thank you for sharing your feelings and thoughts."

Follow through

- Keep to what you have promised to do.
- If you have undertaken to do something, confirm via e-mail or SMS that it has been done.
- Make a note in your diary to follow up on how the person is doing.

Steps in empathic communication

- Reading non-verbal behaviour.
- Recognise feelings in the other.
- Stating our perception of the other's feelings ("It sounds as though you're very upset").
- Legitimising that feeling.
- Respecting your colleague's/subordinate's attempts to cope with the predicament.
- Offering support and partnership: "Let's see what we can do together to ...".

After an opportunity of empathy is presented, you may (if appropriate) offer a gesture or statement of empathy.

Reading and responding to non-verbal behaviour
Non-verbal behaviour is the foundation of human relationships. Much communication is transmitted on a non-verbal level, therefore conscious awareness of non-verbal behaviour is most significant in human interactions. People skilled in empathy are also good at reading non-verbal behaviour, including:

- facial expressions;
- tone of voice (inflection); and
- gestures and the like.

It should be no surprise to learn that empathy contributes to work success.

Effective verbal response

Verbal responses are critical in a counselling process. The following may be helpful in responding empathically:

- **Reflecting accurately**
  An effective listener is also good at finding the right words to sum up what the other feels. The technique is to identify the general feeling, then to try to identify the particular feeling expressed:

  "Do I understand you correctly...?"
  "I can understand how that makes you feel..."
  "It sounds as though you are..."

- **Mirroring**
  One way to practice empathy skills is through "mirroring". When one person makes a complaint, the other repeats it back in his or her own words, trying to capture not just the thought but also the feelings that go with it. The person mirroring checks with the other to make sure that the re-statement is on target, and if not, tries again until it is right – something that seems simple, but is surprisingly tricky to execute. The outcome of being mirrored accurately is not just feeling understood, but having the added sense of being in emotional alignment.[20]

- **Clarifications**
  Clarification entails making certain that you understand correctly what the person has conveyed:

  "I want to make sure that I understand you correctly..."
  "Tell me more about..."

- **Questions**
  When used wisely, questions can be extremely helpful when specific information is needed:

  "How does this make you feel...?"
  "What has this been like for you...?"
  "Can you tell me more about that...?"

MORE WAYS TO PRACTICE EMPATHY SKILLS

- Practice listening attentively to a another person.
- Make sure that you have actually *heard* what the person is saying.
- In answering, try to summarise the essence of what the person has told you.
- Try not to give advice.
- Watch your body language – lean forward – concentrate.
- Don't look at your watch.
- Demonstrate with your body as well as with your words that you understand both the feeling and the content of what the other is saying.
- Don't look as if you are in a hurry.
- Show warmth, caring and interest.

Individuals epitomising empathy

Ronald Reagan
Dalai Lama
Dr Frederick van Zyl Slabbert
Desmond Tutu
Nelson Mandela
Carl Rogers (psychologist)
Others?

A FINAL WORD

Empathy is a powerful interpersonal tool. The core of empathy is the capacity to understand another person's experience from within that person's frame of reference. We are not all equally capable of recognising, managing or effectively responding to our own or others' emotions. Furthermore, people differ in the intensity of emotions they experience. Those who are more volatile may disturb others by acting outside the boundaries of socially acceptable behaviour. Individuals who are less abrasive may feel taken aback when confronted in a less polite manner. It therefore makes sense to enhance our empathic skills, because they are key to building meaningful relationships. When we attempt to understand another person, we practice empathy.

SECTION 2: ACTIVITIES FOR SKILLS DEVELOPMENT

Self-assessment

Individual activities

 Activity 1: Measuring the level of your empathy

What is the level of your empathy? Spend a few minutes benchmarking your empathy level. Give your responses to the statements below honestly. Assign a number to each item, using this scale:

1 = Very seldom or not true of me
2 = Seldom true of me
3 = Sometimes true of me
4 = Often true of me
5 = Very often true of me or true of me

I am good at understanding what other people feel.

1	2	3	4	5

I am a good listener.

1	2	3	4	5

People say that it is easy to confide in me.

1	2	3	4	5

The suffering of people moves me.

1	2	3	4	5

I care deeply about other people, for example, fellow workers.

1	2	3	4	5

Multiply the total by 4 to arrive at a total out of 100.

Empathy scale

10	20	30	40	50	60	70	80	90	100

 **Activity 2**

To what extent are you able to hear someone out without interrupting?

....

....

Describe an incident in which you demonstrated little empathy or a great deal, and explain why you reacted in this way. Describe your behaviour.

....

....

Reflect on what you need to do better to improve your empathy skills.

....

....

What do you think prevents you from being empathic?

....

....

Group activity

Activity 3

Discuss the barriers to empathy.

....

....

What are the key features of empathy?

....

....

What is the difference between empathy, sympathy and pity?

....

....

 **Activity 4**

In dyads, or larger groups, read the following brief scenarios and choose an appropriate empathic response.

Scenario 1

Jill relates to Susan that her husband (Joe) is having an affair with his secretary.

How do you respond to her?

a) I could have told you that Joe is the unfaithful type… you should never have married him.
b) What a mess you have got yourself into now. What do you plan to do?
c) I suggest that you immediately see a divorce attorney.
d) You must be devastated and shocked… Is there anything I can do?

Scenario 2

Your husband, Peter, arrives home obviously upset. He says with a sigh, "I did not get the promotion; Jack got it."

You reply:

a) Too bad, I was bargaining on the extra pay.
b) You certainly have been unlucky lately…
c) Peter, you are just going to have to work harder from now on…
d) What a day you must have had – you must be very disappointed.

Scenario 3

Your son phones you. He excitedly tells you that he has passed his attorney's exams.

You reply:

a) So what are you going to do now…?
b) At last you have achieved something in your life… are you going to have a party tonight and get drunk?
c) I'm very proud of you, you must be feeling very excited!
d) I'll tell your father; I suspect he will be pleased…

Scenario 4

Your 17-year old daughter, Anne, enters the room and tearfully informs you that she is pregnant; and to make matters worse, her boyfriend has left her.

You reply:

a) How could you allow this to happen to you?
b) I knew all along that Cedric was a good-for-nothing.
c) Don't worry, darling, this happens in the best of families.
d) You must be feeling very down and upset at this moment.

 Activity 5

Identify emotions felt by group members. Each member should jot down his or her own emotion as well as the perceived emotions of the group. Cross-check for accuracy.

 Activity 6

Role play basic emotions. Each member is allocated an emotion to role play. Group members have to identify the displayed emotion.

REFERENCES

Anon (2017). *Oxytocin* [Online]. Available: https://en.wikipedia.org/wiki/Oxytocin. [Accessed 26 January, 2017].
Barger, N.J. & Kirby, L. (1998). *WorkTypes*. New York: Warner Books.
Covey, S.R. (1992). *The seven habits of highly effective people.* London: Simon & Schuster
Covey, S.R. (2004). *The 8th habit: From effectiveness to greatness.* London: Simon & Schuster.
Dayton, T. (2007). *Emotional sobriety: From relationship trauma to resilience and balance.* Deerfield Beach, Florida: Health Communications.
Goleman, D. (1995). *Emotional intelligence: why it can matter more than IQ.* New York: Bantam Books.
Goleman, D. (2001). An EI-based theory of performance. In C. Cherniss & D. Goleman (eds.). *The emotionally intelligent workplace.* San Francisco: Jossey Bass, p. 27–44.
Goleman, D. (2014). *Focus: The hidden driver of excellence.* London: Bloomsbury
Hardee, J.T. (2003). *An overview of empathy.* The Permanente Journal. [Online]. Available: https://www.ncbi.nlm.nih.gov/pmc/articles/PMC5571783/ [Accessed 20 May 2009].

Nouwen, H.J.M. (nd). *Out of solitude: Three Meditations on Christian life* [Online]. Available: https://www.goodreads.com/work/quotes/116112-out-of-solitude-three-meditations-on-the-christian-life. [Accessed 7 January 2017].

Rogers, C.R. (1965). *Client-centred therapy*. London: Constable.

Van Niekerk, E.C. (1996). *Paradigms of the mind. Personality theories in perspective.* Cape Town: Oxford University Press.

Wikipedia. (2009). *Empathy*. [Online] Available: https://simple.wikipedia.org/wiki/Empathy [Accessed 7 January 2017].

ENDNOTES

1. Van Niekerk, 2017.
2. Nouwen, 2017.
3. Covey, 1992.
4. Hardee, 2003.
5. Rogers, 1965.
6. Van Niekerk, 1996.
7. cf. Goleman, 2014.
8. Rogers, 1965.
9. Anon, 2017.
10. Wikipedia, 2009.
11. Goleman, 1995:268.
12. Goleman, 2014.
13. Dayton, 2007.
14. Dayton, 2007:33.
15. Goleman, 2001:50.
16. Goleman, 1995.
17. Covey, 2004.
18. Covey, 2004:193.
19. Barger & Kirby, 1998.
20. Goleman, 1996.

Chapter 11

SOCIAL RESPONSIBILITY

Eugene van Niekerk

Divorced from ethics, leadership is reduced to management and politics to mere technique.
–James MacGregor Burns

SECTION 1: OVERVIEW

Social responsibility is essential to the maintenance of a healthy and self-respecting society. Social responsibility is the ethical and moral duty we have to the community and society at large, whether individual, corporation or organisation. All our best-intentioned efforts will come to nothing in the absence of social responsibility. Failed social responsibility will inescapably end in strife among individuals, between individuals and society, and in time, lead to sacrificing the future in order to gratify short-lived needs.

After completing this chapter, you should be able to:

- define social responsibility;
- reflect on some of the benefits of social responsibility;
- understand ways to develop social responsibility;
- assess your own level of social responsibility; and
- understand and implement individual and group activities to enhance social responsibility.

DEFINITION OF SOCIAL RESPONSIBILITY

Social responsibility reflects our ability to act pro-socially – to care for the welfare of others. This aspect of emotional intelligence involves behaving in accordance with our inner convictions and moral compass. It further demonstrates an "other person" sensitivity which promotes a climate in which members of an organisation, community, church, or business can accept one another and develop their potential in the interest of the collective. In sharp distinction is the anti-social type often associated with sociopaths, who flout social convention.[1]

Hughes et al.[2] proffer another perspective. For them, social responsibility entails being accountable for the welfare of the larger group and for the other individuals who live and operate in it. That larger group could be a church organisation, a sports league, a business enterprise, a community, and so on. One demonstrates that he or she is a productive and cooperative member of the social group by contributing to it in a reliable and commendable way. Typically, one would give one's time, energy, input, money, and loyalty to the group and its individual supporters in order to help it accomplish its collective purpose in a way that benefits all its members.

DEVELOPING SOCIAL RESPONSIBILITY

How can social responsibility benefit both psyche and society? According to Stein and Book,[3] the good news about social responsibility is that because it is directed outwards, it is the easiest component of emotional intelligence to change. As attitudes and behaviours towards social responsibility change, it facilitates other skills to 'fall into place'. There is an old saying that goes something like this: "If you feel empty inside you, give to others and you will feel full". By helping others we take on a new focus; a fresh perspective that, in the fullness of time, adds to life. In this respect, consider the Good Samaritan, who helped others with no expectation of a reward at some future date.

A sense of community reflects social responsibility; it suggests "a feeling that members have a belonging, a feeling that members matter to one another and to the group, and a shared faith that member's needs will be met through their commitment to be together".[4] When a sense of community flounders, its members are at increased risk of experiencing a sense of self-alienation, demoralisation, and learned helplessness.[5]

At another level, social responsibility serves to broaden and build social capital, thereby assisting individuals, families, corporations, and communities to flourish. As Hughes et al. (2012) aptly point out, social responsibility allows groups to realise shared goals far beyond what an individual could ever accomplish on their own.

On 3 February 2009, Sha Zukang, Under-Secretary-General to the United Nations, addressed the Civil Society Forum (New York). A few passages from his speech are highlighted below:

The theme you selected highlights social integration as a process of creating an inclusive society where all, regardless of race, colour, religion, gender, age, and physical or intellectual capacity have rights and responsibilities, and where they have a role to play… In an inclusive society, all are protected from discrimination and social exclusion. There is shared responsibility for the welfare and inclusion of all members, especially those at risk of poverty and marginalisation. Victims of extreme poverty, discrimination, new forms of stigmatisation, xenophobia, gender-based violence, abuse within families, can resort to violence as a way of resolving conflict….

> *Today we confront economic slowdown in both developed and developing countries given the global financial crisis... [As] people suffer from poverty and unemployment with rising social tensions, the ranks of people at high risk for exclusion can only grow... Your civil society organisations raise awareness about the importance of promoting social inclusion, through your tireless advocacy and multicultural education...*
>
> *You [members of civil society] can both support government's efforts and help to keep governments accountable for implementing policies that effectively promote social integration.*[6]

CIVIL SOCIETY

'Civil society' is an ancient concept that can be traced back to Greek and Roman times. Historically, the idea was closely tied to the notion of a "politically active citizen".[7] The term is also associated with societies governed by the rule of law that are committed to holding free and fair elections. Civil society is traditionally thought of as that part of society not concerned with formal rule, but holding the government of the day accountable.

The Congress of South African Trade Unions (COSATU), for example, played an important role in developing political and economic resistance to the apartheid regime. Today the trade union movement is recognised in the Constitution of the Republic of South Africa, 1996, and is a dominant force in the present political space.

Institutions of civil society take on many forms and hues, and include business associations, churches, professional associations, non-governmental organisations, women's organisations, academic institutions, coalitions, and advocacy groups. According to Govender,[8] the themes that feature most prominently in local civil society include poverty reduction, environmental issues, HIV/AIDS, and gender equality.

CORPORATE SOCIAL RESPONSIBILITY

In recent years, interest in business ethics has seen a dramatic increase. Major firms' websites reflect their non-economic values under a variety of headings – ethics, codes and social responsibility charters. Given the prevailing *zeitgeist*, corporations often re-envision their ethical considerations and core values. In this respect, consider, for example, BP's "beyond petroleum" environmental slant. The rallying cry behind the new business ethos can be summarised by the slogan: People, Planet, Profit. People refer to fair labour practices; Planet is the communities and regions where the business operates; and Profit is the economic value created by the organisation after deducting the costs of all inputs, including the cost of capital.[9]

Corporate social responsibility (CSR) takes on many forms and shapes. One approach to CSR that is gaining in popularity includes the Shell Foundation's involvement in Flower Valley South Africa. This project has been responsible for setting up an Early Learning

Centre to help educate the community's children, as well as helping to build the work skills of the local adults. Marks and Spencer (UK) are also participating in this project through establishing trade networks within the community.

Other projects include HIV/AIDS educational programmes, and the establishment of educational facilities for illiterate adults. Another CSR approach is providing aid to destitute communities in developing countries. The latter, however, has been criticised for failing to build on the skills of the local population, whereas community-based developmental projects tend to yield more sustainable development.[10]

Many corporations now publish annual reports that cover CSR issues on sustainable development, however these differ in style, format, and evaluation methodology. For these and other reasons, critics often dismiss these reports as misleading, citing examples such as Enron's Corporate Responsibility Annual Report and annual reports from tobacco companies. More importantly, companies are coming under increasing pressure from their own constituents (stakeholders and shareholders) to practice social responsibility.

Non-governmental organisations, too, are applying collective activism around changing corporate behaviour. Notwithstanding some cracks in the corporate wall, CSR is yielding some progress. For example, the Danish parliament passed a law on CSR on 16 December 2008, making it mandatory for the largest Danish companies, investors and state-owned companies to include information on CSR in their financial reports effective 1 January 2009.[11]

COMMUNITY SERVICE

When someone performs an action that benefits his or her community, it is known as community service, and serves as a vital part of social responsibility. Getting involved in a community makes it healthier and livelier, and numerous organisations around the world support community service activities.

Examples of community projects include:

- building homes in low-income areas;
- assisting senior citizens;
- performing habitat restoration;
- helping out in a local library;
- tutoring children with learning disabilities;
- cleaning a park; and
- collecting items for charity such as clothes, food, or furniture.[12]

Médicins Sans Frontières

Doctors Without Borders or Médicins Sans Frontières (MSF) was created in France in 1971. It is a non-profitable organisation comprising members of the medical fraternity. In short,

MSF provides emergency aid to people who are subjected to famine, wars, epidemics, or where health care is required. MSF is not ideological in outlook, helping people irrespective of race, religion or political persuasions. In 1999, MSF was awarded the Nobel Peace Prize.[13]

MSF has been operating in South Africa since 2000, and has been primarily involved in the treatment of HIV/AIDS, including the distribution of antiretroviral (ARV) medicines at the primary health care level. These clinics now support more than 10 000 people on ARV therapy.

Since 2003, MSF has been working closely with the Nelson Mandela Foundation on a programme based in Lusikisiki, one of the most impoverished areas in the Eastern Cape. Universal ARV coverage was achieved by 2005, and in 2006, the Eastern Cape Provincial Health authorities took over responsibility for running the programme. During this same period, MSF opened a programme in Lesotho based on the model implemented in Lusikisiki. Here, a pilot nurse-based programme was initiated to provide HIV/AIDS and TB care. By the end of 2008, nearly 2 000 people had been placed on an ARV treatment programme.

In 2007, MSF established offices in Johannesburg. Its programmes in the region are managed from these offices and include providing logistical support, offering medical expertise, raising funds from the public, and recruiting medical and non-medical staff. MSF is also involved in raising awareness about the medical and humanitarian crises facing vulnerable communities, by sharing information with the media, the local public, government agencies, and non-governmental organisations.

Since 2009, MSF has been involved in assisting with the outbreak of cholera in Zimbabwe and on the borders of South Africa, and has treated more than 45 000 people, representing 75% of all cholera cases.

MSF has also raised awareness about people who have been displaced, and, through lobbying, has positively influenced decision-making related to non-medical care.[14]

Big Brothers Big Sisters SA

Big Brothers Big Sisters South Africa (BBBSSA) is a non-profit organisation whose mission is to mentor and befriend young persons from the ages of 6 to 18 in the Western Cape, Gauteng, and KwaZulu-Natal. Ernest Coulter, a New York clerk of the court, founded the original organisation in 1902.

Big Brothers Big Sisters South Africa was established in 2000, first in the Western Cape, followed by Gauteng in 2002 and Kwa-Zulu-Natal in 2005. South Africa is the first African country to implement this programme.

Prospective mentors undergo training over a three-day period which teaches them skills relating to self-esteem development, relationship building, child development, communication, and themes relating to sexual matters.

BBBSSA has developed partnerships with local organisations and institutions including, among others, the South African Police Service, the National Youth Commission, the Department of Social Work at the University of Johannesburg, and the Wits School of

Education. These training institutions have integrated the BBBSSA programme into their curriculum programmes to enable students to become mentors, or 'Bigs' as they are known.

Big Brothers Big Sisters host "buddy nights", where mentors meet to share their experiences. These evenings also serve as a vehicle to attract prospective volunteers. BBBSSA also recruit by way of flyers, websites, newsletters and by word of mouth.

According to Legong,[15] the BBBSSA programme has positively influenced the developmental status of our youth. An international study conducted in the United States on youth who were involved as "Littles" in the mentorship programme demonstrated the following gains:

- Thirty-two per cent were less likely to engage in violence.
- Forty-six per cent were less likely to use drugs.
- An increase in confidence and self-esteem.
- An increase in their ability to trust (see also www.childrenfirst.org.za).

Individuals and institutions epitomising social responsibility

Bill Gates
Bill Clinton
Princess Diana
The Rupert family
Greenpeace
Others?

A FINAL WORD

Social responsibility lies at the heart of a socially responsive society. Overcoming social amnesia is an unrelenting task, achieved in part through awareness-building and skills development. What transpires at the individual level (micro) is reciprocally determined at the meso (family, organisation) and macro (community, society) levels. At the individual level, training elevates self-efficacy levels (to paraphrase American psychologist Albert Bandura). Self-efficacy is not unrelated to group efficacy. In fact, collective efficacy is anchored in self-efficacy. Collective efficacy is a group or society's collective belief that they can solve their problems. As former president Barack Obama so elegantly reminded us some years ago: "Yes, we can!" This chapter and training programme is a modest step in that direction.

SECTION 2: ACTIVITIES FOR SKILLS DEVELOPMENT

Self-assessment

Individual activities

 Activity 1

Spend a few moments assessing your level of social responsibility. Answer the questions below honestly. Assign a number to each item, using this scale:

1 = Very seldom or not true of me
2 = Seldom true of me
3 = Sometimes true of me
4 = Often true of me
5 = Very often true of me

I enjoy doing things for other people.

1	2	3	4	5

I care deeply for the poor, the suffering and the less privileged.

1	2	3	4	5

I contribute to my community, if only in a small way.

1	2	3	4	5

I donate money – within my financial means – to worthy causes.

1	2	3	4	5

I consider myself a role model in my community.

1	2	3	4	5

Multiply the total by 4 to arrive at a total out of 100.

My level of social responsibility

10	20	30	40	50	60	70	80	90	100

 **Activity 2**

Name community organisations in which you are involved.[16]

....

....

Name the roles you play in these organisations.

....

....

Do you actively participate in any charitable activities? List and describe your roles and activities.

....

....

What have you done recently to help strangers in need?

....

....

Give two examples in which you behaved like a good Samaritan.

....

....

Group activity

Activity 3

Sketch and debate a model of an "ideal typical" society from a social responsibility perspective.

....

....

To what extent does South African society reflect a socially responsible society?

....

....

How does our society compare to that of Denmark or Zimbabwe?

....

....

Own work for personal growth: a to-do list for the next fortnight

Activity 4

How could less-experienced people learn from your knowledge and talent?

....

....

Have you considered starting a mentorship programme, that is, allowing less-privileged individuals or groups to gain from your personal expertise?

....

....

Think of at least one personal contribution that would make your community a better place to live in.

....

....

REFERENCES

Govender, C. (2000). *Trends in civil society in South Africa today* [Online]. Available at: <www.Anc.org.za/andocs/umrabulo13m.html> [Accessed 1 February, 2010].

Hughes, M. & Terrel, B.J. (2012). *Emotional intelligence in action: training and coaching activities for leaders, manager, and teams* (2nd ed.). San Francisco: Pfeiffer.

Kumar, K. (1999). Civil society. In A. Kuper and J. Kuper (eds.). *The social science encyclopaedia*. London: Routledge.

Legong. M. (2009). *Big brothers big sisters: Making a big difference little by little* [Online]. Available at: http://vosesa.org.za/focus/vol2_no1/index.html?article_4.html~content [Accessed 8 February, 2010].

McMillan, D.W. & Chavis, D.M. (1986). Sense of Community. A Definition and Theory. *Journal of Counselling Psychology, 14*(1), 6 -23.

Stein, S. & Book, H. (2001). *The EQ Edge: Emotional intelligence and your success* (2nd ed.). Toronto: Kogan Page.

Stein, S.J. & Book, H. (2011). *The EQ Edge: Emotional Intelligence and Your Success*. Ontario: Wiley.

Wikipedia. (2017). *Corporate social responsibility* [Online]. Available at: www.wikipedia.org/wiki/corporate-social responsibility> [Accessed 14 January, 2017].

Wikipedia. (2010). *Community service* [Online]. Available at: https://en.wikipedia.org/wiki/Community_service. [Accessed 6 February, 2010].

Wikipedia. (2016). *Médecins Sans Frontières* [Online]. Available at: https://en.wikipedia.org/wiki/M%C3%A9decins_Sans_Fronti%C3%A8res [Accessed 4 January, 2017].

Zukang, S. (2009). *Statement to the Civil Society Forum: Social Integration: Building a Society for all* [Online]. Available at: http://www.un.org/en/development/desa/usg/statements/uncategorized/2009/02/statement-to-the-civil-society-forum-social-integration-building-a-society-for-all.html. [Accessed 6 February, 2011].

ENDNOTES

1. Stein & Book, 2011.
2. Hughes et al., 2012.
3. Stein & Book, 2011.
4. McMillan & Chavis, 1986:69.
5. Van Niekerk & Prins, 2010.
6. Zukang, 2009.
7. Kumar, 1999:89.
8. Govender, 2000.
9. Wikipedia, 2017.
10. Wikipedia, 2010.
11. Wikipedia, 2010.
12. Wikipedia, 2010.
13. Wikipedia, 2016.
14. Wikipedia, 2010.
15. Legong, 2009.
16. Stein & Book, 2001.

SECTION D: DECISION-MAKING

Decision-making refers to the manner in which a person applies emotional information; it is the extent to which a person understands the impact that emotions have on decision-making. This includes the ability to withstand or postpone impulses, to remain objective, and thus to prevent rapid actions together with ineffective problem solving.

The following skills are discussed:

Chapter 12:   Problem solving
Chapter 13:   Reality testing
Chapter 14:   Impulse control

Chapter 12

PROBLEM SOLVING

Annette Weyers

A problem is a solution in disguise.
–Adair

SECTION 1: OVERVIEW

Optimal functioning and well-being largely depend on one's ability to solve the range of problems that form part of daily living. Thus, it is to one's advantage to expand one's ability to solve problems. This chapter proposes that the ability to use emotional data will broaden the scope of one's problem solving skills, equipping one to solve problems more effectively and timeously. The capacity to solve problems is further extended when there is collaboration between cognitive abilities and emotional intelligence capacities.

After completing this chapter, you should be able to:

- define problem solving;
- understand the theory informing problem solving;
- describe the benefits of problem solving;
- reflect on ways to improve your own capacity to solve problems;
- identify individuals who epitomise effective problem solving;
- assess your own ability to problem solve; and
- implement individual and group activities to enhance your ability to solve problems.

PROBLEM SOLVING DEFINED

There are various definitions for problem solving, including:

- Problem solving entails finding effective solutions to problems.[1]
- Problem solving entails active efforts to discover what must be done to achieve a goal that is not readily available.[2]
- Problem solving is the ability to find solutions to problems in situations where emotions are involved.
- Problem solving includes the ability to understand how emotions impact decision-making.[3]

THEORY INFORMING PROBLEM SOLVING

Because of a greater focus on cognitive intelligence, there is an almost exclusive emphasis on cognitive abilities when discussing problem solving. The conventional hypothesis is that only analytical intelligence provides accurate information and that emotions simply cloud the issue and create confusion. However, more recently, the vast research on human affect in psychology evidenced the functional purpose of emotions, and it is now "generally accepted that emotions augment rather than interfere with other cognitive capacities".[4] Therefore, it is acknowledged that emotions provide vital information when solving problems, and that cognisance of the role of emotions and how they affect the process of solving problems may promote greater efficiency in finding the most appropriate solution.

Emotion and problem solving

Emotions play a key role in every phase of the process of solving problems, from the first sensation that something is amiss, to every decision, judgement or action that will eventuate in the resolution of a problem.

The adaptive function of emotions is particularly relevant during the process of solving problems, as it inspires actions that will help you to reach the most suitable solution. For example, the sense of unease you experience when considering a specific course of action may act as a red flag, cautioning you to re-evaluate the situation. In a similar vein, feelings of doubt or uncertainty offer an opportunity to reconsider the suitability of certain strategies or decisions you have made. Moreover, emotion as primary source of motivation energises the behaviour needed to resolve a problem. For example, it helps you to sustain your resolve to succeed, to maintain a focused attitude, to prioritise problems, and to redirect your thinking.

However, emotions can also derail the process of problem solving. When problems evoke all-consuming emotions, they may overwhelm you and prevent you from thinking clearly. For example, when flooded by feelings of anxiety or dread you may be tempted to retreat, make hasty decisions, or seize the first solution that comes to mind. Fear of failure may tempt you to avoid a problem or to overlook important aspects. Rage and uncontrollable anger can cloud judgement and direct your attention the wrong way, or prompt you to charge ahead without heeding the warning signs. Thus, uncontrolled emotions can steer you off course and prevent you from attaining a satisfactory resolution. For this reason it is important to recognise your subjective emotional response to a problem, to regulate your emotions, and to harness those emotions, inspiring actions that will advance the successful resolution of problems.

Affect creates different mental sets, which in turn influence response or action tendencies.[5] For example, positive affect has been found to foster cognitive flexibility, which enables you to think about a problem in multiple ways and entertain a wider range of possible outcomes. This in turn inspires innovative action tendencies and greater efficiency in decision-making. This is particularly true when tasks are complex.[6] Thus, addressing problems when in a positive mood correlates with greater success and efficiency.

A skilled problem solver will be able to use and manage not only his or her subjective emotional experiences, but also successfully integrate emotional data and objective facts to find the most beneficial solution.

Problem solving in teams

Teamwork has become prevalent in most organisations, with one of the vital functions of teams being to solve problems that will enable them to complete their tasks. The performance of a team is enhanced by the skilful management of affect. For example, cognisance of the range of emotions experienced by team members and how this influences their attitudes and points of view provides valuable information that helps with the initiation of constructive engagement, the facilitation of an open discussion, and improved cooperation. The honest expression of emotion is encouraged, as it generates valuable information that serves as a guide for further thinking and action. However, emotional expression needs to be regulated, particularly when it involves personal issues that have no bearing on the problem at hand.[7] Problem solving in teams requires careful management of members' emotions, a keen sense of your own subjective emotional reaction, self-regulation, and the ability to generate those emotions that engender constructive behaviour such as sharing knowledge and expertise.

> *Who is better at problem solving: the individual or the group?*
>
> When problems have obvious solutions, groups usually out-perform individuals, however, when problems have less obvious solutions, groups may be somewhat better than their average member, but usually no better than the most talented member.[8]

Note: Working in groups is often less productive, due to a phenomenon called social loafing, referring to instances where individuals exert less effort in the group than they would when they work alone.[9]

Coping methods

The adaptive or coping behaviour people employ when facing daily problems and crises are grouped into two general categories - problem-focused coping and emotion-focused coping.[10]

Problem-focused coping focuses on efforts to alter, reduce or eliminate the source of the problem. These are the people who take action by defining the problem, generating and considering possible solutions, and working systematically to find the best possible solution.[11] This requires rational thinking and self-control. Problem-focused coping skills include confronting the problem, seeking social support, and properly planned solutions.[12]

Emotional-focused coping aims to prevent and regulate negative emotions and to reduce your response to the problem. Examples of this type of coping include avoiding ("I try not to think about the problem too much") or denying ("This is a temporary situation") the problem, seeking emotional support from others, venting emotions to release stress, and positive self-talk.[13]

Which coping strategy do you use?

....

....

Problem solving by computer

Scientists are developing artificial brains in the form of computer systems that not only see, hear and manipulate objects, but also reason and solve problems. These systems are the product of research in artificial intelligence (AI), a field that seeks to develop computers that imitate the process of human perception and thought. For problems such as those involved in making certain kinds of medical diagnoses, computerised expert systems can already perform as well as humans, and sometimes even better.[14]

BENEFITS OF PROBLEM SOLVING SKILLS

The value of problem solving skills is noticeable in both one's personal and work life.

Personal functioning

It is difficult to imagine a world in which we fail to solve any of the myriad of problems we face on a daily basis. We hardly think about how resolving the range of problems we routinely face affects our lives. This includes both the mundane (e.g. what to wear to work) and the more complex problems (e.g. which career path to pursue). In this regard Chaffee[15] aptly remarks, "[t]he quality of your life can be traced in a large measure to your competency as a problem-solver". The greater life satisfaction and quality of life of effective problem solvers can be ascribed to the fact that this competency influences their career, finances, health and relationships positively.[16]

Personal growth is advanced for those who are prepared to confront their problems and who vow to do their best. This is why Chaffee refers to problems as "the crucibles that forge the strength". Those who face adversity and work through their problems emerge "more intelligent, resourceful and resilient".[17] At an Emotional Intelligence Conference in South Africa, this argument was substantiated in a personal conversation with Bar-On. It was evident that individuals who experienced much adversity, for instance Israelis and black South Africans, tended to measure higher than average on his Emotional Intelligence Test (EQ-i).

Success at work

Creative problem solving is a most sought-after skill, therefore employees who are adept problems solvers have an edge in the labour market.[18] This view is supported by Isen,[19] who points out that "problem solving is an ability that is greatly desired by most people and organisations, and society at large – and especially the capacity for innovation or creative problem solving". This skill promotes success at work by:

- increasing your value as a team member;
- improving overall productivity;
- increasing the prospect for promotion;
- enhancing job satisfaction; and
- elevating efficiency.

In view of the fact that effective problem solving has a positive impact on one's personal and work life, this skill can be considered an important contributor to an overall sense of well-being.

What would you consider the greatest benefit of the problem solving competency to be?

....

....

STRATEGIES FOR DEVELOPING PROBLEM SOLVING CAPACITIES

To become a confident and effective problem solver is an attainable goal, as problem solving is a skill that can be learned and developed. This competency is enhanced by gaining an understanding of the process of problem solving, utilising emotional intelligence competencies, and employing problem solving models:

The process of problem solving

A complex problem may appear as an entangled mass of feelings, information, details, perspectives, hazards and choices.[20] Predictably, this causes confusion and uncertainty about how to proceed. It may be tempting simply to ignore the problem, or act impulsively without due consideration; strategies that can be disastrous in the end. Knowledge about the process of problem solving is foundational for a structured and methodical approach to problem solving. The next six phases comprise the process of problem solving:

- To sense a problem.
- To define and formulate the problem as clearly as possible.

- To generate as many solutions as possible (e.g. brainstorming).
- To decide to implement one of the solutions.
- To assess the outcome of the implemented solution.
- To repeat the process if the problem still exists.[21]

Using the phases of the process of problem solving as a template can assist you to think critically about the objective facts and emotions associated with each phase, i.e. it will help you to clarify and unravel the confusion of data surrounding the problem. The identification of the six phases of problem solving also helps you to understand the rationale for the step-by-step methods discussed in this chapter.

In addition to understanding a problem, there are two key factors that are critical in problem solving. Firstly, the acknowledgment that there is a problem, and secondly, a pledge to confront the problem and find a solution. The following strategies may be helpful to reinforce a commitment to find a solution:

- List the benefits: make a list of all the benefits you may derive from solving the problem successfully.
- Formalise your acceptance: you can formalise your commitment by signing a declaration of intent.
- Accept responsibility: choose to resolve the problem.
- Create a "worse-case" scenario: a problem may persist because you ignore the possible implications. This strategy will remind you of the potentially disastrous consequences.
- Identify what is holding you back: identify and describe all the factors that prevent you from addressing the problem.[22]

EMOTIONAL INTELLIGENCE COMPETENCIES

The problem solving competency is augmented when supported by other EI competencies such as flexibility, reality testing, emotional self-awareness, impulse control and emotional expression. It is helpful to identify which of these subscales may hamper your problem solving skills. For example, a lack of impulse control may result in rash decisions and behaviour that can derail the process and eventually reduce your confidence to solve problems. Proficiency in the ability to solve problems is greatly advanced when EI subscales underpin the undertaking of finding an effective solution.

PROBLEM SOLVING MODELS

Two step-by-step problem solving models are now discussed - the cybernetic cycle by Wessels[23] and a model developed by Chaffee.[24] These models provide guidelines to address problems that are more complex. However, although a step-by-step approach is very helpful, Chaffee[25] cautions against a rigid stance, emphasising that effective problem solvers are flexible and creative. They may follow all the steps in a problem solving model, however not necessarily in sequence, and they will often explore various alternative problem solving strategies.

THE CYBERNETIC CYCLE

Problem solving is conducted by applying a simple cycle. The first step is to conduct a thorough situation analysis of the problem by asking, "What does this problem entail?" or "Do I understand the problem?" Following this step, you set goals that may lead to the resolution by asking, "What is the solution to this problem?" The solution to the problem is the goal you want to attain. With the goal set, you have to identify strategies that may assist in the pursuit of the goal, for example, "What do I need to do to reach this goal?" or "What actions are required to reach the goal?" The last step is to evaluate whether the goals have indeed been achieved by asking, "Is the problem solved?" If not, the cycle is repeated.

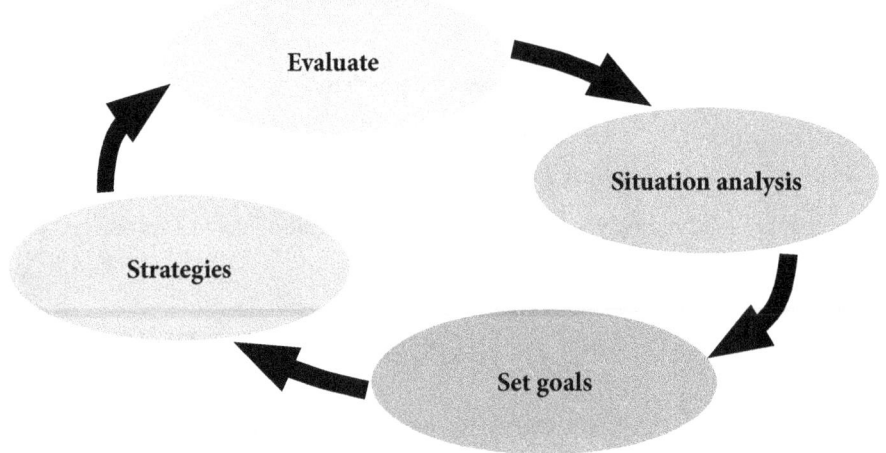

Figure 12.1: The Cybernetic Cycle
Adapted from Wessels[26]

SOLVING COMPLEX PROBLEMS

The proposed model is especially helpful in situations where there is not an obvious solution to a complex problem. The sequential steps provide a framework for a systematic and careful analysis, leading one to work through the problem in an organised way.[27]

Model of problem solving

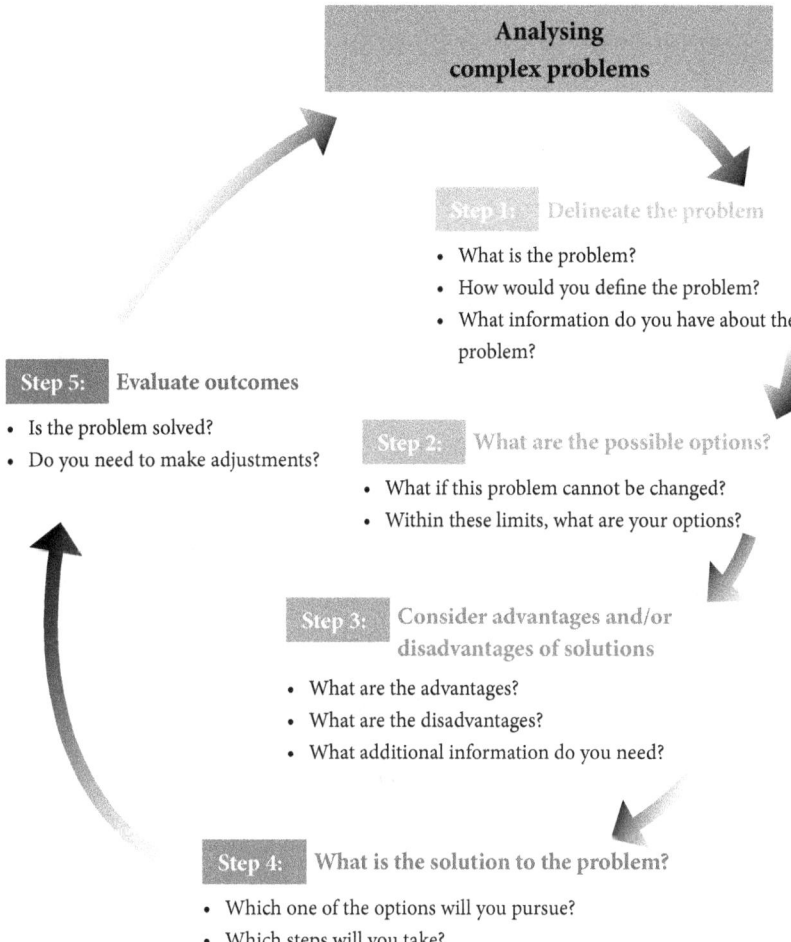

Figure 12.2: Problem Solving Model
Adapted from Chaffee[28]

Step 1: What is the problem?

The first step is to determine exactly what the central issues of the problem are; you may improve your chances of solving the problem if you clearly understand it.[29]

A. What do I know about the problem?
B. What results am I aiming for?
C. How can I define the problem?

Step 2: What are the alternatives?

The boundaries are the limits in the problem situation that one cannot change. Identify the possible actions that can solve the problem.[30]

A. What are the boundaries of the problem situation?
B. What alternatives are possible within these boundaries?

Step 3: What are the advantages or disadvantages of each alternative?

Evaluate the advantages and disadvantages of each possible course of action.[31]

A. What are the advantages of each alternative?
B. What are the disadvantages of each alternative?
C. What additional information do I need to evaluate each alternative?

Step 4: What is the solution?

Decide on a thoughtful course of action based on your analysis of the previous three steps.[32]

A. Which alternative(s) will I pursue?
B. What steps can I take to act on the alternative(s)?

Step 5: How well is the solution working?

Compare the results with your goals. If you are successful, it can provide the foundation for future decisions. If not, consider possible alternatives.[33]

A. What is my evaluation?
B. What adjustments are necessary?

Note: The problem solving steps described above are a left-brain approach, calling for left-brain analytical skills. The so-called right-brain approach calls on us to follow our intuition and go with our gut response. Adept problem solvers use left- and right-brain thinking, which allows for a more holistic approach to problem solving. Intuition is often described as a hunch or an impression. It pays to heed subliminal signals that may hint that something is amiss – an early-warning signal that there is a problem. However, intuition works best when it is methodically explored in a logical way and built on facts. Intuition should never be followed blindly![34]

MORE STRATEGIES

Six thinking hats – looking at the problem from all perspectives

Six Thinking Hats is a powerful technique that helps you to look at important decisions from a number of different perspectives;[35] it helps you to make better decisions by forcing you to move outside your habitual ways of thinking. As such, it helps you to understand the full complexity of the decision, as well as spot issues and opportunities to which you might otherwise be blind.

This tool was created by Edward de Bono in his book, *Six Thinking Hats*. Many successful people think from a very rational, positive viewpoint. This is part of the reason why they are successful. Often, though, they may fail to look at a problem from an emotional, intuitive, creative or negative viewpoint. This can mean that they underestimate resistance to plans, fail to make creative leaps, and do not make essential contingency plans. Similarly, pessimists may be excessively defensive, while people who are more emotional may fail to look at decisions calmly and rationally.

If you look at a problem with the *Six Thinking Hats* technique, you will approach the problem from six different thinking styles. Your decisions and plans will then control for ambition, skill in execution, sensitivity, creativity and good contingency planning. In meetings, this has the benefit of negotiating confrontations that occur when people with different thinking styles discuss the same problem. Each 'thinking hat' is a metaphor for a particular style of thinking. Let's look at each of these hats in turn[36]:

- **White Hat**
  From this vantage point, you would focus on the available data (e.g. facts and figures). Consider the information you have and see what you can learn from it. Revisit the gaps in your knowledge then attempt to either fill them or take account of them. Review past experience and identify a situation with a similar problem. How was the problem addressed? Can we learn from how problems were solved in the past?

- **Red Hat**
  'Wearing' the red hat, you would assess problems using intuition, gut reaction, hunches and emotion. Also, try to think how other people will react emotionally to the problem and its solution. Try to understand the responses of people who are not fully informed and not well versed in your reasoning.

- **Black Hat**
  Using black hat thinking, you would view all the negative aspects of the decision. Look at it cautiously and from a defensive vantage point (often the devil's advocate!). Consider why it might not work. This is important because it highlights the weak links in a plan, allowing you to eliminate them, alter them, or to prepare contingency plans to counter them.

Black hat thinking helps to make your plans 'tougher' and more resilient. It can also assist in identifying fatal flaws and risks before you embark on a course of action. Black hat thinking is one of the real benefits of this technique, as many successful people get so used to thinking positively that often they cannot see problems in advance. This leaves them under-prepared for difficulties.

- **Yellow Hat**
  The yellow hat helps you to think positively. It represents the optimistic viewpoint that helps you to see all the value and benefits of the decision. Yellow hat thinking helps you to retain a positive focus when things look gloomy and difficult.

- **Green Hat**

  The green hat represents creativity. This is where you would develop new concepts and innovative solutions to a problem. It is a freewheeling way of thinking, in which there is little criticism of ideas. A whole range of creativity tools can assist with this process.

- **Blue Hat**

  The blue hat stands for process control, and is 'worn' by people who chair meetings. When things are running into difficulties because ideas are running dry, they may direct the way of thinking (e.g. black hat or white hat thinking) to kindle a renewed attempt to solve the problem.

HOW TO DEAL WITH MULTIPLE PROBLEMS

When you are faced with multiple problems, you may feel overwhelmed, helpless and unsure how to proceed. You may even decide to quit altogether. When facing more than one problem, the key element is to focus on solving one problem at a time. If you have an unhealthy lifestyle and want to change your lifestyle you may need to quit smoking, eat a more balanced diet and exercise regularly. Where do you start? To begin with, choose one area of your lifestyle you want to work on, for example, to stop smoking. Once you have achieved this goal successfully, move on to the next problem.

Incubation

When a problem is complex and a solution seems unattainable, it may be helpful to allow it to "incubate", i.e. set it aside for a while. The solution may suddenly appear when you stop focusing on it. The benefit of incubation may arise from forgetting incorrect ideas that may have been blocking the path to the correct solution.[37]

Individuals epitomising these skills

Bill Gates
Thomas Edison
Albert Einstein
Others?

A FINAL WORD

The ability to solve problems requires more than an understanding of the facts; it also requires the competent management and employment of emotional information. It demands a keen awareness of your own emotional responses and those of other role players, as well as insight into how emotions can hinder or facilitate the process of solving problems. Thus, cognisance of the role of emotions when solving problems forms a vital and important component of this sought after skill.

SECTION 2: ACTIVITIES FOR SKILLS DEVELOPMENT

Self-assessment

Individual activities

Activity 1: Measuring the level of your problem solving ability

What is the level of your problem solving ability? Spend a few minutes benchmarking the level of your problem solving ability. Give your responses to the statement below, assigning a number to each item, using this scale:

1 = Very seldom or not true of me
2 = Seldom true of me
3 = Sometimes true of me
4 = Often true of me
5 = Very often true of me or true of me

When confronted with a problem situation, I break it down into small systematic steps.					
1	2	3	4	5

When somebody approaches me with a problem, I always ask him or her to provide me with all the relevant information.					
1	2	3	4	5

It is always important to see the "big" picture before solving a problem.					
1	2	3	4	5

I enjoy brainstorming with others to solve problems.					
1	2	3	4	5

When solving a problem I always make use of my gut response (intuition).					
1	2	3	4	5

Multiply your score by 4 to arrive at a total out of 100.

Problem-solving ability level scale									
10	20	30	40	50	60	70	80	90	100

Activity 2

Reflect on the recent past and make a list of problems (these need not be major problems) that you have solved successfully.

....

....

What did you do right?

....

....

Will you be able to do it again?

....

....

What did you learn?

....

....

How did you feel when you solved the problem?

....

....

Are there any problems that you find difficult to resolve? Describe how you have attempted to solve the problem, then use the strategies described in this module to help you.

....

....

Group activity

Activity 3

> Daniel is a civil servant who has worked at the Department of Education for 30 years. He decides to take an early retirement as he wants to pursue a lifelong dream of opening a small bookstore. He will use his retirement funds to finance the business. Daniel has no children but his wife does not support him in this undertaking. He does not know where to start and has approached you for help. In your groups, decide what will be the best way to help Daniel. (Use the five-step model discussed in this module.)

Discuss the pros and cons of using intuition in solving problems at work.

....

....

How would you motivate co-workers to develop their problem solving skills? Write an e-mail to circulate to all members of staff.

....

....

Discuss solving the following problem:

Your country is in recession. Your organisation needs to retrench 25% of the staff complement if it wants to survive. The staff is invited to come forward with an approach to the problem.

....

....

Own work for personal growth: a to-do list for the next fortnight

Activity 4

Over the next two weeks, observe your attitude towards problems. Do you avoid problems or do you see problems as a challenge?

....

....

Are there any particular problems that you tend to avoid?

....

....

Are you more successful at solving problems in certain areas of your life than others?

....

....

How do you know when something is a problem?

....

....

Can you think of instances when your emotional response exacerbated the problem instead of solving it?

....

....

How do you motivate yourself to persist in attempts to find a solution?

....

....

What would you consider your strengths/weaknesses when solving problems?

....

....

Which emotions tend to derail your attempts to make a decision?

....

....

Can you think of a situation when positive emotions helped you to solve a problem?

....

....

REFERENCES

Baumgardner, S. & Crothers, M. (2014). *Positive Psychology* (1st ed.). *New Delhi, India*: Pearson.

Berg, Z.C. & Theron, A.L. (2004). *Psychology in the Work Context*. Cape Town: Oxford University Press.

Bergh, Z. 2007. Psychological Disorders. In Z. Bergh and A. Theron (eds.). *Psychology in the Work Context*. Cape Town: Oxford University Press.

Bergh, Z. & Theron, A. (2007). *Psychology in the Work Context*. Cape Town: Oxford University Press.

Bernstein, D.A., Penner, L.A., Clark-Stewart, A. & Roy, E.J. (2006). *Psychology* (7th ed.). New York: Houghton Mifflin Company.

Chaffee, J. (2009). *Thinking Critically* (9th ed.). Boston: Heinle.

De Bono, E. 1996. *Mind Power: Discover the Secrets of Creative Thinking*. London: Dorling Kindersley.

Fredrickson, B.L. (2004). *Gratitude Like Other Positive Emotions, Broadens and Build*. In R.A. Emmons & M.E. McCullough (eds.). *The Psychology of Gratitude*. New York: Oxford University Press.

Hughes, M. & Terrel, J.B. (2012). *Emotional Intelligence in Action* (2nd ed.). San Francisco: Pfeiffer.

Isen, A.M. (2008). Some Ways in Which Positive Affect Influences Decision Making and Problem Solving. In M. Lewis, J.M. Haviland Jones & L. Fledman Barret (eds.). *Handbook of Emotions* (3rd ed.). New York: The Guilford Press.

Jordan, P.J. & Troth, A. (2004). Managing Emotions During Team Problem Solving: Emotional Intelligence and Conflict Resolution. *Human Performance, 17*(2), p. 195 – 218.

Salovey, P., Detweiler-Bedell, B.T., Detweiler-Bedell, J.B. & Mayer, J.D. (2008). *Emotional Intelligence*. In M. Lewis, J.M. Haviland Jones & L. Fledman Barret eds.). *Handbook of Emotions* (3rd ed.). New York: The Guilford Press.

Stein, S. & Book, H. (2011). *The EQ edge: Emotional Intelligence and your Success (3rd ed.)*. San Francisco: Jossey-Bass.

Weiten, W. (2002). *Psychology Themes and Variations* (5th ed.). Belmont: Wadsworth.

Wessels, S.J. (1980). *Stelselontwikkeling en Prestasiemotivering by Eerstejaarstudente by die Universiteit van die Vrystaat*. Ongepubliseerde Proefskrif. Universiteit van die Vrystaat, Bloemfontein.

ENDNOTES

1. Bergh & Theron, 2007:137.
2. Weiten, 2002:243.
3. Stein & Book, 2011:166.
4. Salovey et al., 2008:534.
5. Salovey, 2008; Fredrickson, 2004.
6. Isen, 2008.
7. Jordan & Troth, 2004.
8. Bernstein et al., 2006:304.
9. Bernstein et al., 2006.
10. Bernstein et al., 2006; Berg, 2007; Baumgardner & Crothers, 2014.
11. Bergh, 2007.
12. Bernstein et al., 2006.
13. Bernstein et al., 2006; Baumgardner & Crothers, 2014.
14. Bernstein et al., 2006:299.
15. Chaffee, 2009:80.
16. Stein & Book, 2011.

17 Chaffee, 2009:80.
18 Hughes & Terrel, 2012.
19 Isen, 2008:552.
20 Chaffee, 2009:85.
21 Stein & Book, 2012:169.
22 Chaffee, 2009:85.
23 Wessels, 1980.
24 Chaffee, 2009:97.
25 Chaffee, 2009.
26 Wessels, 1980.
27 Chaffee, 2009:86.
28 Chaffee, 2009:79.
29 Chaffee, 2009:87.
30 Chaffee, 2009:89.
31 Chaffee, 2009:90.
32 Chaffee, 2009: 92.
33 Chaffee, 2009:96.
34 Stein & Book, 2011:173.
35 De Bono, 1996.
36 De Bono, 1996: 66-67.
37 Bernstein et al., 2006:291.

Chapter 13

REALITY TESTING

Eugene van Niekerk

A dream doesn't become reality through magic, it takes sweat, determination and hard work.

—Colin Powel

SECTION 1: OVERVIEW

As you develop your emotional intelligence and the ability to understand and manage your emotions and those of others, you begin to see things in a more realistic light. We have learned to interpret reality against the background of our own life experience, personal desires, needs, distortions and fears. In order to avoid exaggerating the significance of what we are experiencing positively or negatively, we need to develop reality-testing skills that will stand us in good stead.

This chapter assists you to avoid common hazards affecting accurate perception and wise choice: how you think things should be, how you wish they were, distorting reality through self-delusion, self-denial, self-deception, lack of self-knowledge, and naiveté, including the uncritical acceptance of what others profess to be the "truth". Being in contact with the full complexity of reality is certainly no mean feat. It requires not only skill but a whiff of skepticism as well. It compels us to pose awkward questions such as "Who wants me to believe this reality?", "What are their motives?", and "What evidence do I have at my disposal to support my conclusions?"[1]

After completing this chapter, you should be able to:

- define reality testing;
- understand some theory informing reality testing;
- reflect on the benefits of reality testing;
- understand the role that defence mechanisms play in reality testing;
- understand ways to develop reality testing;
- know your own level of reality testing skills; and
- implement individual and group activities to enhance reality testing.

DEFINITION OF REALITY TESTING

For the purposes of this chapter, we define reality as, "The correspondence between what is experienced and what objectively exists. Reality testing involves tuning in to the immediate situation. It is the capacity to see things objectively, the way they are, rather than the way we wish or fear them to be. Testing this degree of correspondence involves a search for objective evidence to confirm, justify, and support feelings, perceptions and thoughts. The emphasis is on pragmatism, objectivity, the adequacy of your perception and authentication of your ideas and thoughts. An important aspect of this component involves the ability to concentrate and focus when trying to assess and cope with situations that arise. Reality testing is associated with a lack of withdrawal from the outside world, a tuning in to the immediate situation, and lucidity and clarity in perception and thought processes. In simple terms, reality testing is the ability to 'size up' correctly the immediate situation".[2]

That we live in a deeply complex society has become a cliché of sorts. We manage life at multiple levels – career, love and family, social, intellectual, physical, and spiritual, and daily face a myriad choices to boot. Coping effectively means navigating ourselves in respect to what we believe to be "true" and "real".

THEORY INFORMING THE REALITY TESTING CONSTRUCT

In his book *Paradigms of Mind*, Van Niekerk[3] reviews George Kelly's notion of mind, where Kelly compares the mind to that of a scientist. To oversimplify, a taste of his theory follows. According to Kelly, individuals develop theories of individual behaviour (people, situations and events) in order to make the world more comprehensible and predictable. Hypotheses (educated hunches) are generated and tested against experiential evidence. Based on this feedback, individuals confirm or reject hypotheses. An example serves to clarify: You meet John at a party. You experience him as extroverted, kind, considerate, polite and well read. You leave the party with some tentative hunches (hypotheses) about John as being pleasant and affable. Two weeks later, you bump into him by accident and he asks you out on a date. You accept. During the course of the evening previous hunches are confirmed and rejected. You begin to see him on a regular basis and find that – give or take a few minor exceptions – your initial predictions are validated. Your theory about John (a number of hypotheses) holds water. You are now able, says Kelly, to predict (roughly) how John will react in a whole range of circumstances. The mind's ability to predict events, notes Kelly, makes the world understandable, and in the process provides a sense of coherence, security and comfort. Kelly's main contention is that the healthy mind has an inbuilt tendency to make sense of its environment by accurately predicting and understanding the nature of reality. Modern life greatly favours this inbuilt tendency. Consider for a moment the important role that reality testing plays in our life:

- Farmers and pilots rely on weather bulletins.
- Politicians depend on opinion polls.
- Doctors predict (diagnose and prognosticate) the course of illness.
- Futurologists plot scenarios informing societal evolution.
- Prophets provide insights into the future.

When we are unable to make sense of our world – when events appear random – we feel unsafe and anxiety levels increase. To underscore, when a woman who has recently detected a lump in her breast visits a doctor, he makes a diagnosis and prognosis – the course and outcome of an illness. When the doctor pronounces the lump benign, the patient is reassured and anxiety abates. The ability to understand and predict our world leads to an increased sense of coherence and a concomitant diminished level of stress and anxiety. Philosophers through the ages have grappled with notions of the "real". German philosopher Jorgen Habermas, for example, seems to suggest that when a number of persons are in agreement (inter-subjective consensus) on the nature of a particular reality, that reality more closely corresponds to the 'real'.

By way of clarification: The DSM-V is referred to as the *Diagnostic and Statistical Manual of Mental Disorders*. This document is widely accepted as the most influential work on the diagnosis and classification of mental disorders.[4] The DSM-V is sometimes good-humouredly referred to as the "bible" of mental health professionals. The manual provides mental health professionals (psychiatrists, psychologists, medical doctors and medical aid insurance companies, among others) with clear and quantifiable guidelines in respect of the classification of disorders.[5]

The DSM-V is continually updated and revised. The burden of deciding the categories of mental disorders and criteria for diagnosis falls on the American Psychiatric Association's (APA) Committee on Nomenclature and Statistics. They are the final arbiters of psychopathology – whether the mind is judged healthy or sick, functional or dysfunctional. Once the committee has reached agreement, that is, inter-subjective consensus, its findings are published in book form. Most mental health professionals adhere to this powerful convention.

When the mind loses touch with reality

In 2013, the APA's Committee on Nomenclature and Statistics updated its criteria on one of the most serious mental disorders [DSM-V], namely schizophrenia.[6] It proclaimed that an individual suffers from this disorder when two (or more) of the following criteria present for a period of a month or more:

- Delusions (belief in something despite lack of evidence).
- Hallucinations (imaginary perceptions).
- Disorganised speech.
- Catatonic behaviour (stupor).
- Emotional flattening (visible lack of emotion).

Untreated sufferers seldom enjoy an ordinary life. More importantly, their ability to distinguish reality from unreality is significantly impaired. Modern psychotropic drugs only treat symptomology, leaving patients short of a cure - banishing these people to the margins of society.[7]

Having said all this, we also need to be mindful of the following.

> ### Beware... reality is elusive!
>
> "... In one sense, we can never see reality directly; we see it only through our own perceptions. Our perceptions are learned from our experience and our society, and they give us a map of our reality, but no matter how accurate that map may be, it is never the whole territory. Improving our reality testing means [discovering] how well our perceptions match those of others and adding detail to our map, but in order to be as accurate as possible, it must also honour the mystery that lies behind all we can ever perceive."[8]

ROLE OF DEFENCE MECHANISMS IN REALITY TESTING

The Austrian psychiatrist and psychoanalyst Sigmund Freud first coined the term "defence mechanism" early in the 20th century. Among others, defence mechanisms psychologically protect the individual against inconvenient truths. Consider how German Jewry reacted to the ascent of Adolph Hitler and Nazi ideology. Psycho-historians suggest that Hitler's rise was so painful to the Jewish collective psyche that despite overwhelming evidence of looming persecution, this community sought psychological refuge in denial. Their inability to read reality accurately gave rise to unspeakable misery and suffering.[9]

Victims of HIV/AIDS often distort reality (through denial) of their AIDS status, and in the process refuse to seek help. Minimisation, a less potent form of denial, is apparently equally dangerous. Alcoholics, smokers and drug addicts often minimise to twist and skew reality, lessening the anxiety associated with predictable health outcomes. True recovery is seemingly possible only once individuals have come to terms with the reality of their addictive status.

Other mechanisms of defence take on many forms. Indolent (work-shy) students (at times) blame their lecturers for poor performance – a form of rationalisation. A defence mechanism such as regression can sometimes alleviate anxiety. In the wake of a recent marriage, a young mother – let us call her Janet – passes through a "psychological time machine" to regress to a point where she experiences less responsibility – her childhood. Scripting a less demanding role for her allows for temporary respite from marital and maternal pressures, but at some personal cost – inability to face reality head-on. While regression affords us a relatively safe haven, our ability to grow psychologically (build mental muscle) accordingly suffers.

> ## Other defence mechanisms
>
> **Projection**
> Attributing repressed motives, feelings, or wishes to others:
>
> Keniwe is unfairly passed over for promotion. She denies that she is angry about this, but is certain that her boss is annoyed with her.
>
> **Identification**
> Taking on the characteristics of someone else to avoid feeling incompetent:
>
> Anne, low in self-esteem and unclear about her identity, takes on the mannerisms and dress of a famous woman actor.
>
> **Intellectualisation**
> Thinking abstractly about stressful problems as a way of detaching oneself from them:
>
> When Joe is informed of his retrenchment, he rationally and dispassionately discusses the recently-released unemployment statistics and their implications for social cohesion. This defence mechanism is often referred as intellectualisation.
>
> **Reaction formation**
> Expression of exaggerated ideas and emotions that are the opposite of one's repressed beliefs and feelings:
>
> Outwardly Jonathan is very complimentary to his rival, David, whom he dislikes intensely. Despite on-the-surface-congeniality, they are bitter rivals for the position of company CEO.
>
> **Displacement**
> Shifting repressed motives from an original to a substitute object:
>
> Angry with his boss but afraid to confront him, John returns home and takes his frustrations out on his wife, with unhappy domestic outcomes.
>
> **Sublimation**
> Redirecting repressed motives and feelings into more socially acceptable channels:
>
> Chantelle exercises intensely in the gym and plays all kinds of sport to re-channel her deep personal anger (negative destructive energy) following two failed marriages.[10]

DEVELOPING REALITY TESTING

People with a strong capacity for reality testing see the world around them in an objective, clear-eyed manner. They are quick to recognise where problems exist, and can perceive opportunities when they come into sight. Those who have weaker reality testing skills either 'keep their heads in the sand' to avoid facing problems, or can see (and magnify) only risks and, as a result, are unable to take advantage of opportunities.[11]

Well-developed reality testing skills are more likely to help us avoid unexpected loss or disappointment since we more readily anticipate its coming. Reality-testing skills promote harmonious interpersonal relations. Harmony, after all, is a value deeply embedded in our culture.

Consider how a crucial decision affects life's quality, for example:

• Who to marry.	• Who to confide in.
• What career to follow.	• Where to invest your hard earned money.
• Who to trust.	

> ### 'Love is blind' – the story of Lindi
>
> Most of you are familiar with the phrase, 'love is blind'. Many romantic relationships begin with mutual infatuation and a blind spot for the other's faults and shortcomings. Let us eavesdrop on a conversation between mother and daughter. Lindi is responding to her mother, who is very concerned about Lindi's intention of marrying her new boyfriend, Joe, whom she met a few weekends ago at a party.
>
> "I realise you think that I'm being hasty in my decision to marry Joe, but I really love him. We talked over the weekend about his drinking, drug addiction and his many jobs. He placed all his cards on the table and I respect him for his honesty. He told me that he thinks people just do not understand him and he is ready to make a fresh start.
>
> He told me that despite three failed marriages he has at last found true love. He also confessed that he comes from a home in which he was a victim of molestation, and in addition to that, both parents were alcoholics. He promised me that he has given up drink and drugs and that he has found the Lord."
>
> *What do you think of Lindi's reality testing skills? What are the possible implications for her future happiness? Discuss.*

HOW A LEADER TESTS REALITY – THE "CEO DISEASE"

Self-delusion is a powerful trap – not one into which a business leader should fall. In their book, *Primal Leaders*, Daniel Goleman et al.[12] discuss an emergent phenomenon increasingly apparent within leadership circles – the "CEO disease". More than anyone else, a leader should be privy to all relevant information at hand before arriving at a decision, yet there is a tendency, the authors argue, for leaders to receive only (or mostly) good news. Apparently, the CEO disease is fed by a tendency to want to please the boss (sycophancy) resulting in a distorted view of reality.

According to Goleman et al., leaders who receive only positive information about their own leadership styles as a form of self-evaluation are much less effective than leaders who receive both positive and negative feedback. More recently, in an effort to provide feedback that is more objective, organisations have begun to implement a 360-degree feedback technique. With the 360-degree format, the CEO now receives feedback from superiors, peers, and sub-ordinates – overall, more accurate feedback vital to a leader's continued growth and effectiveness.[13]

The mind manufactures mental maps that correspond (to a greater or lesser degree) with "objective" reality. A privately-constructed world inevitably includes bias, that is, we tend to exaggerate the significance of what we experience positively or negatively. This happens against the background of our own life experience and history, and colours our perception of the current situation. Very often, we use only three out of the five senses to construct our experience of reality. Therefore, it is often helpful to verify what we see, hear, feel and sense. Likewise, it is very helpful to check our reasoning processes to confirm that the conclusions we arrive at actually follow logically from all the information available to us. When we are unsuccessful in this, we are not assessing reality adequately enough to achieve the results we pursue. Re-evaluating our perceptions on a regular basis is yet another avenue to develop our reality testing skills further.[14]

Reality testing requires a healthy mind

Healthy minds not only function optimally, but they are also generally more in touch with reality. The healthy mind is also an alert mind, and is able to view and weigh up problems from various perspectives ("multi-perspectives") and make fresh connections from existing knowledge and information. The healthy mind has a broad thought stream that nourishes conscious awareness.

In contrast, the "blunted" mind suffers from thought "poverty" (clouded consciousness), sometimes referred to as "a head full of cotton wool". High stress levels, together with an unhealthy life style – poor eating habits, sleep deprivation, alcohol abuse, and smoking – often lead to a less than alert mind.

Intuition – another way of knowing

The intuitive mind is a sacred gift, and the rational mind is a faithful servant. We have created a society that honours the servant and has forgotten the gift.

– Albert Einstein

Intuition has been associated with folk medicine for decades. Of late, intuition has come under renewed scientific scrutiny, enjoying newfound scholarly respect. According to Daniel Goleman,[15] there are too many things that a person cannot predict by relying on hard data alone. Goleman – who has made a study of how the intuitive brain functions – writes that intuition serves as an important tool in coming to grips with complex issues. Intuitive learning (also referred to as tacit or silent learning) takes place in the primitive zone of the brain – the basic ganglia – outside the reach of words. The amygdala (the brain's storage site of emotions associated with memory) is similarly involved in intuitive learning. The amygdala's circuitry runs down into the gastrointestinal tract, which literally creates a "gut feeling".[16]

According to Goleman, we need to practice intuition regularly if it is to become a skill that we can trust. More business leaders have come to acknowledge the value of going beyond the data to rely on their own instincts. Even if a business plan looks good based on hard data alone, if it does not "feel right", they proceed with the utmost caution – or not at all.[17] For these executives, intuition serves as yet another means by which valuable information may be gathered. Goleman cautions, however, that placing all our trust in intuition alone can lead to ineffective decision-making. He notes that intuition works best when it is backed up with other kinds of information, including consulting experts and bringing hard data under scrutiny. The following pointers serve to refine our decision-making abilities further:

- Differentiate between hearsay and facts.
- Invest in serious thought before you arrive at a decision.
- Make sure that you have hard evidence at hand to support your view of a person, proposition or situation.
- Consider approaching a neutral party for their objective assessment.
- Check that you are not viewing the person or situation through either too dark or overly rose-tinted lenses.
- Attempt to distance yourself from your own prejudices – this is an advanced life skill requiring practice and superior (self) insight.
- Test your own beliefs or points of view against the agreement of others you know. In other words, is there general agreement among those you poll in respect of your own view of reality?
- Scrutinise a problem from various perspectives before reaching a conclusion.

Individuals epitomising reality testing skills

Dr. Hans Blix (chief negotiator: International Atomic Energy Board)
Helen Zille
Helen Suzman
Others?

A FINAL WORD

Individuals who lack reality testing skills often blunder through life triggering one calamity after another. An inability to exercise sound judgment may, for example, lead them to fall victim to "get rich quick" schemes (without carefully exploring the implications), impulsively leave a job, leave a small child unattended in a car, recklessly squander personal resources, and more. Such persons, naïve to the ramifications of their actions, often engage in wishful thinking, and hope that things will somehow work out. On another level, impulse-driven individuals are often slave to the whim of the moment – lashing out at the boss without forethought, regularly overdrawing on their personal bank account, misusing credit card facilities, and otherwise recklessly indulging themselves – invariably with dire consequences.

SECTION 2: ACTIVITIES FOR SKILLS DEVELOPMENT

Self-assessment

Individual activity

 Activity 1

Spend a few moments assessing your reality testing skills. Give your responses to the statements below honestly. Assign a number to each item, using this scale:

1 = Very seldom or not true of me
2 = Seldom true of me
3 = Sometimes true of me
4 = Often true of me
5 = Very often true of me or true of me

While I may occasionally indulge in daydreaming, my feet are usually firmly on the ground – I am well grounded in the "real" world.

1	2	3	4	5

I do not live in a make-believe world.

1	2	3	4	5

I have the capacity to view things "objectively" – the way they are, rather than the way I wish or fear them to be.

1	2	3	4	5

When an individual tells me his or her side of events, I do not just accept it at face value, I ask for the evidence.

1	2	3	4	5

I am aware of my own prejudices that may distort the way I view reality.

1	2	3	4	5

Multiply the total by 4 to arrive at a total out of 100.

Reality testing scale

10	20	30	40	50	60	70	80	90	100

Activity 2

In your opinion, why is reality testing important? What insights have you gained from this chapter?

....

....

Describe how you go about making important decisions in life. Think back on the most important decisions you have had to make in your life so far. How did you go about making those decisions?

....

....

When sizing up a situation, do you think that you are more often on base or off base? Provide examples when you were on base and examples when you were off base.

....

....

When summing up a situation, are you more inclined to use your rational left brain or your intuitive right brain? Do you make use of both hemispheres in problem solving? Can you think of examples in your personal life? (Einstein, for example, said that most of his greatest insights came to him in the shower, while others say that jogging gives them greater perspective, and so on.)

....

....

You have recently been diagnosed with Type 2 diabetes. View the problem from different perspectives. (You may want to consider the problem from a biological, psychological, social and spiritual perspective. Can you think of any other examples?)

The boiling frog and reality

If you drop a frog into boiling water, it will instinctively jump out. However, if you place a frog in a pot of cool water and gradually increase the temperature, the frog will not notice that the water is getting hotter. It will sit there until the water boils – and will boil with it. The fate of that poached frog is not unlike that of some leaders who settle into a routine or let convenient practices solidify into habits – and allow inertia to set in.

Are you a boiling frog? Have you become complacent lately? What type of feedback are you receiving from your environment?[18]

Group activity

 Activity 3

What are some of the prejudices that you hold in respect of people from different cultures, professions, religions, and so on? (Think, for example, of possible prejudice towards Jews, Afrikaners, Afro-Americans, black South Africans, gays, Catholics, Muslims, boxers, and so on.)

How do these influence your perceptions in your day-to-day life?

REFERENCES

American Psychiatric Association (APA). (2013). *Diagnostic and statistical manual of mental disorders* (5th ed.). Washington, DC: APA.

Breger, L. (2000). *Freud: darkness in the midst of vision.* New York: John Wiley.

Goleman, D. (2011). *The brain and emotional intelligence: New insights.* Northampton, MA: More Than Sound.

Goleman, D., Boyatzis, R. & Mckee. A. (2013). *Primal Leadership.* London: Little Brown.

Hughes, M., Patterson, L. & Terrel, J. (2012). *Emotional intelligence in action: Training and coaching activities for leaders and managers.* San Francisco: Pfeiffer.

Morris, C.G. (1996). *Psychology: An Introduction.* New York: Prentice Hall.

Sadock, B.J. & Sadock, V.A. (2000). *Kaplan & Sadock's comprehensive textbook of psychiatry.* New York: Lippincott.

Shorter, E. (1997). *A History of Psychiatry: From the era of the asylum to the age of Prozac.* New York: John Wiley.

Stein, S. & Book, H. (2011). *The EQ edge. Emotional intelligence and your success.* Toronto: Kogan Page.

Van Niekerk, E.C. (1996). *Paradigms of mind. Personality in perspective.* Cape Town: Oxford University Press.

Van Niekerk, E.C. (2016). *Mind Alive.* (Unpublished Manuscript). Cape Town.

ENDNOTES

1. Hughes, Patterson & Terrel, 2012.
2. Stein & Book, 2011.
3. Van Niekerk, 1996.
4. Coleman, 2013.
5. Shorter, 1997.
6. APA, 2013.
7. Sadock & Sadock, 2000.
8. Hughes, Patterson & Terrel, 2012.
9. Breger, 2000.
10. Morris, 1996.
11. Stein & Book, 2011.
12. Goleman et al., 2013.
13. Goleman et al., 2013.
14. Hughes, Patterson & Terrel, 2012.
15. Goleman et al., 2013.
16. Goleman, 2011.
17. Goleman et al., 2013.
18. Goleman et al., 2013:26.

Chapter 14

IMPULSE CONTROL

Annette Prins

Industry, thrift and self-control are not sought because they create wealth, but because they create character.

– Calvin Coolidge

SECTION 1: OVERVIEW

Impulses are urges compelling action:[1] "They exist beyond logic and spring from our subconscious minds with persistence and intensity. They pulsate with primal urgency and are fueled by psychological or physiological factors." Impulses may be helpful (helping us escape from an attack) or harmful (if they lead to the destruction of property or hurt people). A lack of impulse control can diminish efficiency and cause much misery, thus we need to contemplate the consequences of our actions before rushing into them.

Self-control is the most basic of the self-management competencies, which hold the key to managing stress and anger, controlling impulses and helping us to remain motivated in the face of setbacks.[2]

Inappropriate or excessive emotion could prove detrimental to a career,[3] thus self-regulation, which is the ability to manage both positive and negative emotions, control impulses, deal effectively with stress, and stay clear-minded, is crucial. Emotional self-control builds on emotional self-awareness; while emotional self-awareness asks: "How aware are you of your emotions?", emotional self-control wants to know: "How effective are you at controlling your emotions and impulses?"

"To become an emotional capitalist – to create wealth in the fullest sense of the word – you must take the decision to accept personal responsibility and become self-reliant. Self-responsibility is the core quality of the fully mature, fully functioning individual."[4]

After completing this chapter, you should be able to:

- define impulse control;
- understand some theory underpinning the construct of impulse control;
- reflect on some benefits of impulse control;
- understand ways to develop impulse control;
- identify individuals epitomising impulse control;
- assess your own level of impulse control; and
- implement individual and group activities to enhance impulse control.

DEFINITION OF IMPULSE CONTROL

"Impulse control is the ability to resist or delay an impulse, drive or temptation to act and involves avoiding rash behaviors and decision making."[5] In addition, self-control is "the ability to remain composed in spite of our emotional state".[6]

Impulse control "…entails a capacity for accepting one's aggressive impulses, being composed, and controlling aggression, hostility, and irresponsible behavior".[7] Problems in impulse control are manifested by low frustration tolerance, impulsiveness, anger control problems, abusiveness, loss of self-control, and explosive and unpredictable behaviour.

Impulse control is, in fact, "not taking a particular action aimed at short-term gratification in order to avoid possible long-term consequences".[8] In order to manage an impulse, a mental representation of the possible consequences of such action needs to be made in the working memory in order to contain the impulsive action. Impulse control therefore involves the suppression of approach behaviour. (See Chapter 2.)

In conclusion, emotional self-control is our ability to:

- resist or delay an impulse or temptation to act;
- control aggressive, hostile and irresponsible behaviour;
- act in a predictable way; and
- understand how we can go about managing destructive emotions.

Our attention now turns to theory related to impulse control.

THEORY UNDERPINNING THE CONSTRUCT OF IMPULSE CONTROL

"Our top down mind takes more time to deliberate on what it is presented with, taking things one at a time and applying more thoughtful analysis".[9]

Impulsivity may be explained by a broad range of factors, including psycho-dynamic, psychosocial and biological factors, the scope of which falls outside the ambit of the current text. The interested reader is referred to Sadock et al.[10] for a more in-depth discussion.

If we wish to function at a higher level of effectiveness it is essential that we control and resist our harmful impulses.[11] If, for example, a person becomes demonstrably angry in the workplace/home it may damage relationships. Individuals with Type A personalities are constantly on the move, action-orientated, like to multi-task, and are not much concerned with controlling their urges. They frequently view these traits as the ones that rocketed them to the top of the career ladder, and believe them to be essential to success. They pay scant attention to the carcasses falling by the wayside. Furthermore, these individuals are prone to illnesses, including an increased risk of cardio-vascular disease. These risks also hold economic implications for the workplace.

According to Ferguson and Kelly,[12] emotions have a definite place in the world of work; they provide for passion, vision, enthusiasm, and compassion. People do not, however, have equal control over their emotions. Some voice their emotions too loudly and too often, or simply "blow up". Too intense or inappropriately-expressed emotions can disconnect key players in a team. An example would be the EFF party in South Africa, which in 2016/7 repeatedly disrupted parliamentary proceedings. Dressed in red overalls they ran amok, with a concomitant disruption of orderly procedures. This gave rise to negative press coverage, which was detrimental to a country in dire need of economic support and a positive evaluation of its political and economic stability. Emotions may, however, be used to focus and inspire others in pursuit of an ideal. Even anger, if well timed and well controlled, may function to alert people to mistakes and problems. Emotional self-control, note Ferguson and Kelly,[13] "...is extremely important and has a profound impact on the bottom line".

Effective impulse control does not equal stifling or even disregarding your gut feeling. It is, however, the ability to look before you leap – to manage wisely and coolly a range of volatile emotions and urges.[14]

Controlling yourself does not equal suppressing emotions, but rather implies that individuals with this ability are better able to use their emotions effectively and, when appropriate, express them in a constructive manner.[15] Others, such as Adler, countered this by advancing the argument that individuals are creative beings, able to create their own unique lifestyles, and should therefore take responsibility for their behaviours and personalities. Newman[16] holds the view that successful leaders have a strong sense of internal accountability in the different spheres of their lives, from personal to work.

Both impulsive behaviour and indecision through procrastination are forms of behaviour which have the intention of avoiding responsibility and thoughtful choice. Plato believed that we house an ongoing battle between the adult and child in ourselves. "The child in you remains controlled by fear and insecurity and wants to remain dependent on other adults. The adult part of you wants to assert mastery over the fears that sabotage independent, creative thought and action."[17]

In addition, Watson and Idinopulos[18] state that all human beings harbour destructive elements, despite many pursuing the good life in a disciplined manner. Outwardly, respectability is projected, "guided by reason and civility", however on the inside, human beings are often besieged by angry, lustful, and hurtful impulses. We inadvertently house both Dr. Jekyll and Mr. Hyde. Part of being resilient is reflected in our acceptance of the dualities in our personalities (such as being soft and hard; cruel and kind; thoughtful and impulsive; hardworking and lazy), rather than negating these dualities. The art lies in channeling primitive instincts into so called "higher purposes". According to the authors, "[h]igh ideals and civility resonate positively with people's saintly side. Their minds nod acceptance to those virtues that civilisation honours: humility, kindness, decency, fairness…". People try to instill these qualities in themselves and then to project them on the outside. These qualities include, *inter alia*, being principled and controlled. They attempt to steer their lives by love and reason, but temptations are ever present; part of our not-so-nice reality. We may, at times, be hijacked by our anger, frustration, and selfish desires, losing control and flaring up. Selfish desires may seduce even the best among us, while ambitions and needs cry out to be fulfilled.[19]

Good values may give way to the urges of greed; people may believe that they are due certain privileges by virtue of, *inter alia*, their hard work. They may take short cuts to increasing their bank balances and other privileges. When it pays off and they aren't caught out, they relax and let go of their moral compasses, giving in to their immediate desires. The process grows increasingly easier as they become immune to the discomfort that accompanies underhand transactions, and they begin to view themselves as above the laws and rules governing others' behaviour.[20] This is prevalent in political circles where corruption is under cover.

Examples?

At work

Mersino[21] contends that negative emotions can poison and even cripple a team, especially when coming from a leader. When a great deal is at stake for both an organisation and a team, emotions may get out of control. Larger projects are typically managed against aggressive deadlines, with dire financial implications if they are not met according to schedule. Particularly when things are being done for the first time, estimates may be unrealistic; delivering becomes a personal success or failure for the project leader.

An example may be some of the student population, who were led by their Student Representative Councils in tertiary institutions across South Africa, who demanded that "Fees must fall" in 2016. Victory was seen as non-negotiable and negative emotions, including anger, rage, disappointment, and fear, led to the destruction of university property, the disruption of the academic year, and the closing down of campuses, amongst other outcomes.

These emotions need to be monitored and managed expertly so that the functioning of the whole tertiary system is not undermined, and the key is to respond, not react. Responding is a thoughtful and considered response, whereas a reaction is an immediate response triggered by the (emotional) amygdala to something it perceives is threatening. This means that the survival response triggered by the amygdala in the emotional brain needs to be calmed down so that the neocortex can come up with a more rational and appropriate response. Managing these emotions does not, however, mean that they are suppressed, negated or dismissed, but rather that they are managed in a way that does not cripple the team in its workings. Working under pressure may bring out both the worst and the best in us. "Any tiny crack in our emotional foundation is brought to light, and often, when exposed to heat and pressure, will result in unpleasant side effects."[22] It is therefore acknowledged that we may all carry the seeds of psychopathology, but that they may be revealed only when we are exposed to intense pressure. Our underlying emotional nature may thereby be revealed.

If a project manager, for example, cannot control his or her emotions, they may gain a reputation of being "out of control", which may have repercussions when working with people both in and outside of the team. In turn, this may have implications for gaining and retaining the best resources. Worse may happen when team members set out to sabotage the project quietly. When people "lose it" on the job and it holds negative consequences for progress, it may, for example, lead to disciplinary hearings and investigations that may be very embarrassing for a project leader. When angered, a leader should, *inter alia*, first allow time to calm down rather than reacting inappropriately from a position of anger so as to evaluate alternative routes more rationally. The underlying relationship and the undercurrents must also be attended to and not ignored, to avoid the possibility of unruly or inappropriate behavior in a toxic environment.[23]

Self-control should also be applied sensitively in relation to positive emotions when it is inappropriate to express them, such as when someone is promoted and a competing colleague is not. Both highs and lows need to be controlled so that the expression thereof is appropriate for the context. Emotional hijacking or breakdown is an involuntary response to an emotional situation. This is due to a primitive neurological survival system acting in response to threat, and is a more intense reaction than the normal fight-and-flight response.[24] An extreme form may be road rage, where an individual may become so outraged that he or she acts in an unpredictable and out of control manner.

A husband is called by his pregnant wife to take her to hospital to give birth to their first child. In a state of heightened vigilance, he races home. A taxi driver, however, obstructs the road by lazily chatting to a friend in another taxi. No hooting or signs get them to move – they laugh and mock him. He loses it, grabs his hockey stick and charges the taxis...

Mersino[25] describes a few examples of emotional breakdowns:

- Angry tirades where people explode with anger and come down on a co-worker.

- Door slamming, such as when a person does not get his way.

- Angry e-mail when reacting and not thoughtfully responding.

- Withdrawal and isolation; avoiding people.

- Holding grudges or getting even – especially after unwelcome decisions, having received negative feedback or criticism.

- Criticising with the intention of hurting the other, frequently emanating from feelings of insecurity.

- Sarcasm or inappropriate humour, especially when we do not want to confront a situation or person directly.
- Playing the victim. This is yet another reaction indicative of a possible emotional breakdown. In this instance, people blame others for their mistakes, and do not accept responsibility for their own actions or reactions.

Attention now turns to the personality characteristics of a person with low impulse control.

Personality characteristics of a person with low impulse control

People who have difficulty in controlling their emotions often exhibit the following personality profile. They are:

- hot headed and impatient;
- impulsive;
- low in frustration tolerance – easily become impatient and aggressive;
- unpredictable in terms of their responses;
- poor decision makers when under pressure;
- prone to spending money unwisely;
- unable or find it difficult to sustain long-term relationships;
- easily carried away by the moment, frequently to their detriment; and
- possibly subject to outbursts of anger.[26]

Such behaviour may have negative consequences, such as:

- being less adept at establishing worthwhile social contacts;
- tending to be stubborn and indecisive;
- yielding more readily to temptations and frustration;
- being more vulnerable to stress;
- behaving in thoughtless, arbitrary and compulsive ways;
- finding it difficult to control anger and rage reactions;
- readily giving way to abusive outbursts, and explosive and unpredictable behaviour;
- reduced ability to think clearly and focus on the task at hand;
- suffer from psychological and physical distress or illness;
- poor interpersonal relationships; and
- poor impulse control – lacking the discipline to resist time-wasting distractions and pleasures.

In conditions such as conduct disorder, oppositional defiant disorder, kleptomania etc., individuals have an "inability to resist an intense impulse, drive or temptation to perform a particular act that is obviously harmful to self or others, or both". The individual may experience mounting arousal and tension, at times mingled with anticipatory pleasure.[27]

Completion of the act brings immediate relief and gratification. This may be followed by remorse, regret, guilt and dread.

The most debilitating form of impulsivity is attention deficit (hyperactivity) disorder in adults.

Attention deficit hyperactivity disorder (ADHD) in adults

A diagnosis of ADHD requires a comprehensive evaluation by a licensed clinician, such as a paediatrician, psychologist, or psychiatrist with expertise in ADHD.
ADHD is a brain disorder marked by an ongoing pattern of inattention and/or hyperactivity-impulsivity that interferes with functioning or development.

- **Inattention** means a person wanders off task, lacks persistence, has difficulty sustaining focus, and is disorganised, and these problems are not due to defiance or a lack of comprehension.
- **Hyperactivity** means a person seems to move about constantly, including in situations in which it is not appropriate, or excessively fidgets, taps, or talks. In adults, it may be extreme restlessness or wearing others out with constant activity.
- **Impulsivity** means a person makes hasty interpretations that occur in the moment without first thinking about them, which may hold high potential for harm, a or a desire for immediate rewards or an inability to delay gratification. An impulsive person may be socially intrusive and excessively interrupt others, or make important decisions without considering the long-term consequences.

A range of specialised interventions including medication and psychotherapy aims to help contain the person to lead a functional life. A professional counsellor or therapist can help an adult with ADHD learn how to organise his or her life with tools such as:

- keeping routines;
- making lists for different tasks and activities;
- using a calendar for scheduling events;
- using reminder notes;
- assigning a special place for keys, bills, and paperwork; and
- breaking down large tasks into more manageable, smaller steps so that completing each part of the task provides a sense of accomplishment.[28]

IMPROVING IMPULSE CONTROL

While emotions are both important and needed, they have to be regulated,[29] as uncontrolled emotion may hamper the process of pursuing goals. A loss of respect and credibility follow from overly emotional reactions, while badly-timed anger may negatively influence morale at work and at home.

We can become our own best assets by mastering the art of self-discipline.[30] Self-discipline, in contrast to impulsiveness, "...enables humans to be punctual, to act with perseverance, to be industrious, to rise above pettiness, to focus efforts on important matters and produce desired results". A good life is lived only with a good amount of discipline.

Tracy[31] suggests a direct relationship between the number of positive emotions we enjoy and independence, control, and responsibility. Building emotional capital, it is argued, is directly related to the level of responsibility we are able to manage, thus we build emotional capital via impulse control.

Cherniss and Adler[32] refer to "flow", a condition where individuals experience an intense absorption in a task that they find interesting and optimally challenging. This state, inducing superior performance, is brought about by enjoyment of the task at hand. It has been demonstrated that people in flow work most efficiently. While flow may be induced by a range of activities, from reaching the summit of Mount Everest to working on a favourite project, the advantage is that people work more happily and efficiently when in flow. It has been found that, on average, people experience flow for about half of their working day. However, large differences present between individuals; those who are able to spend more time in flow become those who excel. The pathway to flow is via self-control and acute self-awareness.[33] It would seem that individuals who control their impulses are therefore more likely to experience flow.

DEVELOPING IMPULSE CONTROL

The best way to gain impulse control is via our logical thinking processes and the ABCs discussed in Chapter 16 on stress management.[34] They speak of the so-called "impulse gate", which needs to function to keep impulses in check, have them cool off, and be open to free impulses and volatile emotions only when they have cooled down sufficiently. When this gate is not intact and swings to and fro, unchecked impulses and emotions escape and often cause much damage to others and the self.

Impulse control starts with the habit of viewing our own actions and inactions and measuring them up against the goals we've set for ourselves.[35] Do these actions measure up? We need to accept our "primitive instincts" and use them to our advantage in an artful manner. "Inspecting and correcting" our own behaviour therefore lies at the core of mastering impulsiveness. Self-discipline reflects two main components – self-evaluation (against a set of virtues) and habit building. If we allow our basic instincts to run rampant, it will bring unwelcome reactions our way. We need to "...harness dangerous, natural instincts and direct them to useful purposes, rather than trying to negate them".[36]

Therefore, the building of impulse control entails the identifying and analysing of dysfunctional behaviour and then changing such behaviour.[37] Controlling of impulses requires emotional self-awareness and the ability to trade immediate satisfaction, seeking for a more thoughtful response aimed at longer term or strategic gratification. The aftermath of impulsive behaviour may not be worth the momentary satisfaction.

Lynn[38] notes that emotional breakdowns may be preceded by specific triggers that act as catalysts for a breakdown. Such triggers may include, for example, an activating event that leaves us vulnerable, as described in the case of the road rage incident. The cycle may be broken by identifying the potential triggers and cognitively managing the situation. Some triggers may include the moods and attitudes of other individuals or groups; dwelling on issues and pre-empting consequences ("working yourself up"); hot buttons; illness; unpleasant physical conditions; and so on.

Mersino[39] presents an excellent overview and suggests the following to reduce your vulnerability to emotional triggers:

- Be alert to moods and attitudes that resonate with hurtful experiences in your personal past and affect you negatively.
- Avoid an unhealthy physical environment; illness and fatigue increases our vulnerability for emotional breakdown.
- Be aware of prethinking/foreshadowing, which is the tendency to expect the worst, such as a project being terminated. (This does not preclude the healthy skepticism needed to functionally steer a project.)
- Be cognisant of criticism and blame, particularly when we feel we are not at fault and are treated unfairly, as this can leave us feeling deflated and depressed.
- Avoid unhealthy thinking patterns, where distorted and irrational thinking can move us into a negative emotional space, sabotaging ourselves.
- Reach out and seek support when in need of it.

The following techniques to improve self-management may be considered:

Techniques to improve self-control

1. **Enhance your self-awareness**, which is key to self-control.
2. **Use HALT**, which stands for hungry, angry, lonely and tired. These make us vulnerable to emotional breakdowns.
3. **The physical environment** – how comfortable is it? If you are a work-from-home professional, stay in touch or go work in public spaces at times.
4. **Personal health** – pay careful attention to the different aspects of staying healthy.
5. **Self-renewal** – invest in training and development to stay ahead in your subject.
6. **Avoid long work weeks** that decrease your resilience.
7. **Seek support** from a mentor, friend, co-worker, manager etc.
8. **Manage and reduce your stress level** – see Chapter 16.

9. **Sounding board** – find someone with whom you can talk.
10. **Time out** – be kind to yourself and take time out when possible.
11. **Release an emotional charge** by writing a letter/email that you do not intend to send as an emotional release.
12. **Humour** – use this appropriately to defuse tension; hang out with someone really funny.
13. **Take care of yourself**, including time off for vacations, weekends, exercise, illness etc.
14. **Emotional dashboard** – keep track of how you feel – see the chapter on self-awareness.
15. **Don't strive to be perfect** – strive for excellence and attempt to do your best in every situation.
16. **Plan and prepare ahead.** This contributes to calmness and confidence when you have check listed the things to do and prepared accordingly.[40]

> *Role play an emotionally laden incident where you reacted with intense and inappropriate behaviour. How might you approach it differently?*

BENEFITS DERIVED FROM ENHANCED IMPULSE CONTROL

The control of impulsive behaviour contributes to increased productivity and self-regard.[41] "It is liberating and empowering to our determination and higher-order reasoning to overcome compelling urges."

"Impulse control involves understanding the appropriate times and ways to act on emotions and impulses, and the importance of thinking before acting."[42] Donald Trump, newly elected president of the USA in 2017, had to make a transition from an outspoken individual to a president of a country where impulsive outspokenness unleashed much negative reaction from the public.

It is well known that excessive stress gives rise to a variety of physical, emotional, cognitive and behavioural symptoms. Uncontrolled heightened stress may entice an individual into impulsive reactions, staining a once respected character and putting a career in jeopardy.

In certain instances, including managing air and ground traffic, retaining composure in tense situations may be of the utmost importance. It was found that traffic officers in New York who could retain their composure in tense situations reported the fewest incidents escalating into violence.[43]

Consider Ané, a usually contained, refined and very professional senior staff member at a leading tertiary institution. When student numbers increased exponentially, together with an increase in work load, the student composition changed dramatically. In addition, the "Fees must Fall" campaign with its concomitant unrest jeopardised her staff's safety. As a result, her hearing became impaired and she experienced great pain from a previous back injury. This coincided with a change in management and new ways of doing things. She became increasingly overburdened and agitated. One day, she "lost it" and verbally and inappropriately attacked her line manager. Discuss.

Chronic increased stress may contribute to the development of chronic illness. For many American organisations, employee illness is contributing to bottom-line issues, and thus needs to be monitored and managed via staff wellness programmes. People under stress are furthermore not able to produce at maximum output level as a result of, for example, problems with concentration, memory, and decision-making.[44]

A well-known experiment is one in which four-year old children were tested for impulsiveness.[45] They could either eat a marshmallow immediately – which would be acceptable – or await the return of the experimenter, when they would receive an extra marshmallow as a reward. The researchers found that one third could not control their impulse to eat the marshmallow immediately. Those who could, however, were followed up in a longitudinal study over a period of 12 years. The children presented as follows:

- They were more successful.
- They had better-developed social skills.
- They had better-developed coping skills.
- Academically they were the better achieving students, scoring higher in both their grades and the SATs.

Stein and Book[46] further note the following benefits:

- Individuals with good impulse control first think and then respond, rather than just responding reflexively. This allows "mental space" for comparing and assessing alternatives so that behaviour is both reasoned and well-considered.
- Impulse control allows for informed and wise decision-making, giving rise to responsible behaviour.
- If plans are made and implemented after weighing alternatives and reflection, they have a better chance of success.

- Calmly planning verbal responses and behaviour, and remaining unperturbed despite challenging circumstances, will help an individual steer their relationships and life more successfully.

- Individuals with sufficient impulse control tend to not take undue risks flowing from insufficient knowledge, as they carefully consider the possible outcomes.

Note: Controlling impulsiveness does not necessarily imply that you are inflexible or unable to act spontaneously.

Individuals epitomising impulse control

Astronauts
Physicists
Pilots
Others?

A FINAL WORD

I can resist everything except temptation.
–Oscar Wilde[47]

Little seems to be more offensive to a career or an intimate, close relationship than the expression of inappropriate or excessive emotion. A lack of impulse control can cause an individual a great deal of misery. Self-regulation is the ability to manage both positive and negative emotions, controlling impulses, dealing effectively with stress, and staying clear minded. Self-management competencies hold the key to managing stress and anger, controlling impulses, and helping you to remain motivated in the face of setbacks in pursuit of important goals.

SECTION 2: ACTIVITIES FOR SKILLS DEVELOPMENT

Self-assessment

Individual activities

 **Activity 1**

Spend a few moments assessing your level of impulse control. Respond to the statements below honestly. Assign a number to each item, using this scale:

1 = Very seldom or not true of me
2 = Seldom true of me
3 = Sometimes true of me
4 = Often true of me
5 = Very often true of me or true of me

I tend to act quickly before thoroughly thinking things through.

1	2	3	4	5

People view me as an impatient person.

1	2	3	4	5

I tend to shop on impulse.

1	2	3	4	5

I tend to show signs at others when driving if they obstruct me.

1	2	3	4	5

I control negative emotions such as anger, anxiety and depression.

1	2	3	4	5

Multiply your score by 4 to arrive at a total out of 100.

Impulse control scale

10	20	30	40	50	60	70	80	90	100

 **Activity 2**

What satisfaction do you experience from acting impulsively? What feels good about it in the moment?

....

....

What do you regret about acting impulsively?

....

....

Describe a recent example of good or poor impulse or emotional control in your life. What were the consequences?

....

....

Group activity

 **Activity 3**

> The new dean of a faculty is finding his feet. In order to gain some insight into the politics of his new workplace, he chit chats with staff members who are willing to do so. The other staff members soon become wary. They note favouritism and that the rules are bent for those let into his inner circle. They observe that confidentiality is no longer a trademark of the faculty. Trust declines and factions develop. The former positive atmosphere at work becomes toxic. Discuss the situation.

Advise Mr Khumalo, Head of the Advisory Board, on how to manage this situation.

....

....

Own work for personal growth: a to-do list for the next fortnight

 **Activity 4: Tips for developing impulse control**

Ferguson and Kelly[48] propose the following:

- Seek feedback on your emotional style (seek a candid confidante who will tell you what others say about you – do you anger too easily, get upset too easily, or are you too sensitive?).
- Reason with yourself – are you logical in your interpretation of the current situation? If not, you may set into motion an unrealistic understanding of the situation, further perpetuating unruly emotions. (See Chapter 14 on reality testing.)
- Reason or double-check with a trusted colleague or friend who may act as a sounding board against which you may view your concerns, such as the possibility that your job may be in jeopardy.
- Learn how to pause – your gut feeling should be complemented by a cognitive appraisal or by involving extra sources of information so as to inhibit unappraised actions.
- Avoid taking major decisions when experiencing intense emotions, as a lack of appropriate emotional reactions may lead to poor decision-making. Decisions made when under pressure may not be advantageous – rather take time out and negotiate for responding later.
- Avoid becoming over-stimulated by pacing your day according to your preferences where possible, such as planning time for problem management, or devising means to distract your attention from inflammatory moments or situations.
- Choose an appropriate companion, preferably not part of the team or organisation (and therefore not also in the hot seat), with whom you can vent your feelings, since repressing them is not recommended.
- Do not use the instant method of e-mailing to communicate your intense feelings. First allow yourself some time to cool down and rethink what you really want to say, and decide if it is worth your while to do so.
- Attempt to bring some work-life balance into your life. If your whole existence rests on your job, too much is at stake and you may become overly emotional about it. Redirect some time for friends, family, and hobbies.
- Develop a phrase that you can rehearse and unbundle when you realise that you are getting tensed up. For example, "I need time to consider your viewpoint carefully and will get back to you on the matter as soon as I have thought it through."

REFERENCES

Bar-On, R. (2002). *Bar-On emotional quotient inventory: A measure of emotional intelligence.* New York: Multi-Health Systems.

Brondolo, E., Jelliffe, T., Quinn, C.J., Tunick, W. & Melhado, E. (1996). Correlates of risk for conflict among New York City traffic agents. In G.R. van den Bos & E.Q. Bulatoa (eds.). *Violence on the job: Identifying risks and developing solutions.* Washington DC: American Psychological Association.

Cherniss, C. & Adler, M. (2005). *Promoting emotional intelligence in organizations.* Alexandria: ASTD Press.

Ferguson, R. & Kelly, M. (2005). *Enhancing emotional intelligence. Leadership tips from the executive coach.* Raleigh, NC: Mark Kelly Books.

Goleman, D. (1995a). *Emotional intelligence: why it can matter more than IQ.* New York: Bantam Books.

Goleman, D. (1995b). What's your emotional intelligence quotient? You'll soon find out. *Utne Reader,* November–December.

Goleman, D. (2014). *Focus: the hidden driver of excellence.* London: Bloomsbury.

Hughes, M. & Terrel, B.J. (2012). *Emotional intelligence in action: training and coaching activities for leaders, manager, and teams* (2nd ed.). San Francisco: Pfeiffer.

Lane, R.D. (2000). Levels of emotional awareness: Neurological, psychological, and social perspectives. In R. Bar-On & J.D.A. Parker (eds.). *The handbook of emotional intelligence: Theory, development, assessment, and application at home, school, and in the workplace.* San Francisco: Jossey-Bass, p. 186.

Multi-Health Systems Inc. (2011). *The complete EQ-i 2.0 experience.* Toronto: Multi-Health Systems Inc.

Multi-Health Systems Inc & Jopie van Rooyen Psychometrics. (2011). *The complete EQ-i 2.0 experience.* Toronto: Multi-Health Systems Inc.

Mersino, A.C. (2013). *Emotional intelligence for project managers: the people skills you need to achieve outstanding results* (2nd ed.). New York: American Management Association.

Newman, M. (2007). *Emotional capitalists. The new leaders.* Chichester: John Wiley & Sons.

Prins, A. (2010a). *Emotional intelligence and leadership: A work wellness perspective.* Saarbrücken: VDM Verlag Dr Müller.

Prins, A. (2010b). *Wellness in the workplace.* (Unpublished presentation). Bloemfontein: University of the Free State.

Prins, A., Van Niekerk, E.C. & Weyers, A. (2007). *Emotional intelligence.* Unpublished workbook. Bloemfontein: Talent and Wellness.

Prins, A., Van Niekerk, E.C. & Weyers, A. (2011). *Emotional Intelligence: Tipping point in workplace excellence.* Randburg: Knowres.

Quist, J.F., Kennedy, J.L. & Lombroso, P.J. (2001). Genetics of childhood disorders: XXIII. ADHD, Part 7: The serotonin system. *Journal of the American Academy of Child & Adolescent Psychiatry,* 40(2), 253-256.

Sadock, B.J., Sadock, V.A. & Ruiz, P. (2015). *Kaplan & Sadock's synopsis of psychiatry: behavioral sciences/ clinical psychiatry* (11th ed.). Philadelphia: Wolters Kluwer.

Stein, S.J. & Book, H.E. (2011). *The EQ Edge: Emotional Intelligence and your success* (3rd ed.). San Francisco: Jossey-Bass.

Watson, C.E. & Idinopulos, T.A. (2007). *Are you your own worst enemy? The nine inner strengths you need to overcome self-defeating tendencies at work.* Oxford: Greenwood World Publishing.

ENDNOTES

1. Hughes & Terrel, 2012:91.
2. Cherniss & Adler, 2005:18.
3. Ferguson & Kelly, 2005:4.
4. Newman, 2007:35.
5. MHS & JvR, 2011:9.
6. Mersino, 2013:63.
7. Bar-On, 2002:18.
8. Lane, 2000:172.
9. Goleman, 2014:26.
10. Sadock et al., 2015:608.
11. Hughes & Terrel, 2012:92.
12. Ferguson & Kelly, 2005:40.
13. Ferguson & Kelly, 2005:42.
14. Stein & Book, 2011:177.
15. Cherniss & Adler, 2005:19.
16. Newman, 2007:35.
17. Newman, 2007:37.
18. Watson & Idinopulos, 2007:121.
19. Watson & Idinopulos, 2007.
20. Watson & Idinopulos, 2007:143.
21. Mersino, 2013:64.
22. Mersino, 2013:64.
23. Mersino, 2013.
24. Goleman, 1995.
25. Mersino, 2013:69.
26. Stein & Book, 2011:175.
27. Sadock et al., 2015:608.
28. Quist, Kennedy & Lombroso, 2001.
29. Ferguson & Kelly, 2005:4.
30. Watson & Idinopulos, 2007:117.
31. Newman, 2007:36.
32. Cherniss & Adler, 2005:19.
33. Cherniss & Adler, 2005.
34. Stein & Book, 2011:179.
35. Watson & Idinopulos, 2007:117.
36. Watson & Idinopulos, 2007:123.
37. Hughes & Terrell, 2012:92.
38. Mersino, 2013:70.
39. Mersino, 2013:70.
40. Mersino, 2013: 87-92.
41. Hughes & Terrell, 2012:93.
42. MHS & JvR, 2011:15.
43. Brondolo et al., 1996.
44. WHO/World Economic Forum Report in Prins, 2010.
45. Stein & Book, 2011:180-181.
46. Stein & Book, 2011:177-178.
47. Prins et al., 2011.
48. Ferguson & Kelly, 2005:42–47.

SECTION E : STRESS MANAGEMENT

Stress management refers to how well you cope with emotions that come with change and unknown and unpredictable circumstances, whilst being hopeful regarding the future and resilient when confronted by setbacks and obstacles.

The following skills are discussed:

Chapter 15: Flexibility
Chapter 16: Stress tolerance
Chapter 17: Optimism

Chapter 15

FLEXIBILITY

Annette Prins

Flexible individuals are resilient, able to withstand pressures without breaking, akin to a well rooted willow in a storm. If an individual or organisation is well rooted into their values it provides a guide for actions in line with their strengths, purpose and credibility.[1]

SECTION 1: OVERVIEW

As we all know by now, change is the only constant of our time. Change is necessary for innovation and staying ahead of the competition.[2] Flexibility helps one to adapt to these "unfamiliar, unpredictable and fluid circumstances" without rigidity.[3] Adapting to change and viewing it as a challenge rather than a threat, thriving on change, and being able to adjust to new requirements is of the utmost importance to survive in a modern society. Flexible individuals are indeed able to change their thoughts when there are indications that they might be wrong.

Flexibility is an emotional intelligence (EI) skill which helps you to tap into your fears, such as the fear of losing control or being pushed around by others, together with damaging self-talk. There is "a direct connection between feeling afraid and becoming less flexible".[4] A lesser degree of self-esteem will also co-vary with rigidity, since the individual has a greater need to "save face", and cannot be shown to be wrong or "giving in".

Flexibility is furthermore dependent on an individual's ability to manage stressful situations. You need to deal with impediments like these if you wish to embark on a route to greater innate flexibility. When acted out as an emotional intelligence skill, flexibility is applied together with problem solving, independence and impulse control to enhance emotional functioning.[5] In the emotionally intelligent individual, flexibility is engaged with full regard for others and without compromising values. Individuals whose behaviour is securely rooted in a strong value system can be flexible without discarding these values.

After completing this chapter, you should be able to:

- define both flexibility and inflexibility;
- understand some of the theory informing thinking on flexibility;
- understand why improving your flexibility makes sense;
- understand the causes and consequences of both rigid and flexible behaviour;
- develop flexibility;
- reflect on benefits derived from enhanced flexibility;
- identify individuals epitomising these skills;
- benchmark your own level of flexibility; and
- implement individual and group activities to enhance flexibility.

DEFINITION OF FLEXIBILITY

Flexibility represents the "ability to adjust your emotions, thoughts and behaviour to changing situations and conditions. This component of emotional intelligence applies to your overall ability to adapt to unfamiliar, unpredictable, and dynamic circumstances. Flexible people are agile, synergistic, and capable of reacting to change without rigidity. These people are able to change their minds when evidence suggests that they are mistaken. They are generally open to and tolerant of different ideas, orientations, ways and practices. Their capacity to shift thoughts and behaviour is not arbitrary and whimsical, but rather in concert with shifting feedback they get from their environment. Individuals who lack this capacity tend to be rigid and obstinate. They adapt poorly to new situations and have little capacity to take advantage of new opportunities".[6]

"Flexibility requires that you are able to modify your thoughts, emotions, and behaviours in response to change."[7]

Adaptability and plasticity indicate the ability to change an attitude and behaviour comfortably, and therefore to respond fittingly to changing circumstances.[8]

Inflexibility

Typical of inflexible individuals is an unthinking habit, a fear of failure, the inclination to do just the minimum, postponement, and reliance on old ways and methods to solve problems.[9] They avoid challenges and opportunities because of their fear of failure. The less they do, the less able they are; the less they attempt to do things, the more avoidance is practiced and the lower their self-esteem becomes. This circle of behaviour therefore has an immobilising effect on the individual.

Inflexible individuals are resistant to change. They struggle to adapt or are incapable of doing so at all. "They cling to old behaviours in novel situations, even though their actions are clearly insufficient and ineffective."[10] Flexibility is also securely tied to reality testing. An individual who cannot accurately read or assess his or her environment will not be able to pick up the signs leading to an appropriate and adaptable response.

In its most extreme form, inflexibility is seen in the schizophrenic with catatonic features, marked by a catatonic stupor with decreased reactivity to the environment, together with a reduction in spontaneous movement and activity, at times also including mutism. Catatonic negativism includes a seemingly motiveless resistance to both instructions and attempts to be moved; a rigid posture against all efforts to be moved; and even catatonic posturing, reflecting in an inappropriate and bizarre posture.[11] This seemingly results from anxiety and an attempt to keep the environment "as is".

THEORY INFORMING THINKING ON THE FLEXIBILITY CONSTRUCT

An "open system is more likely to grow and adapt than is a closed system".[12] This holds true for individuals, teams, organisations, and governments. Being open to honest and accurate feedback can provide information on how one hinders or helps processes. An absence thereof may, *inter alia*, contribute to arrogance, bad judgements, and poor leadership. Requesting and welcoming candid feedback in order to evaluate one's strengths and limitations constitutes a pathway to accurate self-assessment.

According to Gill,[13] "[p]sychological flexibility, a meta-cognitive skill, is the ability to be aware of your thoughts, feelings and urges, diffuse those that are unproductive, and choose appropriate responses". Flexibility requires us to "[b]reak free of entrenched ways and mindless routine".[14] Mindless routine may contribute to work being done both well and timeously, but typically reflects an inability to stand back and evaluate the current situation or practice, rushing on without taking time to evaluate the current state of things critically and imaginatively.

Millions of people are trapped by set ways of seeing and doing things.[15] They find safety and security in the "old ways" of doing things. They would rather continue along these lines than try out new ways, for fear of failure and the criticism and embarrassment that may follow. This may contribute to a loss of excitement, and feeling dissatisfied and unfulfilled. Many individuals consequently become stale, frozen, dull, bored, and cynical, not pushing their own limits in an upward spiral of enthusiasm and the excitement of challenge and self-actualisation. "Their minds appear to be asleep, their zest for living extinguished" (ibid). In conforming to past practices, they mindlessly continue to do things in the same old way. The discovery of new truths and possibilities which would help them to improve things, as well as the thrill of new discoveries, elude them, dulling their imagination so that work becomes a dreary routine.

Ingrid is imaginative, bright and likes exploring new ideas in the tertiary education system. She explores using mind-maps in the accounting area. Others say it is impossible. However, she follows her instinct and uses all new measures available to stimulate insightful learning with her students. The students love it and she loves teaching them! The one innovation in her teaching leads to another.

Emily, on the other hand, is requested to initiate a new programme at work. She is not quite certain how to do so and ponders on it. Suddenly, she has a bright, new, creative idea! Energised, she starts planning. However, doubt slowly sets in... What if this isn't such a bright idea? What if they lose money? She cannot take that chance! Rather stick to the old way. She cannot lose face, cannot risk her position and the esteem she has gained over time. She sighs, then diligently starts to plan anew... according to the well-trodden old rules. Face-saving, once again, wins the day.

Nurturing environments enhance psychological flexibility.[16] Those individuals less rigidly attached to their beliefs tend to be more tolerant and less critical and complaining of others. Since they judge less, they are less inclined to hurt and punish and more inclined to "praise, support, attend to, and care for others". Such individuals focus less on feeling good than on behaving in accordance with their values.

The Center for Creative Leadership in Greensboro, North Carolina, USA,[17] studied the reasons leaders do not progress as expected, and found that rather than being due to their cognitive abilities, the two most common characteristics failing them were their rigidity and poor relationships.

The downside of flexibility

The downside of flexibility may include that flexible individuals might be defined as unreliable, fickle and manipulative.[18] They may also be viewed as individuals who might consider compromising their values when required to do so by authority figures. This picture, however, does not hold true for the emotionally intelligent. Flexibility needs to link with problem solving, independence and impulse control[19] whilst holding on to one's values. Inflexible people's thinking may be dominated by timelines, rather than the bigger picture.

A case in point, where people did in fact relinquish their value systems in order to satisfy their greed, is the Enron situation, one of the biggest scandals to shake the USA in recent years. A firm started off with very good intentions and values, however these became eroded over time and management forgot what had initially driven them. Corruption, cheating, lying, and the blurring of facts became the order of the day. Borders became diffuse, and the whole "reich" came to a downfall, affecting thousands of lives. This is certainly not what is meant by the EI skill of flexibility!

On the opposite side of the spectrum, the former CEO of Pick 'n Pay South Africa, Raymond Ackerman, on vacating his position in 2010 at the age of 79, stated that his organisation had gone to great heights owing to his never forgetting a university professor stressing, on the very first day of his B.Com degree, the importance of taking good care of your customers. The money will flow of necessity, he said, however if the first and overriding aim is to make money, the business may not make it. In this case, the CEO of this very successful business had never let go of his principles in favour of becoming "flexible" with regard to his value system… and it paid off.

IMPROVING YOUR FLEXIBILITY

Managing change

We live in a complex, radically changing and turbulent world. The inflexible person may want to stunt growth by keeping things the way they are rather than embracing change and scanning for new opportunities.[20] However, massive changes, as reflected in turbulent "technical innovation, global competition, and pressures of institutional investors" dominate the global workplace.[21] "[I]nnovation drives progress – and profit."[22] People are continually making changes; they dream up and apply new ideas. Not all are successful, but some are astonishingly successful! In competitive economies, those who are the quickest to take advantage of the latest innovations and improvements tend to get better results and returns on, for example, marketing. A case in point is Bill Gates, who was not interested in the Internet, thinking it was too slow to be of real consequence. A competitor, however, created Netscape, dramatically changing Internet access to make it quick and simple. Microsoft then lagged behind with regard to this new, cutting-edge technology. Instead of turning a blind eye, Gates "turned on a dime".[23] He was not concerned with his public image and his previously confessed lack of belief in the Internet but, governed by the future, he altered his position to move forward, something successful leaders are not afraid to do. For individuals to really perform at a superior level, they need to be change catalysts. This is necessary to mobilise others towards change. Change catalysts require the skills needed both to support employees, and to anticipate and manage resistance.

Change, although needed, is often intimidating because of its disruption of organisations and the stress it causes staff. It may entail things such as technological innovation, new services, new problem-solving techniques, or new ways to motivate staff. When change is not well managed, it may elicit resistance. Much communication is required so that employees are well informed, otherwise even more problems may be created. Change and innovation, when guided by emotional intelligence, are more likely to be effective and sustainable.[24] Stimulating innovation and leading people in new directions requires courage, creativity, and wisdom, together with good communication and flexibility.

"Change is the greatest constant in our fast-paced world. The ability to adapt to change is a predominant characteristic of successful people. It allows them to avoid or take advantage promptly of the critical factors affecting any situation in which they are involved, rather than getting caught up in an ego-dominated struggle of how it should be."[25] An example may be the 2008/2009 collapse of the property market in the USA. Criteria for approving loans were relaxed and loans were readily extended, even to those who were less financially credible. This behaviour continued even when the first signs of disaster appeared. Rather than flexing and re-evaluating their position, banks were inflexible in their ways long enough for a recession to set in that afflicted most of the world's economy.

At times individuals also get caught up in power struggles, not wanting to let go of their prior positions, even if time shows it to be risky or less appropriate. Inflexible people may then stick to prior plans despite mounting evidence against them, alienating co-workers and losing their trust, and frequently also their position in the market.

Had there not been so much flux in our increasingly demanding world, the need for flexibility would have been less prominent. Many books on the topic of flexibility line the shelves in bookstores, indicating people's struggle to learn a variety of skills and techniques to equip them for the turbulent ride in an ever-changing modern society.[26] Present-day teenagers may expect to change their careers up to six times before they retire.[27] They will therefore need to upgrade their skills consistently so that they can keep up with progress. New jobs not even contemplated at present will be part of their future.

At a personal level

Flexible people can "smoothly handle multiple demands, shifting priorities and rapid change".[28] At an individual level, many people who are referred to counsellors suffer from inflexibility. They have, in many respects, chosen a particular behavioural response and apply this behaviour steadfastly and with diligence. When they realise it does not elicit the expected results, they do more of the same thing... and again, and again, with the same non-result. This may increase anxiety since they believe they have no alternatives to resort to. The same pattern of behaviour appears in relationships between parents and children, married couples, and in the workplace. An example may be a mother "cracking down" on her son who does not study. She argues and complains and deprives the child of things he enjoys, but he does not respond as she had hoped. She then continues in the same manner, doing more of the same thing. And so does the child. The behaviour gets them nowhere. Rather than motivating the child, the increased levels of control, discipline or curfew decrease the motivation of the child to take control and steer his or her life effectively. A married couple may likewise revert to an inflexible stance in an attempt to protect themselves from further hurt and anxiety, repetitively doing "more of the same thing".

In such cases, counsellors may assist by helping the individuals to take on a meta-perspective, that is, viewing the behaviour "from above", distancing themselves from the situation to observe the repetitive cycle of dysfunctional behaviour. In so doing, they may recognise the dysfunctional behaviour and choose a more functional approach.

Studies indicate that individuals who become more caring (and forgiving) towards themselves tend also to become more caring with others.[29] Biglan[30] argues that therapies with a mindful focus such as acceptance and commitment therapy (ACT) demonstrate that "when people are helped to adopt this type of acceptance, they become more flexible in making their way in the world". He notes that research has demonstrated a variety of benefits derived with regards to problems such as "anxiety, depression, diabetes, etc. Thus, evidence shows that when people become more accepting of their own thoughts and feelings, they become more caring toward others".

In the workplace

Leadership

Traditionally, consistency was a signature characteristic of leadership.[31] When an executive director made a decision, "that decision was defended by everyone in the organization - from top to bottom - even when contradicted by the data. Changing your mind (or altering course) was perceived as an unbearable weakness". A modern day example may be South Africa in 2016/2017, where the President of the country had 875 accusations of fraud, corruption and money laundering against him. Despite this and many other allegations concerning his appropriateness for office, the ANC supported him despite the exponential detrimental effect for the country. This tunnel vision was retained despite all contradictory evidence. This is true for many despots around the world; many in Africa will, despite all evidence, not relinquish their power.

Employees who are flexible tend to respond reflectively rather than reactively, which leads to the perception that they have greater control and more behavioural choices at their disposal.[32] This ability contributes to resilience, improves levels of attention, and decreases burnout. Flatter and less bureaucratic corporate structures create a platform for self-managed teams. In research with 395 MBA students, it was found that psychological flexibility is important in self-managed teams for several reasons. Firstly, leadership in self-managed teams is shared, rather than concentrated in one person. Individuals with higher psychological flexibility have more attention sources available and more readily notice how much control they have in a given situation. They are also less involved in avoidance behaviour and learn by trial and error, and are better equipped to influence a team's goals, behaviour, culture, and maintenance.

Coping in the modern-day workplace requires self-discipline, patience and flexibility. Many organisations downsize, and the individuals who are retained in the shrunken organisation are more visible and accountable. They need a broader scope of interpersonal skills to manage a wider range of customers, peers and subordinates, and they need to be more adept at managing relationships and feelings – their own and those of others.[33] Real passion for the envisaged change, high levels of self-confidence, the ability to innovate, initiate, and influence others, and being adept at leadership, are required to implement change successfully. Such employees need to "read" organisations well and be highly adaptable.[34]

Flexibility is essential for coping when the unexpected occurs, when circumstances change, or where old ways simply no longer suffice.

DEVELOPING FLEXIBILITY

At a personal level

Flexibility can be learned. Individuals can be taught how to be more flexible by helping them to become aware of their feelings and thoughts, and to take control of their behaviour by "basing their actions on values and goals rather than their internal events".[35]

To increase flexibility, an individual needs to learn to reinterpret unfamiliar, unpredictable, unexpected, and fluid situations that tend to elicit doom and gloom or catastrophic thinking. However, people tend to want to remain in their particular comfort zones, and it takes a great deal of discipline to move on the inflexibility–flexibility continuum. People become overly attached to known ways of thinking and behaving.[36]

One has to keep one's mind active and allow it to continually grow, as the human brain is able to continuously evolve in its ability to thoughtfully analyse and imagine, even into ripe old age.[37] This is dependent on one's use and exercise of "this magnificent gift".[38] Mental powers and spiritual qualities, it is argued, are perfected through constant use, and especially by challenge. One should let go of spending time on inconsequential things that sap one's time and creative inclination.

"Remember that the mind will waste away like body muscles if not exercised regularly. Do the same things day after day, don't experience new challenges, remove the possibility of challenge, and limit what you read or see and the people you encounter – this is the perfect prescription for rigidity and narrowness of thought, and a sure, quick way to obsolescence."[39] Further, "a great tragedy occurs when a person's mind dies while the rest of the body lives on" (ibid). People's enthusiasm for life seems to decline as cynicism increases and as mental alertness declines. Their joy of life diminishes together with an inability to enjoy things of beauty and to see the humour in things. However, "[t]he possibilities for making ongoing change and improvement by tapping into our creative energies reside within each of us. We are meant to be active, creative beings".[40]

All of civilisation's achievements came into being through the actions of human beings. Two powers drive us, namely our curiosity and our drive for self-determination. Human beings are free to make a choice between being active or passive. We can therefore explore by using our curiosity or allow our minds to rest in peace. We can be "active, thinking individuals or passive observers of our surroundings".[41]

In the workplace

The world of work[42] offers endless opportunities to thoughtful men and women to apply their imagination and problem-solving skills in order to be clever and imaginative. For this to happen, an individual needs to "eliminate the assumptions and habits that choke off creative ideas".[43] The creative person has learnt the secret of defeating the powers chaining him or her to monotony, mindless conformity, and repetition.

In the workplace, individuals need to take advantage of new information as it occurs, evaluate it, and adjust in order to retain a worthwhile market share. Important to note, however, is that flexibility does not equal impulsiveness. The latter tends to act in an arbitrary manner, without thinking things through sufficiently or taking all new evidence into consideration.[44]

An effective way to break with entrenched ideas and methods is to set specific improvement goals.[45] The following guidelines are provided in this regard:

- Identify problems to be solved in your particular business unit.
- Contemplate improvements in how the unit performs its functions.
- Identify problems with your own performance.
- Consider improvements you could make in order to be a better performer.

At work, you can, for example, improve your productivity by seeking out new and better methods to problem solve and get work done. A case in point would be to use an index card and do the following:

- Write down the six most important things you need to do the following day.
- Prioritise them from 1 to 6 in order of importance.
- The following day, keep the card in your pocket and start work on the first item.
- Keep to this item until you are done with it.
- Then take on number 2 on the list, until finished.
- Then start on number 3, etc., in the same way. Take the card out every 15 minutes to remind you of what you are busy with.

Do not be concerned if you take the whole day on the first item; you will at least have dealt with the most important of the items. If, working in this way, you are unable to deal with these, you would not in any event have dealt with them in another way. Such a system assists one to decide what is really important. Take a few minutes of every day to decide what needs to be done the following day.[46]

BENEFITS DERIVED FROM ENHANCED FLEXIBILITY

Flexible people tend to be open and tolerant, agile and adaptable. They are usually less dogmatic and allow for the fact that they may not always be correct; they would rather be happy than correct.

Strengthening your flexibility skills should certainly have at least the following results:

- Enhance your ability to work successfully with and within an ever-changing world.

- Expand your life satisfaction and happiness by more effectively managing changing situations and relationships, rather than "seeking to force a reality not supported by the circumstances".[47]
- More freedom, less defensiveness, less having to be "right", therefore less stressing about less important matters.

Individuals epitomising flexibility

The Chinese government and their economic changes
Barack Obama
Trevor Noah
Others?

A FINAL WORD

Modern man lives in an ever-changing environment. Flexibility is the component of emotional intelligence that that helps one adapt to the current dynamics, unpredictability and the unfamiliar confronting us.[48] Flexibility makes us "willing or ready to yield to the influence of others (tractable; manageable), and characterised by ready capability for modification or change by plasticity, pliancy, variability and often by consequent adaptability to new situations".[49] Flexibility is underscored by problem solving, independence and impulse control.

Flexibility may also be equated to being supple, elastic, resilient and springy; those who cannot keep up with the pace of change will fall by the wayside. Flexible people, in contrast, are agile, synergistic, and capable of reacting to change without undue rigidity. Flexibility is therefore indicative of our overall ability to adapt to the unfamiliar, unpredictable and dynamic circumstances of modern living.

SECTION 2: ACTIVITIES FOR SKILLS DEVELOPMENT

Self-assessment

Individual activities

 Activity 1: Level of flexibility

What is the level of your flexibility? Spend a few minutes assessing this. Give your responses to the statements below honestly. Assign a number to each item, using this scale:

1 = Very seldom or not true of me
2 = Seldom true of me
3 = Sometimes true of me
4 = Often true of me
5 = Very often true of me or true of me

I have no difficulty dealing with change.

1	2	3	4	5

I experience no difficulty changing my opinions about something.

1	2	3	4	5

I have the willpower and discipline to change old habits.

1	2	3	4	5

I have the ability to adjust to a foreign culture and country.

1	2	3	4	5

I don't have difficulty in beginning new ventures.

1	2	3	4	5

Multiply your score by 4 to arrive at a total out of 100.

Flexibility scale

10	20	30	40	50	60	70	80	90	100

 Activity 2: (Individual – 5 minutes)

To what extent is your day driven by routine? How frequently do you change the way in which you go to work, or the order in which you do routine things?

....

....

Do you enjoy trying out new things or new ways of doing things? If you tend to be avoidant, try, in retrospect, to identify why you have been acting in that way. Was it, for example, owing to a fear of failure, fear of losing face, fear of losing control, fear of criticism? Attempt to find the pattern governing your behaviour. Can you dispute these? If not, consult with a professional therapist.

....

....

How do you feel about change? Respond to the scenarios listed below.

Changing an aspect of yourself:

....

....

Changing a less efficient habit:

....

....

Continual change at work such as new PC programmes, moving offices, turnover:

....

....

Do you avoid trying out new things? If so, why?

....

....

How up-to-date are you with the latest trends in music, fashion, cars, books, and so on?

....

....

How do you avoid being mediocre?

....

....

Rethink what you do on a day-to-day basis. What holds you back from performing better? What limits you, bores you, make you feel dissatisfied?

....

....

Group activity

 **Activity 3**

Discuss: What improvement have you made in the way you do things at work of late?

....

....

An important change needs to be implemented at your organisation. Choose a group leader.

Quest for the group leader:[50]

- Create excitement and curiosity.
- See every obstacle as a challenge to be overcome.
- Remember change for the sake of change is inefficient. Is this change you wish to implement change for the sake of real improvement?
- Remember that survival sometimes demands of us to change.
- Keep in mind that your staff will execute change better if they help create the change (get them involved).
- Might there be a better way to do things than at present?
- Innovation requires a team to work together.

Task

Leader: Introduce the proposed change to your staff.
Group: Criticise or assess the leader using the cues provided above.

Own work for personal growth: a to-do list for the next fortnight

Activity 4

1. Request feedback from people close to you on:
   - your general level of flexibility; and
   - which areas they find you less flexible/too flexible.
2. Is there any specific area that you view as important for you to change?
   - Why?
   - How will things be different for you if you are able to turn this around?
   - How will you set about the change? Which steps will you consider implementing?
3. Consider taking an interest in one new thing. What would it be? How will you evaluate whether you are successfully mastering the new interest?
4. When last did you participate in a fun thing spontaneously, or something you are not a master at? What "crazy" thing would you like to do but have always resisted trying?

> We can change the patterns of our lives by deciding to change our script and by finding meaning in a different life plan.[51]

5. Enhance creativity via curiosity. Curiosity helps us to not become complacent.
   - How would you view your general level of curiosity?
   - What might you do to enhance your curiosity? What stimulates you? What fires your enthusiasm?

REFERENCES

American Psychiatric Association. (2013). *Diagnostic and statistical manual of mental disorders* (5th ed.). Washington, DC: APA.

Bharwaney, G. (2006). *Emotionally intelligent living. Strategies for increasing your EQ.* (Rev ed.). Carmarthen: Crown House Publishing Limited.

Biglan, A. (2009). The role of advocacy organizations in reducing negative externalities. *Journal of Organizational Behavior Management, 29*(3-4), 215-230.

Cherniss, C. & Adler, M. (2005). *Promoting emotional intelligence in organizations.* Alexandria: ASTD Press.

Ferguson, R. & Kelly, M. (2005). *Enhancing emotional intelligence. Leadership tips from the executive coach.* Raleigh, NC: Mark Kelly Books.

Gill, C. (2010). *Psychological flexibility* [Online]. Available: <www.mbs.edu/go/news/don-t-get-angry-get-psychological-flexibility) > [Accessed 20 March, 2010].

Gill, L.J., Ramsey, P.L. & Leberman, S.I. (2015). A Systems Approach to Developing Emotional Intelligence Using the Self-awareness Engine of Growth Model. *Systemic Practice and Action Research 28*(6),575–594. DOI 10.1007/s11213-015-9345-4

Hughes, M., Patterson, L. & Terrell, B.J. (2005). *Emotional intelligence in action: Training and coaching activities for leaders and managers.* San Francisco: Pfeiffer.

Hughes, M. & Terrel, B.J. (2012). *Emotional intelligence in action: training and coaching activities for leaders, manager, and teams* (2nd ed.). San Francisco: Pfeiffer.

Multi-Health Systems Inc & Jopie van Rooyen Psychometrics. (2011). *The complete EQ-i 2.0 experience.* Toronto: Multi-Health Systems Inc.

Multi-Health Systems Inc. (2011). *The complete EQ-i 2.0 experience.* Toronto: Multi-Health Systems Inc.

Plug, C., Meyer, W.F., Louw, D.A. & Gouws, L.A. (1987). *Psigologie-woordeboek.* Johannesburg: McGraw-Hill.

Stein, S. & Book, H. (2001). *The EQ Edge: Emotional intelligence and your success* (2nd ed.). Toronto: Kogan Page.

Stein, S.J. & Book, H.E. (2011). *The EQ Edge: Emotional Intelligence and your success* (3rd ed.). San Francisco: Jossey Bass.

Steiner, C. (1999). *Achieving emotional literacy. A personal programme to increase your emotional intelligence.* London: Bloomsbury.

Watson, C.E. & Idinopulos, T.A. (2007). *Are you your own worst enemy? The nine inner strengths you need to overcome self-defeating tendencies at work.* Oxford: Greenwood World Publishing.

ENDNOTES

1. Hughes & Terryl, 2012.
2. MHS & JvR, 2011:16.
3. Stein & Book, 2011:19.
4. Hughes & Terryl, 2012:98.
5. MHS & JvR, 2011.
6. Stein & Book, 2011:187.
7. MHS & JvR, 2011:16.
8. Plug, Meyer, Louw & Gouws, 1987.
9. Watson & Idinopulos, 2007.

10 Stein & Book, 2011:192.
11 American Psychiatric Association, 2013:119.
12 Ferguson & Kelly, 2005:24.
13 Gill, 2010:1.
14 Watson & Idinopulos, 2007:78.
15 Watson & Idinopulos, 2007.
16 Biglan, 2009:1.
17 Bharwaney, 2006:134.
18 Hughes & Terryl, 2012.
19 MHS, 2011.
20 Hughes & Terryl, 2012.
21 Cherniss & Adler, 2005:3.
22 Ferguson & Kelly, 2005:160.
23 Stein & Book, 2011:189.
24 Ferguson & Kelly, 2005:160.
25 Hughes & Terryl, 2012:97.
26 Hughes et al., 2005:97.
27 Stein & Book, 2001:163.
28 Stein & Book, 2001:165.
29 Biglan, 2009:1.
30 Biglan, 2009.
31 Stein & Book, 2011:188, 189.
32 Gill, 2010:1.
33 Cherniss & Adler, 2005:3.
34 Cherniss & Adler, 2005:32.
35 Gill, 2010:2.
36 Stein & Book, 2011:191.
37 Watson & Idinopulos, 2007.
38 Watson & Idinopulos, 2007:116.
39 Watson & Idinopulos, 2007:116.
40 Watson & Idinopulos, 2007:80.
41 Watson & Idinopulos, 2007:83.
42 Watson & Idinopulos, 2007:830.
43 Watson & Idinopulos, 2007:84.
44 Stein & Book, 2011:192.
45 Watson & Idinopulos, 2007:81.
46 Watson & Idinopulos, 2007:129.
47 Hughes & Terryl, 2012.
48 Stein & Book, 2011.
49 Webster's, 1993.
50 Ferguson & Kelly, 2005:160-161.
51 Steiner, 1999:123.

Chapter 16

STRESS TOLERANCE

Eugene van Niekerk

We can easily manage if we will only take, each day, the burden appointed to it. But the load will be too heavy for us if we carry yesterday's burden over again today, and then add the burden of the morrow before we are required to bear it.

–John Newton

SECTION 1: OVERVIEW

Psychologists estimate that more than 70% of us are liable to fall prey to debilitating depression/stress at some stage in our life. For many, such an experience will seriously challenge our ability to live a gratifying and rewarding life. Equally distressing (if not more so) is that the interface between stress and our body can give rise to lifestyle diseases such as chronic pain, diabetes 2, and cardio-vascular disease, which can be life-shortening.[1]

Our ability to manage stress is important because it bears a direct relationship to our ability to process information, utilise memory functions, make decisions, pursue life goals, make critical judgments, and work innovatively and creatively. Working intelligently with our emotions also requires the ability to manage stress.

Often we lose sight of the fact that optimal stress can be **eustress** – that is, good for us. Some individuals find that stress actually raises their energy levels, and in addition helps them focus their minds better on their work or their sports activities. Stress thresholds differ greatly. For example, some people experience high stress tolerance thresholds and can absorb a high stress load before they begin to experience breakdown. However, even the most stress-resistant individuals (consider here an elite group of specially-trained combat soldiers) are apt to succumb when their levels remain chronically elevated.[2]

 After completing this chapter, you should be able to:

- define stress;
- understand some theory informing our thinking on stress;
- reflect on some of the benefits of stress tolerance;
- understand ways to develop stress tolerance;
- assess your own level of stress tolerance; and
- implement and understand individual and group activities to enhance stress tolerance.

DEFINITION OF STRESS

> *"Stress is a negative emotional experience accompanied by predictable biochemical, physiological, cognitive, and behavioural changes."*[3]
>
> *"Stress… is the persistent and recurrent feeling of sadness; being overwhelmed; physical, emotional and mental exhaustion; extreme anxiety or tension; anger or rage; irritability; or a general feeling of being out of control."*[4]
>
> *"Stress is a state we experience when there is a mismatch between perceived demands and perceived ability to cope. It is the balance between how we view demands and how we think we can cope with those demands that determine whether we feel no stress, distressed or eustressed."*[5]
>
> *"Stress is a state of physical or psychological strain that imposes demands for adjustment upon the individual. Stress may be internal or environmental, brief or persistent. If excessive or prolonged, it may overtax the individual's resources and lead to a breakdown of organised functioning, or decomposition. Types of situations that produce stress include frustrations, deprivations, conflicts, and pressures, all of which may arise from internal or external sources."*[6]

THEORY OF THE STRESS CONSTRUCT

Richard Lazarus, a South African born American psychologist, provides a definition of stress that has widespread appeal.[7] According to him, stress is understood best as a transaction between an individual and their environment. How we appraise or perceive a stressor plays an important role in whether the stressor triggers the stress response. That said, we concede that some stressors are universally stressful, such as the death of a loved one, losing your job, earthquakes, floods, experiencing bankruptcy and the like.

According to Lazarus, an individual typically assesses a threat posed by a situation or event. If the individual views his personal resources as inadequate to the challenge, various levels of stress are experienced. Lazarus refers to this as primary appraisal, which typically refers to an individual's ongoing assessment of danger faced and perceived personal resources available.

More specifically, primary appraisal asks the question: "Am I in danger?" This question may lead to three possible outcomes, namely "loss", "threat", or "challenge". For example, when John loses his job in a large multinational corporation, he may view the event as a threat or a loss. Such an interpretation may elicit varying degrees of anxiety. Alternatively, John may interpret this setback as a challenge and enjoy the fruits of personal growth. Factors that may influence this appraisal include previous experiences in similar situations, perceived social support, self-efficacy, and the availability of material resources. Secondary appraisal refers to the ongoing assessment of resources available for coping.

Stress is typically acute when we have deadlines to meet, argue with a spouse or a colleague, or work long hours. Alternatively, chronic stress is the outcome when we suffer from a long-term illness, are unhappily married, or experience job disengagement. Chronic stress and burnout often reflect a loss of self-esteem, severe lethargy, impaired cognitive ability, and emotional exhaustion, including depression, fear, and sadness. As already mentioned, stress is not necessarily bad for us; in fact, it is an integral part of living. Conflict, pain, challenges, and struggles in many respects are fundamental to enjoying a full and meaningful life.

To cite an apt maxim: "Modern life promotes a mind less focused." To a greater or lesser degree, we are all subject to frustration, such as failing to realise a cherished goal, or alternatively experiencing some form of conflict occurring within the family, at work, or on an interpersonal level. That said, the pressures of life are ever present, requiring us to be good stress managers. Rapid change is also closely associated with stress.

Many of us are "…crunched for time, deluged by information, and paralysed by the weight of many choices". So writes Daniel Pink in his book *A Whole New Mind*. He added that "…when we rise from our slumber and flick on the lights, we know we will spend much of the day paddling through a torrent of data and information".[8]

While the mind/brain continuum blossoms in the face of environmental stimulation, it is also true that mental over-stimulation contributes to an over-aroused nervous system. Psychologist David Lewis proposes that change is associated with physical, mental and social problems. The findings of his research led him to coin the phrase: Information Fatigue Syndrome. This leads to difficulties in memorising, a shortened attention span, free-floating anxiety, and poor decision-making. In the classic book, *Future Shock,* by sociologist and futurist Alvin Toffler, Toffler defines this term as "too much change in too short a period of time", a syndrome comprising severe physical and psychological afflictions.

Places of employment are notoriously stressful; a negative work climate often serves to promote stress and job dissatisfaction. Work overload may, in a similar vein, lead to emotional exhaustion and in extreme cases even result in psychological burnout. Other sources of stress within the work environment include role ambiguity, e.g. not knowing one's work role, inadequate career prospects, job insecurity, and over- or under-employment.[9]

Certain personality typologies are similarly associated with stress. Consider the type A personality; they are highly competitive in all domains of life, including work, friendship, recreation, and love. Time urgency, anger outbursts, and a constant need to take control of situations characterise type As. Given their particularly stressful lifestyle, these people are thought to be vulnerable to heart disease, accidents, and interpersonal conflict. In contrast, type B personalities generally demonstrate an easy-going demeanor. Many of the unhealthy traits observed in type A personalities are absent in type B personalities.

An unhealthy lifestyle also carries the risk of unwanted stress, suggests Gauiltiere.[10] People exposed to continuously stressful lifestyles often reflect the following profile:

- Always in a hurry.
- Short-tempered.
- Constantly anxious.
- Use adrenaline or caffeine to sleep less and get more work done.
- Harbour unrealistically high expectations.
- Deny their feelings.
- Take life too seriously.
- Have a self-critical attitude.
- Expect perfection.

SYMPTOMS OF STRESS

Butler and Hope[11] cite the following changes that may be signs of stress:

Feelings
- Lowered self-esteem
- Fear
- Anxiety or feelings of panic
- Worried about health

Thoughts
- Forgetfulness
- Concentration problems
- Indecisiveness
- Worrying unnecessarily
- Brooding on problems
- Anticipating the worst

Behaviour
- Working longer and longer hours
- Bringing work home on weekends
- Avoiding tackling problems
- Losing touch with friends
- Blaming others for problems

Sensations
- Aches and pains
- Tension – especially neck and shoulders
- Disrupted sleep patterns
- Appetite for food – increased or decreased

Psycho-spiritual
- Loss of meaning of life
- Absence of crystallised value system
- Unarticulated life goals
- Absence of faith in something larger than oneself (for example, God)

THE CASE FOR IMPROVING STRESS TOLERANCE

*Do not let your difficulties fill you with anxiety, after all it is only in
the darkest nights that stars shine more brightly*
–Abu-Tabil

Research suggests that under conditions of chronic stress, the stress hormone cortisol can cause shrinkage in an area of the brain called the hippocampus, which houses much of the brain's memory functions. Furthermore, stress causes the neurons in the brain to fire two to three times faster than normal. When brain activity is increased, it causes us to think faster and our emotions to intensify. Memory and critical thinking faculties are impaired as a result, leading to impulsivity and irrational decision-making, which often incur further stress.[12]

Stress can contribute directly and indirectly to mental and physical disorders. Most health professionals concede that many, and in fact most, diseases, are stress-related. Stress compromises the immune system and makes us vulnerable to conditions including hypertension, cardio-vascular disease, cancer, and, of course, depression. For example, one recent study found that men whose blood pressure increased with stress had a 72% rise in the risk of a stroke. Additional physical ailments associated with stress include headaches, heartburn, acne, asthma, diabetes, fibromyalgia, and infertility. Stress may also affect the clinical profile of disorders such as cancer, asthma, diabetes, and cardio-vascular disease, as well as symptoms such as chronic pain and high blood pressure.[13]

Misery teaches you the value of joy. It reveals to you the gravitas of human life.
–Abhijit Naskar

Scientists tell us that about 60 to 90% of individuals who experience stress, especially chronic stress, also suffer from depression. Furthermore, stress can dull the mind and prevent us from developing our inner potential. Stress in the workplace lowers motivation and productivity and leads to decreased job satisfaction.[14]

PHYSIOLOGY OF STRESS

When you interpret a situation, an event, an occurrence or a problem as a threat to your well-being, your body goes on "red alert", and chemical messengers including adrenaline, noradrenalin and cortisol are released into the bloodstream. Breathing rates intensify, thereby providing the brain and muscles with more oxygen; the heart rate increases (increasing blood volume in arteries by as much as 400%, increasing the danger of arterial wear and tear); blood pressure rises; sugars and fats are released into the blood stream for extra energy; muscles tense up; flow of saliva decreases; and perspiration surges. Needless to say, it is difficult to function optimally under such circumstances.[15]

However, many of the demands we face in present-day society are not of necessity life threatening, but pose threats and challenges to our sense of self-esteem, psychological security, and well-being. These demands are often emotional rather than physical by nature.

DEVELOPING STRESS TOLERANCE

What is stress tolerance? According to Corsini, stress tolerance can be defined as "the capacity to withstand pressures and strains, the ability to function effectively under conditions of stress, [and] the quality and the quantity of stress that an [individual] can endure".[16]

Can you strengthen your resilience to stress and actively increase what may be called your hardiness? Indeed, you can. Stress tolerance can be learned. Once learned, it offers relief and improved health in both the short and the long term. That in turn allows us to become more flexible and adaptive when further severe challenges come our way.

Below we examine some strategies that increase stress hardiness.

AT THE PHYSICAL LEVEL

Lifestyle

- Psychologists estimate that no less than 50% of early deaths in Western society are due to leading an unhealthy lifestyle.
- If you heed the following advice, your ability to deal with stressful events will improve dramatically:
    - Sleep at least eight hours a night.
    - Eat three meals a day, including a sound breakfast.
    - Don't smoke.
    - Drink alcohol moderately.
    - Exercise (even walking) three days a week for 20 minutes.

In their recent book, Rock and Page[17] extol the virtue of a healthy lifestyle. In their opinion, a healthy lifestyle is associated with quality of life and well-being. Exercise, they say, delays the effects of ageing, helps us sleep better, helps us to enjoy longevity, and combats depression.

While scientists are not yet certain as to why people require sleep, a good night's rest is essential for good health and functionality. Consider for a moment the last time you experienced sleep deprivation. Were you able to perform at your best mentally and physically? Were you able to think clearly? What was your memory like?

Diet and nutrition

The media regularly report findings on diet and nutrition. While these findings are sometimes conflicting, most findings support the following contentions. A well-balanced diet includes a variety of vegetables and whole foods, especially fruits, fibre and protein. Such a diet increases energy levels and strengthens the mind and body. Rock and Page[18] also advise avoiding processed and deep-fried foods. They provide a citation from the Mayo Clinic that is worthy of repetition: "Research has shown and clinical experience has confirmed that what you eat deeply affects your health [including stress levels]."

Biological stress triggers

As mentioned above, diet is related to the stress response. Coffee, tea, chocolates, fizzy drinks, and appetite suppressants are liable to act as biological stress triggers. It is said that excessive coffee and cola drinks are liable to cause palpitations (rapid heartbeat), and can lead to irritability, testiness, and general nervousness.

AT THE PSYCHOLOGICAL LEVEL

Herbert Benson, founding president of the Body-Mind Institute at Harvard University, and his colleague, Aggie Casey (in Casey & Benson),[19] pioneered a wellness programme that addresses, among others, our ability to manage stress at the psychological level. We summarise below what they and other scholars have to say in this regard.

Psychological stress triggers

You will recall Arnold Lazarus' stress theory, covered in section 1 of this chapter. There we learnt that the stress response is usually activated by an event that we interpret as a threat – such thinking most typically elicits the stress response.

Casey and Benson[20] further propose three other stress experiences that serve as psychological triggers:

- A major change that affects a large group of people – a tsunami or a large earthquake, for example.
- Life events that cause a major upheaval in our personal life, including the death of a loved one, loss of a job, car accident, divorce, financial problems, etc.
- Small stressors called daily hassles,[21] which include irritating demands, troubled interpersonal relationships, traffic jams, computer breakdowns, and power failures, among others.

Our thinking style not only influences our emotions (sadness, lack of energy), but also impacts on us somatically. For example, negative thoughts can make us vulnerable to bodily symptoms that include aches and pains, especially in the neck and lower back region. This may set in motion an unhealthy lifestyle of habits that include overeating, smoking, alcohol misuse, and sleep deprivation, compromising quality of life.

We all experience life subjectively, explain Casey and Benson.[22] This is well illustrated by thinking of a couple ambling down a busy boulevard. Objectively, the boulevard presents as a shared set of facts, yet each individual experiences the boulevard differently. The take-home message is this: we interpret our world differently because our underlying expectations and beliefs shape our thoughts. It's as if we view the world through multi-hued lenses – some rose-tinted, while others take on a somewhat darker hue.

Can you remember what you were thinking this morning when taking a shower? What were you feeling? We are often led to believe that thinking – the rational mind – is oppositional to the feeling mind. In reality, thoughts are intimately connected to emotions. For example, if you were thinking about a recent setback or crisis, chances are that you will experience negative emotion – anxiety, worry, possibly even anger or guilt. On the other hand, if you think about something positive – a recent promotion for example – it is not inconceivable that you will be awash with positive emotion, such as satisfaction, or even joy.

The ABC of our emotions

Albert Ellis, noted American psychologist, developed a theory to explain the relationship between events and feelings. He proposed that the real causes of our feelings are not events in themselves but the beliefs we entertain in respect of these events. Ellis argues a simple model to help us better understand emotions. Below follows a vignette to demonstrate its underlying principle.

It is three o'clock in the morning. Helena is sound asleep in her double-storey house. Suddenly there is a noise down below in her sitting room. Upon hearing the noise, she fears that a burglar is attempting to break into the house.

This belief translates into a visceral (bodily) response – palpitations, a cold sweat, and an inability to move. She experiences raw panic and expects the worst. After a protracted silence, she remembers that she did not close the sitting room window – the cat had probably entered through the open window, and upset the vase on the table. With this realisation, her mind and body return to emotional equilibrium.

- 'A's are the *activating events* – in the situation described above, the noise in the sitting room was the activating event.
- 'B's are Helena's *beliefs* about the sounds coming from the sitting room.
- 'C's are emotional *consequences*. In this example, these were Helena's feelings of fear.

Our thoughts allow us to make sense of the world in which we live. Our upbringing is coloured by cultural and religious experiences, therefore we are inclined to make different interpretations of events that befall us. Interpretations usually lead to emotional and physical responses. Many of the thoughts we experience are called automatic thoughts, which are ideas "triggered by a particular stimulus that leads to a specific emotional response".[23]

Let us clarify by way of illustration. Something happens or we notice something that triggers a thought. Particular types of thoughts tend to lead to certain emotions. When

Delray thinks, "I'm being treated unfairly and won't stand for it…", the chances are that she will experience anger. On the other hand, when Joanne thinks thoughts such as, "I'm in danger and won't be able to cope", the chances are that she will experience fear or anxiety. When Joe's self-talk is filled with thoughts such as, "Everything is hopeless, no-one likes me…", depression is usually not far away.

How to identify automatic thoughts[24]

Certain words serve as telltale signs for the presence of automatic thoughts:

- Should
- Must
- Ought
- Never
- Always

Examples of automatic thoughts:

- "I'm hopeless."
- "Things will never change."
- "Nothing ever changes."
- "I can't take this anymore."
- "Oh, no!"
- "How could I be this stupid?"
- "This always happens to me."
- "I'll never get anywhere in life."

The best way to deal with automatic thoughts includes a two-step process: first, create awareness, i.e. recognise dysfunctional thoughts as they occur. Then determine what provoked the automatic thought(s). Dr Aaron Beck (1976) is an American psychiatrist known as the father of dysfunctional thinking. He identified categories of cognitive (thinking) distortions. Below follow some of the better-known types of thinking distortions.

Catastrophising: A preoccupation with worst-case scenarios – jumping to a conclusion in response to a minor event. Jack experiences a headache and fears he is the victim of a brain tumour.

Minimising: A thought pattern closely related to catastrophising. Minimising takes many forms. When Jill fails to acknowledge her personal strengths, she is practicing a form of minimising.

All-or-nothing thinking: This kind of thinking does not allow us to view situations and events on a continuum, which enables us to think in shades of grey. Thembi thinks in all-or-nothing terms when she views herself or her actions in absolutes. She is either an abject failure or a total success. No in-between thinking is possible or allowed.

Labelling: When Angela describes herself as "dumb", "stupid", "wicked" or "boring", she is in effect using a cognitive distortion called labelling. It is a distortion because humans are far too complex for simple labels to capture their behaviour.

Dwelling on the negative: Janet attends a fancy wedding, where someone accidentally spills wine on her dress. She confides to a friend that her whole evening has been spoilt.

Unfavourable comparisons: Joe berates himself most of the time. He also constantly compares himself unfavourably to others. By doing this, he ensures the maintenance of low self-esteem.

"Shoulds" and "musts": This takes the form of self-criticism by concentrating on all the things you *should* be doing instead of what you're doing at the time. For example, if you are enjoying a day at the beach and all you can think is, "I should be working", you diminish any possible enjoyment you could be getting from the beach experience. By simply saying, "I should be working", you make it into a bothersome inconvenience and thereby make it less likely that you will actually motivate yourself to work.

Mind-reading: We assume that we know what people are thinking about us. If we have a conversation with someone and they correct us about something, we may automatically think, "He thinks I'm stupid!"

Fortune telling: When we assume that we can predict the future, we are guilty of fortune telling. Jonathan is unemployed and his mind is filled with dysfunctional expectations (predictions). He thinks, "There's no way that I will get a job in the present economic climate". Fortune telling controls his behaviour to such an extent that he fails to apply for any positions.

Personalising: You blame yourself for something that is not entirely your fault. After the market crash, Paul's business goes under and he is declared insolvent. He blames himself entirely for this state of affairs. A more rational analysis would suggest that at worst, Paul is only partially to blame for this parlous situation.

Blaming: Blaming is the opposite of personalising. In personalising, we take all the blame and responsibility for our difficulties, whereas in blaming we point the finger at somebody else for something that we have caused: "My drinking problems are due to an unhappy childhood."

Janet's wedding day

It is the day before Janet's wedding and she is apprehensive. The wedding will be held outside in the gardens of a wine estate. While the weather forecast predicts fine weather, Janet is convinced that the weather will not be favourable, and persuades herself that if the weather is not perfect, the entire day will be a disaster. While studying herself in the mirror, she is convinced that a tiny spot on her forehead entirely mars her appearance, and that the wedding photos will reflect her as wan and pale.

Name Janet's cognitive distortions, based on the sketch above. Then identify some of your personal thinking distortions.

Changing thinking habits

Cognitive behaviour therapy (CBT) focuses on better ways to manage our thought processes. Most of us are unaware of the nature of our automatic thoughts, and CBT helps us to become aware of this process and the effect that our automatic thoughts have. If we are constantly angry, sad, upset, or hurt, our automatic thoughts are where the problem begins. According to CBT, it's not the situation that is the problem, it's the automatic thoughts we're experiencing in the situation that create the notion of a problem.

Cognitive restructuring is a process in which we become aware of negative self-defeating thoughts, challenging their assumptions and reframing them. It is important to note that changing our thinking habits requires practice, much like learning to play a musical instrument. Your initial attempts may feel awkward, but that changes with practice. Daniel Goleman[25] explains that as we practice new thinking habits (over an eight-week period), these mental processes will lead to the establishment of fresh neural pathways in our brain that support long-term behavioural change.

Changing one's thinking habits is reflected in a three-step process, as set out below:

1. Identify self-defeating (cognitive distortion) thoughts.
2. Replace the distorted thoughts with a more functional or realistic thought – often referred to as reframing.
3. Note how you feel.[26]

Changing the way we think is best facilitated by making use of a dysfunctional thought log. This is an easy and effective way to become aware of how our thoughts influence our emotions and feelings. The thought log captures situations and events that most typically trigger automatic thoughts. Once you have worked through the four scenarios in the thought log, you can write your own stress events and practice how to reframe automatic thoughts into adaptive responses. To be repetitious: it is again emphasised that permanent change is possible, but it requires time and practice on our part.

Table 16.1: Dysfunctional thought log

Situation	Physical signs and feelings	Automatic thoughts	Cognitive distortions	Adaptive response	Outcome
Your manager wants to see you in his office.	Heart rate quickens; hands become sweaty; feel dizzy.	"Oh no!" I am sure he wants to fire me. How am I going to explain this to my wife? My life is ruined – I am so ashamed!	Jumping to conclusions. Fortune telling. Catastrophising.	There is no evidence that the manager wants to fire you. Possibly he needs to ask you something.	Calmed down – more in control.
Caught up in traffic jam on a hot summer's day.	Rapid shallow (chest) breathing. Frustration – blow hooter.	"I can't stand this… this always happens to me! I'll never get to work today!"	Catastrophising. Generalisation. Magnification.	Yes, it is inconvenient. However, it's not the end of the world. Let's listen to some calming music.	Frustration level drops, anger subsides – more relaxed.
Near collision after motorist fails to stop at intersection.	Anger/rage – grinding of teeth, pounding heart, flushed face…	"That is so rude and dangerous. Today's drivers are all stupid and ignorant!"	Generalisation. Catastrophising.	None of us is perfect. The motorist was probably absent-minded. Luckily, no accident occurred.	Anger subsides, physiology returns to equilibrium.
Stepped on a scale and it read 110 kg. I have been trying to diet to get it down to 80 kg.	Sad. Frustrated. Ashamed.	I will never be able to lose weight! I should be able to lose the weight – what's wrong with me?	Catastrophising.	Although I am a little overweight, there are still attractive things about me. Many others have been successful. Why can't I be one of the success stories?	Feeling more composed. Plan – revise my diet and increase exercise.
Write your own stress events and reactions in these spaces.					

Breathing awareness: the anchor point for stress management

As a preamble to stress management techniques we will briefly overview 'breath', which is fundamental to relaxation. According to stress experts, proper breathing techniques form an essential part of stress management. When we take a breath, we take in oxygen and release the waste product, carbon dioxide. When we fail to breathe correctly, it can lead to symptoms that include headaches, panic attacks, fatigue, muscle tension, and even depression. Deep and slow breathing sends messages to the brain that lower stress hormone levels such as adrenalin and cortisol, enhancing psychological and physical well-being in the process.[27]

Newborn babies typify healthy breathing: they breathe deeply, slowly, and rhythmically, and fill their lungs to full capacity. Unfortunately, as we grow up, most of us – unless properly trained – will by force of habit become shallow chest breathers.

In her book *The Stress Management Handbook*, Dr. Lori Leyden-Rubenstein[28] furnishes us with some interesting statistics on our breathing styles; we take in about 24 000 breaths a day, these breaths are predominantly shallow, moving on average only 500 cubic centimeters of oxygen through the lungs, filling some 20 per cent of the lungs with oxygen. Importantly, this deprives the body of energy. On the other hand, diaphragmatic or belly breathing represents slow and rhythmic breathing that fills the lungs to full capacity – moving some 4 000 to 5 000 cubic centimeters of oxygen through the lungs. Abdominal breathing boasts many advantages. It invokes the relaxation response, releases beta-endorphins, and allows for a greater awareness of stress-provoking thoughts while simultaneously increasing mental clarity.

Diaphragmatic breathing, says Rubenstein, is also associated with other advantages, including:

- decreased heart rate;
- reduced blood sugar levels;
- diminished tension and fatigue;
- decreased perception of pain;
- higher levels of physical relaxation;
- improved mental alertness;
- improved emotional stability; and
- increased self-confidence.

Alpha and beta brain waves

During the brain's normal (problem solving) awake state low beta brain waves most typically dominate. On the other hand, high anxiety, anger or rage is characteristic of high beta brain wave activity as measured/quantified by an electro-encephalogram (EEG) device.

Meditation amplifies the alpha wave characteristic of normal awake but relaxed individuals. High beta waves on an EEG are characteristic of high (chaotic) deep spikes (think of stormy seas). In contrast, low beta and especially alpha waves reflect smoother superficial spikes. For examples see Lawlis and Wikipedia.[29, 30]

Mindfulness meditation

In a recent article, Van Niekerk[31] poses the question: 'Can the mind heal?'

Below follow a few pertinent extracts:

"Some 40 people sit in blissful silence. They are meditating with their eyes closed, focussing on the breath moving in and out of their bodies. According to Kabat Zinn, one of the world's leading authorities on mind-body medicine, these people suffer various illnesses including cardio-vascular disease, hypertension, general anxiety disorders, cancer, diabetes, colitis and chronic pain. According to him, most people who make this practice mindful meditation (MM) a part of their daily routine report a lessening of their symptoms."

Holistic approaches to health, such as mind/body medicine, have practical implications for patients. It means that we are able to exert higher levels of control over our thoughts and emotions (such as stress, fear, depression, pessimism and anger) and in the process help us stay healthy and recover more rapidly from illness."

Mind-body medicine suggests that there is much to be gained if health professionals go beyond attending to physical disease and in addition demonstrate sensitivity to mental, social, and spiritual influences'"

Goleman suggests that there is growing evidence that mind/body approaches (e.g. meditation) can significantly ease the frequency of symptoms associated with illness. For instance, they can reduce high blood pressure in the case of hypertension, diminish nausea following chemotherapy, provide relief for those suffering from angina, speed up recovery from surgery, and help strengthen the immune system, making the body less vulnerable to disease.[32]

At its root, what is mindfulness meditation? According to its founder, Jon Kabat-Zinn, mindfulness meditation (MM) "is awareness that arrives through paying attention, on purpose, in the present moment, non-judgementally (operative word). It is knowing what is on your mind".[33]

Mindful meditation is, according to research in the field, probably the most effective means of coping with stress and stress-related concerns. After an extensive review of the literature (meta-analysis), two internationally respected scholars, Edenfield and Saeed, concluded: "In summary, a greater mindfulness in one's way of living has consistently been shown to result in less emotional distress, more positive states of mind and overall improved quality of life. The ability to effectively regulate internal emotional experiences through mindful awareness and acceptance may result in greater long-term psychological wellbeing."[34]

There are many approaches to mindfulness meditation. The author has chosen a rudimentary approach to accommodate a beginner/novice, which is based on a book written by Dr. Richard O'Connor (2005).[35] He suggests the following steps to achieving mindfulness relaxation:

- Choose a quiet place where you will not be interrupted. Turn off the phone, TV and stereo. If you have pets close the door.
- You may either sit in a chair or lie on a bed – as long as you are comfortable.
- Close your eyes, and start to breathe slowly and deeply. Not so deeply that you strain yourself, just comfortably.
- Focus on your breathing. It is normal if thoughts enter your mind. Do not let that concern you. Gently let the thoughts pass and return to your breathing. You may want to visualise these distracting thoughts rising to the surface of a calm pool of water. The thoughts rise, burst, and disappear. Return your attention to your breathing.
- Do not judge yourself. It is important to note that distracting thoughts is part of the process of meditation.
- When you come to the end of the session, open your eyes. Stay seated or lying on your bed and appreciate the calm state you are experiencing.

A few comments are in order. Do not use an alarm; you may glance at a clock/watch from time to time to see how much longer you intend to meditate. Many want to know how long they should meditate. There are no set rules in this respect. You may want to begin with only ten minutes a day. Many meditate for 30 to 40 minutes. Others again give preference to mindful meditation called the "body scan". Some individuals like to end their meditation with loving thoughts towards other people. This practice is called loving-kindness meditation. Mindfulness meditation audiobooks/CDs read by Jon Kabat-Zinn are available online at Amazon.com. These supports are particularly helpful for beginners.[36]

Interested readers are also referred to the following sources for more in-depth coverage:

- Pickert, K. The Mindful Revolution. Time Feb 23, 2014 Vol 184 (no4) pp 32-38.
- 'Mindful' can be accessed at the following internet address: http:/mindful.org. An on-line magazine

The use of imagery

Close your eyes and imagine any one of the following scenes.

- A beautiful garden.
- Ocean scene at sunset.
- Mountain scene.
- A stream in a secluded forest.
- Choose your own mental image.

Using imagery can break negative mental cycles and replace them with positive thoughts and feelings. First, place yourself in a state of deep relaxation. Then, in your mind's eye, begin to imagine a scene that you find very relaxing. The scene can be one described above or be one of your own choosing.

In *The Wellness Book*, two academics attached to the Harvard Body-Mind Institute, Herbert Benson and Eileen Stuart (1992), provide useful information for using imagery as a stress relief technique. According to them, a state of deep relaxation and imagery interact naturally; the state of calm invites the forming of mental images, while images further create a sense of serenity and quietude. This practice relieves not only anxiety but also pain and emotional stress.[37]

Make your own mental video

The following 'uncomfortable' situations often create stress and apprehension:

- Asking your boss for a promotion or a raise.
- Taking up a sensitive issue with a colleague.
- Standing your ground at a meeting.
- Making an apology for inappropriate behaviour.
- Add your own uncomfortable or challenging situation.

To paraphrase UCLA's Professor Jeffery Schwartz (author of *The Mind and the Brain*): "If you can imagine it, you can create it." You must first be able to clearly visualise the objective you wish to achieve. Close your eyes and see yourself going through the steps leading to a desired goal, as if you were viewing a video. View it in as much detail as possible. You can rehearse your mental video repeatedly and sharpen the images. More than a static visualisation, this learning method actually programmes your neural circuitry step-by-step, so when you begin the action steps, you have already created a "highway" (footprints in the brain) along which the neurons can travel. As Donald Hebb, the Canadian pioneer psychologist reminds us, "Neurons that fire together wire together".[38]

Famous athletes use visualisation techniques to improve their performance, and you can do the same. In fact, the more clearly you scrutinise your video, the more motivated you become. John Kehoe (1996), author of *Mind Power into the 21st Century*, adds a further dimension to the video technique. He calls this 'seeding'. Instead of adding words to the soundtrack, you add feelings to accompany the movie. For example, you are to make an important presentation to secure a project for your company. Much is at stake. You mentally rehearse your talk a number of times, but instead of creating only pictures, you also add emotions to your film. In seeding, you are therefore also concerned with the emotion of whatever you are visualising. After a rehearsal, you may, for example, say to yourself, "I have delivered a perfect presentation". You then invoke positive feelings, including joy, elation and excitement. To quote Kehoe: "… feel it in your guts and make the feelings a part of you."[39]

Psycho-spiritual stress

Psycho-spiritual stress (also referred to as existential angst - see the works of Martin Hedegger) is suggestive of experiencing life as devoid of meaning. The meaningless syndrome often results in psycho-spiritual stress. People who experience this condition often lack insight and knowledge of the (deeper) self, and more specifically, their personal values, interests, and goals. This condition is often reflected by a sense of apathy (a sense of inner emptiness) and fear of taking initiative in the affairs of life. According to Victor Frankl, existential angst syndrome is linked to our post-industrial consumer society, including an over-emphasis on technology and materialism. Unhappiness in our work (job disengagement) can take on a form of psycho-spiritual stress – an "existential work vacuum".[40]

How do we address spiritual stress? By means of developing increased levels of awareness of the inner self. Such an exercise may include value and interest crystallisation, clarifying life goals, practicing gratitude, and taking calculated risks.

We close with two citations on the healthy personality.

To experience a healthy mind is to have the personal skills that characterise a rich and balanced personality. A healthy mind includes, but is not limited to, "…a state of successful performance of mental function, resulting in productive activities, fulfilling relationships with people, and the ability to adapt to change and to cope with adversity" (Keyes & Lopez, in Van Niekerk, 2006).[41]

A study in resilience – the story of a man called Abraham

People become extremely stressed when they fail to succeed in life. Consider the true story of a man called Abraham who overcame many failures and mishaps. "He lost his job; suffered defeat in a campaign for the legislature; faced failure in business; won an election for the legislature; lost his sweetheart to a fatal disease; experienced a nervous breakdown; lost an election as speaker in the legislature; lost in the race for congressional nomination; won an election to congress; lost re-nomination; was rejected as a land officer; lost an election for the senate; lost in a race for the vice-president nomination; and suffered a second defeat in a senate election. Two years after his last defeat, Abraham Lincoln was elected President of the United States."[42]

Individuals epitomising stress tolerance

Rudy Giuliani (New York mayor at the time of the 11 September 2001 Twin Towers attacks).

Captain Chesley Sullenberger (airline pilot who landed his Airbus safely on the Hudson River in New York on 15 January 2009).

Anne Frank (fearless – life-affirming spirit in the face of Nazi cruelty and danger).

Beyers Naudé (composed resolve in the face of injustice).

Others?

A FINAL WORD

You may feel as though the stress in your life is out of control, but remember that you can always control your response to stress. Managing stress is all about taking control; being in charge of your thoughts, your emotions, your schedule, your environment, and the way you deal with problems. Stress management involves changing the stressful situation when you can, changing your reaction when you cannot change the stressful situation, taking care of yourself, and making time for rest and relaxation.

Emotional intelligence skills – including our ability to manage stress – finds growing resonance in the face of demanding interpersonal relationships, a taxing corporate environment, and a fractured global economy. The most important factor that identifies the individual high in emotional intelligence is the ability to calm down under pressure of circumstance. While personal levels of resilience vary considerably among individuals, it is our emotional intelligence that assists us to preserve our sense of equanimity, come what may.

SECTION 2: ACTIVITIES FOR SKILLS DEVELOPMENT

Self-assessment

Individual activities

 Activity 1

Spend a few moments assessing your stress tolerance skills. Answer the questions below honestly. The point is not to "look good", but to gain an indication of where you stand in terms of this important emotional intelligence competency. Assign a number to each item, using this scale:

1 = Very seldom or not true of me
2 = Seldom true of me
3 = Sometimes true of me
4 = Often true of me
5 = Very often true of me or true of me

I can stay calm under stressful situations.

1	2	3	4	5

Overall, I lead a healthy lifestyle.

1	2	3	4	5

I have an optimistic approach to life.

1	2	3	4	5

For the most part, I view problems and setbacks as a challenge.

1	2	3	4	5

I seldom become irritable.

1	2	3	4	5

Multiply your score by 4 to arrive at a total out of 100.

Stress tolerance scale

10	20	30	40	50	60	70	80	90	100

Activity 2: Stress awareness exercise

A useful approach is to recognise early stress warning signs.

Over the next seven days, record when you experience the stress response. Establish what circumstances or events trigger the stress response.

Time   Stressful event   Physical and emotional feelings

Name and describe your stressors at the following levels:

Personal level:

Social level:

Spiritual level:

Choose stress management techniques to address the stressors cited above.

My stress management techniques include the following:

Group activity

Activity 3

Think of a demanding, unpleasant or unexpected situation that has arisen recently at work. It may be a deadline that looms when you are already snowed under, a lost promotion, or the prospect of losing your job.

With regard to the above-mentioned incident, record your physical, mental, and emotional reactions.

Now think of a similar situation that has arisen in your personal life, such as encountering problems with a significant other, parents, or children. Again, record your physical, mental and emotional reactions.

Think back to several recent stressful incidents and make a note of the event that sparked the stress. Do these events form a pattern, revealing your vulnerability to stress; that is, are they mainly work- or family-related?

How do you deal with stress at present? Also, list methods that are not effective that you would like to change.

....

....

Are there stress tactics that you have learned from this book that you can apply to improve your stress tolerance? What are they?

....

....

Own work for personal growth: a to-do list for the next fortnight

Activity 4

Reflect on your career. Conjure up in your mind's eye a continuum or scale with values ranging from 1 to 10. Where do you place yourself on this scale in respect of the level of your job-satisfaction? If your job satisfaction reflects "below average", how do you intend addressing this problem? How does the level of your job satisfaction influence your stress level? Explain.

....

....

Consider for a moment your work stress level on a scale from 1 to 10. Are you happy with your stress level? Where would you like it to be?

....

....

If your work stress level were uncomfortably high, how would you go about bringing it down to more acceptable levels?

....

....

What are your career (efficacy) expectations going forward?

....

....

Keep a personal log of your moods for five consecutive work days (see Chapter 4 on self-awareness). What does your 'mood log' tell you about your state of mind and your stress levels?

....

....

Do you enjoy having a 'game plan' in life or do you take every day as it comes? Why?

....

....

REFERENCES

Benson, H. & Stuart, E. (1992). *The wellness book: The comprehensive guide to maintaining health and treating stress related illness.* New York: Simon & Schuster.

Butler, G. & Hope, T. (2000). *Manage your mind – The mental fitness guide.* Oxford: Oxford University Press.

Casey, A. & Beson, H. (2004). *Mind Your Heart.* New York: Free Press.

Charlesworth, E.A. & Nathan, R.G. (2001). *Stress management – a comprehensive guide to wellness.* London: Souvenir Press.

Cherewatenko, V.S. & Perry, P. (2003). *The stress cure.* New York: Harper Collins.

Corsini, R. (2002). *The dictionary of psychology.* New York: Brunner & Rutledge.

Davis, M., Eshelman, E.R. & McKay, M. (2000). *The relaxation & stress reduction workbook.* Oakland, CA: New Harbinger Publications.

Edenfield, T.M. & Saeed, S.A. (2012). An update on mindfulness meditation as a self-help treatment for anxiety and depression. *Psychology Research and Behavior Management,* 5, 131–141. http://doi.org/10.2147/PRBM.S34937, p. 136.

Gaultiere, B. 2001. *Optimal stress.* [Online]. Available at: <http://www.vietchristian.com/lifehelps/optimalstress.asp> [Accessed 26 October, 2009].

Goldstein, R.M. (ed.). (1984). *Longman's dictionary of psychology and psychiatry.* New York: Longman.

Goleman, D. (2002). An EI-based theory of performance. In C. Cherniss & D. Goleman (eds.). *The emotionally intelligent workplace.* San Francisco: Jossey Bass.

Kabat-Zinn, J. 2017. *Defining Mindfulness.* [Online] Available at: https://www.mindful.org/jon-kabat-zinn-defining-mindfulness/ [Accessed 15 January, 2018].

Kahn, A.P. & Fawcett, J. (2009). *The A to Z of mental health: A comprehensive guide to understanding mental illness.* New York: Checkmark Books

Kehoe, J. (1996). *Mind power into the 21st century.* Vancouver: Zoetic Inc.

Lawlis, F. (2009). *Retraining The Brain.* New York: Penguin Group.

Lazarus, A. & Folkman, S. (1984). *Stress, appraisal and coping.* New York: Springer.

Leyde-Rubenstein, L. (1998). *The stress management handbook: Strategies for health and inner peace.* New Canaan, CT: Keats Publishing Inc.

Looker, T. & Gregson, O. (2003). *Managing stress.* London: Hodder Headline.

O'Connor, R. (2005). *Undoing perpetual stress.* New York: Berkley Books.

Pickert, K. (2014). The mindful revolution. *Time,* 183(4), 32-38.

Pink, D.H. (2005). *A whole new mind. Why right-brain will rule the world.* London: Penguin Books.

Rock, D. & Page, L. (2009). *Coaching with the brain in mind: Foundations for practice.* Upper Saddle River, NJ: Wiley.

Schwartz, J.M. (2003). *The mind & the brain: Neuroplasticity and the power of mental force.* New York: Harper Collins.

Taylor, S.E. (1999). *Health psychology.* Singapore: McGraw-Hill.

Van Niekerk, E.C. (2005). Strategic briefing: conversations on stress in the workplace. *HR Future,* October, 15–17.

Van Niekerk, E.C. (2006). *The healthy mind.* Unpublished manuscript. Bloemfontein.

Van Niekerk, E.C. (2009). Contextualising modern society. In E. van Niekerk & J. Hay (eds.). *Handbook of youth counselling.* Sandton: Heinemann.

Van Niekerk, E.C.(2017). *Can Mind Heal?* Unpublished Manuscript. Cape Town.

Wikipedia. (2017). *Alpha Wave.* [Online] Available at: https://en.wikipedia.org/wiki/Alpha-wave. [Accessed 5 January, 2017].

Yalom, I.D. (2017). *The Gift of Therapy: An open letter to a new generation of therapists and their patients.* New York: Harper.

ENDNOTES

1. Lawlis, 2009.
2. Kahn & Fawcett, 2009.
3. Taylor, 1999.
4. Cherewatenko & Perry, 2003.
5. Looker & Gregson, 2003.
6. Goldstein, 1984.
7. Lazarus & Folkman, 1984.
8. Pink, 2005.
9. Van Niekerk, 2009.
10. Gauiltiere, 2001.
11. Butler & Hope, 2000.
12. Van Niekerk, 2005.
13. Van Niekerk, 2005.
14. O'Connor, 2005.
15. Van Niekerk, 2005.
16. Corsini, 2002:951.
17. Rock & Page, 2009.
18. Rock & Page, 2009:125.
19. Casey & Benson, 2004.
20. Ibid.
21. Lazarus & Folkman, 1984.
22. Casey & Benson, 2004.
23. Corsini, 2002:85.
24. Casey & Benson, 2004.
25. Goleman, 2002.
26. Casey & Benson, 2004.
27. Davis, Eshelman & McKay, 2000.
28. Leyden-Rubenstein, 1998.
29. Lawlis, 2009.
30. Wikipedia, 2017.
31. Van Niekerk, 2017.
32. Goleman, 2002:1-2.
33. Kabat-Zinn, 2017.
34. Edenfield & Saeed, 2012.
35. O'Connor, 2005.
36. Ibid.
37. Benson & Stuart, 1992.
38. Schwartz, 2003:252.
39. Kehoe, 1996:22.
40. c.f. Yalom, 2017.
41. Van Niekerk, 2006:1.
42. Charlesworth & Nathan, 2001:292.

Chapter 17

OPTIMISM

Annette Prins

A pessimist sees the difficulty in every opportunity;
an optimist the opportunity in every difficulty.
—Winston Churchill

SECTION 1: OVERVIEW

Optimism constitutes a positive attitude and outlook on life. Researchers have only in recent years started looking rigorously into the possibility of an optimistic orientation to life being beneficial.[1] Many results have since supported this notion. From the perspective of psychology and neuroscience, optimism "may be so essential to our survival that it is hard-wired into our most complex organ, the brain".[2] Optimism biases both human and non-human thought. The optimism bias is "the inclination to overestimate the encountering of positive events and to overestimating the likelihood of experiencing negative events".[3] This bias helps protect us from viewing the difficulties held in store for us with their accompanying limited options. It helps reduce stress and anxiety, improves mental and physical well-being, and enhances our motivation to act and be productive. A self-fulfilling prophesy is a cause rather than a forecast of an event, since "people's behavior is determined by their subjective perception of reality rather than by objective reality".[4] Predictions may influence outcome as they might very well change behaviour.[5]

Chang[6] argues that optimism and pessimism represent unipolar dimensions and not opposites on a continuum. The opposite of optimism is thus a lack of optimism and not pessimism.

Optimists tend to look forward to a fulfilling life with good things coming their way. Pessimists, however, expect a more bleak future and vigilantly wait for the inevitable bad things to happen. Optimists believe that good events are both regular and long lasting, while bad events are less frequent and temporary in nature.[7] Folk wisdom has long held that this difference among people reflects in numerous aspects of their lives, and contemporary research has indeed confirmed much of what was believed in common folklore.[8]

After completing this chapter, you should be able to:

- define optimism;
- understand the theory informing thinking on the optimism construct;
- reflect on some benefits of being optimistic;
- understand ways to develop optimism;
- identify optimistic individuals;
- assess your own level of optimism; and
- implement individual and group activities to enhance optimism.

DEFINITION OF OPTIMISM

Optimists hold positive expectations of their future, such as expecting to do well in life, having good relationships, and being productive, happy and healthy.[9]

Martinuzzi[10] describes optimism as "...an emotional competence that can help boost productivity, enhance employee morale, overcome conflict, and have a positive impact on the bottom line".

Stein and Book[11] contend that "optimism is the ability to look at the brighter side of life and to maintain a positive attitude even in the face of adversity". In this way, optimists are able to retain their hopefulness and resilience in the face of setbacks.

THEORY OF THE OPTIMISM CONSTRUCT

Taylor argues that some theories about why optimism influences well-being include its relationship to positive emotions, active problem solving, seeking social support and personal control.[12] A significant amount of research supports the notion that optimists are better equipped to handle stress and reduce vulnerability. Optimism is studied from different perspectives within the positive psychology paradigm. According to some theorists, optimists and pessimists vary in a number of ways that influence their lives. They differ, for example, in how they approach challenges and problems, including the manner in which they cope with adversity.

Ferguson and Kelly[13] hold the view that optimism is both a disposition and something one can learn, however some people learn it more easily. Optimism, according to the authors, opens one's eyes to opportunities and to seeing the potential in others. It also energises the individual with regards to problems and challenges. Optimism further protects against the influence of negative affect, since optimistic individuals see failures as temporary setbacks, as will be explained later on in more depth. Optimism furthermore sits well with leadership, as people would rather follow an optimist than a pessimist.

Optimism does not imply a weakness in reality testing, i.e. believing that things will turn out for the best despite indicators of the opposite. Life consists of real challenges that are exacerbated by risky behaviour, which need to be managed and overcome. "True optimism is a comprehensive and hopeful but realistic approach to daily living."[14] This implies not blind optimism, but the ability to check your thinking and stop saying destructive things about yourself and the world around you. This is especially true in the face of personal setbacks.

Expectancy-value models of motivation – Carver and Scheier[15]

This theory states that behaviour is organised around the pursuit of goals, i.e. people focus on pursuing goals that they view as desirable and try to avoid those that are undesirable. The greater the value of the goal is for the individual, the greater the motivation to obtain the goal. Likewise, with no (important) goal to pursue, people have little motivation to act.

Secondly, expectancy of success is important. Where there is a lack of confidence that the goal may be reached, little energy will be applied in pursuit of such a goal. Optimists who would, on average, have confidence that the goal may be reached, will apply their minds and energy in pursuit of the goals. Lane[16] refers to these types of behaviour as the emotionally intelligent approach and avoidance behaviour. Impulse control, for example, refers to refraining from behaviour that aims at short-term gratification, such as being lazy or giving up studying (by keeping in mind the negative consequences that may follow from such behaviour, such as not obtaining a degree and therefore not being able to support oneself or a family financially).

Persistence, on the other hand, relates to managing negative emotional responses when obstacles present themselves. Persistence assumes an awareness of negative emotions and refraining from acting on them (for example, feeling like physically attacking your rude line manager but realising that he is a stepping stone to furthering your career in the organisation, and then persisting in civil behaviour). Pessimists, on the other hand, would be more doubtful about the possibility of reaching their goals, inducing hesitancy in pursuing them. Optimists will assume that there will be a way around the adversity, while pessimists much more readily anticipate failure.

Learned optimism vs. learned helplessness

Learned helplessness is defined by the thought that nothing you can do will alter the circumstances. When facing adversity, animals tend to become passive and no longer attempt to escape if earlier experience has made them believe no escape is possible. Researchers attempted to identify when individuals will not become helpless by observing how people interpreted bad events. They found that those who believed the setbacks were temporary, changeable and local did not become helpless, e.g. if, in a failed relationship, they believed they could approach it differently next time round, they could do something about it and that it was only a single situation, they quickly bounced back. People who believe something is going to last forever and undermine everything, and there is nothing they can do about it, become helpless.[17]

An individual's expectancies of the future link with how the causes of past events are explained. Optimists use "adaptive causal attributions to explain negative experiences or events", and make "external, variable, and specific attributions" for failure-like events rather than "the internal, stable and global attributions" of pessimists. The optimist therefore explains negative events by taking account of others' roles as well as the environment in negative outcomes (external attribution), and believes that the negative event is unlikely to re-occur (variable attribution). The optimist therefore somehow cognitively distances themself from past negative outcomes of importance.

Table 18.1: Optimism versus pessimism

Optimist	Pessimist
Our cultural backgrounds make it challenging to find common ground for building a relationship. **(External attribution)**	I messed up the chance of building a good relationship. **(Internal attribution)**
I had a good relationship with my previous line managers. **(Variable attribution)**	I don't seem to have what it takes to have good relationships with authority figures. **(Stable attribution)**
I am going to be more sensitive to culture in future relationships. **(Specific attribution)**	I am a failure in all relationships. **(Global attribution)**

Can you think of an example demonstrating this principle?

....

....

If the causes of unfavourable events are seen as stable features, pessimists will believe the causes are enduring and are therefore likely to recur in the future. However, when it is assumed that the causes are unstable, the future may look brighter. Likewise, if explanations for past failures are global and touch all aspects of an individual's life, the expectancy will be that many areas of the individual's life will attract unfavourable outcomes as a result of the causal forces being widely spread. Flexible versus rigid explanatory styles uphold optimistic and pessimistic viewpoints.[18] Optimism links with self-regard, interpersonal relationships and reality testing.[19]

BENEFITS DERIVED FROM ENHANCED OPTIMISM

A whole range of positives seem to emerge from an optimistic attitude to life.

Optimism and subjective well-being

Adversity elicits a range of emotions.[20] These may include positive emotions such as eagerness and excitement, as well as negative emotions such as anxiety, depression and anger. People's natural optimism or pessimism seems influential in how these emotions present; optimists expect positive outcomes even in the face of adversity, with their emotions leaning to the positive, while the opposite holds true for pessimists. Pessimists, for example, seem to experience more distress after adverse events, while optimistic mothers, for example, show resistance to the development of depressive symptoms after childbirth. In bypass surgery[21] it was found that optimists show a negative relationship with distress prior to surgery, and a positive relationship with life satisfaction after surgery.

Optimism, pessimism and coping

As referred to earlier on, Seligman uncovered three major attitudes distinguishing the optimist from the pessimist.[22] "First, they view downturns in their lives as temporary blips on the radar. The bad time won't last forever. The situation will turn around. They don't feel doomed. Basically, they see troubles and difficulties as delayed successes, rather than outright and conclusive defeats. Second, they tend to view the misfortune as situational and specific and not as yet another manifestation of a longstanding and inescapable doom. That way even a really bad experience can be examined and dealt with individually - it isn't the last straw. Third, optimists don't immediately shoulder all the blame. If the examination turns up external causes, they take these into consideration.

"This is in contrast to the three P's of pessimists: Permanence, Pervasiveness and Personalising. Pessimists will tend to experience each and every setback as just the latest in a long line of past and (quite probably) future failures that they are fated to suffer. Any lapse will be seen as yet another example of how they screw up everything all the time. Why do bad things keep happening? Because pessimists decide that their own incompetence or ineffectiveness is to blame.

"The optimist turns those three P's around by disputing inappropriate self-blame and feelings of helplessness." This in turn influences coping.

The physiology of optimists versus pessimists seems to differ, with pessimists demonstrating higher levels of blood pressure and inflammation.[23] Fox,[24] after looking into brain chemistry, asserted that optimistic individuals tend to selectively attend to approach/pleasurable stimuli, while pessimists tend to rather be controlled by fear/avoidance. Optimists are driven by a higher activation in the left prefrontal cortex, enabling them to feel more pleasure, which motivates them to approach potentially pleasurable activities, stay with tasks longer, and sustain pleasurable feelings longer. Pessimists exhibit less activation in the left prefrontal cortex and amygdala.

Do optimists and pessimists differ in their coping strategies?

It has been found that optimists persevere in their efforts to tackle serious adversity, while pessimists use escapism techniques such as focusing on temporary distractions and wishing the adversity away.[25] They are therefore less problem focused and apply less energy in an attempt to solve the problem. Optimists also seem to positively reframe adverse situations that cannot be changed, and to accept reality more readily. They make less use of denial or attempts to distance themselves from the problem; instead, they tend to accept reality as it is, attempting to find the best in negative circumstances and to learn something from the experience. Optimists therefore use more problem-centred coping mechanisms and are more future-orientated than pessimists.

Pessimists show a greater tendency to disengage from the goals associated with adverse conditions, while optimists aim to find something beneficial in adverse circumstances and to learn something in the process. In contrast, pessimists lean towards overt denial, and may indulge in substance abuse and other strategies that decrease their awareness of the problem. This approach to coping is also carried over into the workplace, where optimists exhibit more problem-focused coping than pessimists. Pessimists lean more towards emotion-focused coping and escapism such as indulging in sleeping, eating, drinking, and even avoiding people or seeking their support. Optimists, in general, make use of approach methods of coping, while pessimists use avoidance coping. Coping and well-being both seem to correlate with optimism; optimists indulge in proactively managing their future well-being via active coping, humour, and constructive thinking. They are less focused on the negative aspects of their experiences, with a resultant reduction in stressful emotions and physical symptoms. Pessimists tend more readily to catastrophise, avoid, and give up on adverse events.

Ms. A is a pessimist, and Ms. B an optimist. Both hear from their physician that they have high cholesterol levels.

Discuss how Ms. A and Ms. B may differ in their approach to tackling the problem.

Optimism and physical well-being

Much research has been done in relation to optimism and physical health. According to a study of 1,000 healthy people over 50 years,[26] pessimists die younger than optimists. Many of these deaths were accidental in nature, indicating that pessimists may take more risks than optimists.

Cardio-vascular disease

Seligman,[27] in summarising a range of studies on optimism and cardio-vascular disease (CVD), concludes that optimism strongly correlates with CVD. This holds true even when correction is done for other influencing variables including obesity, smoking, alcohol consumption, heightened cholesterol and hypertension. This also holds true when correcting for depression, perceived stress etc., as well as when optimism is measured in different ways. He argues that high optimism, relative to average optimism and pessimism, protects individuals, whilst pessimism hurts people when compared to the average.

Infectious diseases

Hefferon[28] referred to Cohen et al.'s experiment where 334 participants were exposed to a common cold and observed over a two week period. Those experiencing positive emotions showed less symptoms than their more pessimistic counterparts.

Cancer and all-cause mortality

According to Seligman's[29] overview of cancer literature, results lean quite heavily in the direction of pessimism as a risk factor for developing cancer. He also states that highly optimistic people may indeed have a lower risk for cancer as well as death from all causes.

Why are optimists less vulnerable to disease?[30]

1. Optimists tend to be active and follow healthier lifestyles, believing their actions matter. Pessimists more readily believe they are helpless and nothing they do will bring change, therefore they resort to passive helplessness.

2. Optimists seem to have richer and stronger social bonds, love and support.

3. Biological mechanisms such as the immune system are indicated, with optimists having more infection-fighting white blood cells than pessimists.

4. Furthermore, a pathological circulatory response is seen in response to repeated stress. Pessimists seem to give up and suffer more stress, while optimists cope better with stress. Repeated stress episodes mobilise cortisol production with its concomitant exacerbation of damage to the walls of blood vessels, promoting arteriosclerosis.

According to Hefferon,[31] health assets include subjective, biological and functional assets that may be applied towards positive health. These include aspects such as positive emotions, purpose and engagement, positive achievements, relationships and optimism. Optimism and positive emotions form part of the top coping mechanisms researched in relation to health and well-being. Hefferon holds the opinion that optimists attend casually to presenting risks, but focus vigilantly when real danger looms. Optimists also take active steps to ensure the positive quality of their future, such as increasing exercise or lowering their saturated fat intake, body fat, etc. during periods of rehabilitation in cardiac rehabilitation programmes.[32] Pessimists, in contrast, exhibit "giving up" behaviour and tend to avoid focusing on the problem by, for example, indulging in excessive drug or alcohol use, actively dimming awareness of failure and problems. Their approach to adversity may include (as has already been discussed) self-defeating behaviour, less persistence, avoidance coping such as excessive sleeping, and, in more extreme cases, may even include an impulse to escape from life via suicide.

Mr. T (pessimist) and Mr. B (optimist) are both at risk for CVD due to a family history involving the illness.

How do you assume they may differ in their behaviour in relation to safeguarding themselves?

In summary, Snyder and Lopez[33] and Martinuzzi[34] quote researchers claiming that learned optimism predicts:

- healthier relationships;
- better mental and physical health and longevity;
- better academic or work performance;
- superior athletic performance;
- more productive work records;
- greater satisfaction at the interpersonal level;
- more effective coping with life stressors;
- less vulnerability to depression; and
- superior physical health.

Optimism at work

National Church Life Survey (NCLS) research on leadership - how to build a culture of optimism - states that hope is one of the strongest motivations for change. "An optimistic outlook communicates that change and growth are possible and are more likely to generate positive outcomes – it puts the focus onto the possibilities rather than the problems." Thus, whilst people should be realistic in their appraisal, they also need to understand that "moving forward will be best achieved by focusing on what they have and what they can do, rather than what they lack or what may appear beyond them". Optimism needs to be part of the leadership culture rather than simply a characteristic of one person. Shared optimism may promote personal growth, including a willingness to try out new approaches, which may, if successful, further enhance optimism and personal well-being. Enthusiasm to take another step is encouraged by small wins. Leadership aiming to develop a culture of optimism is more likely to contribute to healthy churches (organisations) and healthy leaders.[35]

Martinuzzi concurs that nowhere is optimism more important than in leading an organisation,[36] as effective leaders have a transforming effect on the people they lead. They are able to sketch a future that instils hope and optimism, and can convince people that they can achieve beyond what they believed possible. Their optimism generates energy and commitment in pursuing objectives. Innovation is underscored by optimism that opens up avenues in pursuing new ideas and possibilities, which may include challenging the current status quo, risk-taking, some adventure, and the expectation of success.

Discuss how, in South Africa, the replacement of President Zuma with Mr Ramaphosa influenced optimism among citizens in 2018.

DEVELOPING OPTIMISM

Firstly, we need to have some understanding of where optimism and pessimism come from. Several authors[37] agree on the following influential factors, some of which are also referred to by Seligman and colleagues:

- Optimism seems to be subject to genetic influences.
- Infants experiencing their social world as predictable develop a sense of basic trust, whereas infants experiencing the world as unpredictable tend to develop a basic mistrust in others.
- Secure childhood attachment is believed to contribute to optimism. In contrast, insecurity of adult attachment relates to pessimism.
- The learning environment that a child has been exposed to is another influential factor.
- Parents who role model optimism and provide for safe, coherent environments tend to promote a learned optimism style in their children. Such parents may provide explanations in relation to negative events that still make children feel good about themselves (external, variable and specific attributions), and after positive outcomes make them feel extra special (internal, stable and global attributions). They teach their children adaptive excusing of failures. Pessimistic children, in contrast, often have pessimistic parents.
- Childhood trauma such as parental death, abuse, incest, etc. may contribute to the development of pessimism.
- Exposure to too much violence, such as excessive TV watching, can also induce learned helplessness and resultant pessimism.

The quality of optimism/pessimism is relatively pervasive and permanent.[38] Genetically determined qualities seem fundamental to personality make-up and exert a virtually unending influence on an individual's life. Further, an early formulated world-view provides a foundation for how life events are viewed; the firmer the held view, the more enduring its influence will be. If pessimism is securely embedded in an individual, is change possible?

Bringing about change

A group of techniques collectively known as cognitive-behavioural therapies may be used to shape a pessimist's behaviour in a more positive direction. Pessimists tend to distort reality unduly in their minds, indulging in a pessimistic interior monologue, inducing anxious and depressive thoughts that cause negative affect. This sets people up to not pursue their goals with the vigour required for success. Cognitive therapies attempt to diminish negative and anxiety-provoking thoughts and thereby reduce distress, allowing for more effort. Automatic thoughts are identified and challenged.

Other techniques include training in personal efficacy in an attempt to enhance individuals' particular competencies via, for example, assertiveness or social skills training. Problem solving is another technique where clear obtainable goals and sub-goals are set, together with decision-making abilities, in pursuit of these goals. Enhancing success helps build optimism, however unquestioning optimism is not the goal of such therapies.

The dangers of blind optimism

There is, of course, a downside to optimism, as it may cause individuals to try and control situations that are biologically not controllable.[39] This may lead to increases in stress, disappointment and depression. The blindly optimistic person may fail to take into account the downside of a situation, for example most gamblers have false expectations about their ability to win money through luck.

The point is that optimism always needs to be grounded in reality and some form of action. Martin Seligman[40] uses the term "flexible optimism" – optimism grounded in reality – and distinguishes it from "blind optimism". For the blind optimist, success can be achieved against incredible odds. Blind optimists often make use of defence mechanisms, such as denial of reality.

Such individuals should be assisted to accept situations that cannot be changed and to be more flexible in setting new goals if the initial ones were unobtainable.

Individuals epitomising optimism

Dr Albert Schweitzer
Gary Player
Minkie van der Westhuizen
Serena and Venus Williams
Others?

A FINAL WORD

Positive mental health is indeed "a presence", namely the presence of positive emotion, engagement, meaning, positive relations and accomplishment.[41] It is not merely the absence of pathology, but rather the presence of flourishing.

Optimists look on the bright side of life and tend to maintain a positive attitude, even in the face of adversity. Optimism energises the individual with regard to problems and challenges, and helps one to focus on opportunities and see the potential both in situations and other individuals, and energetically pursue goals. Failures are seen as temporary rather than as enduring setbacks. Pessimists, on the other hand, are doubtful about the possibility of reaching their goals, inducing hesitancy in pursuing these goals. Optimists will assume that there will be a way around the adversity, while pessimists may much more readily anticipate failure. Optimism, furthermore, sits well with leadership, since people would rather follow an optimist than a pessimist.

SECTION 2: ACTIVITIES FOR SKILLS DEVELOPMENT

Self-assessment

Individual activities

Activity 1

Spend a few moments assessing your level of optimism. Respond to the statements below honestly. Assign a number to each item, using this scale:

1 = Very seldom or not true of me
2 = Seldom true of me
3 = Sometimes true of me
4 = Often true of me
5 = Very often true of me

Overall, my friends and family see me as an optimist.				
1	2	3	4	5

I usually look on the bright side of life.				
1	2	3	4	5

Despite setbacks in life, I believe things will turn out all right in the end.				
1	2	3	4	5

I tend to remain optimistic, even when things go wrong.				
1	2	3	4	5

Even in the darkest moments, I see light at the end of the tunnel.				
1	2	3	4	5

Multiply your score by 4 to arrive at a total out of 100.

Optimism scale									
10	20	30	40	50	60	70	80	90	100

 ## Activity 2

You failed an important exam. How did you explain it to yourself? What type of attributions did you make? Stable/unstable, variable/permanent, or specific/ global? Repeat this exercise a few times in an attempt to identify your typical attribution style. Can you dispute any pessimistic attributions you made?

....

....

Group activity

 ## Activity 3

Think of someone you consider to be a pessimistic employee. A conflict develops between the employee and his or her line manager. How will the pessimist approach the problem (taking cognisance of what you have learnt about pessimism)?

....

....

Identify an optimistic employee. Using the same occurrence as in the question above, how might the optimist tackle the problem?

....

....

Can you think of other examples? Discuss.

....

....

Own work for personal growth: a to-do list for the next fortnight

Activity 4

Compare the advantages and disadvantages of optimism and pessimism.

Optimism	Pessimism

Where on the continuum of optimism versus pessimism do you operate as a rule? Where would you feel comfortable being?

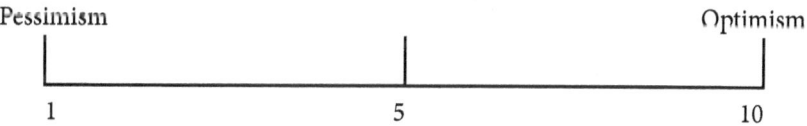

Pessimism   Optimism

1   5   10

Use the cybernetic cycle model (in Chapter 13) to evaluate and set goals, and then apply the strategies below to enhance your level of optimism. Evaluate after four months how successful you have been. Consider the following strategies to enhance your level of optimism:

1. Go back to the sections on thinking skills and problem solving and actively practice these skills. If you struggle, seek professional assistance.
2. Decide to read at least two books on successful people during the next year.
3. Talk to both optimistic and pessimistic people – ask them about their outlook.
4. Check your e-mails and compare the number of negative to positive words.
5. Request feedback from co-workers, family, and significant others as to the level of positivity versus negativity that you tend to project.

Use the tips provided by Martinuzzi,[42] who suggests the following:

1. Avoid negative environments: seek the company of positive individuals in your business.
2. Celebrate your strengths: focus on your strengths, not your weaknesses.
3. Take care of your spiritual and emotional well-being: regularly expose yourself to inspirational material such as the biographies of successful people.
4. Manage or ignore what you cannot change: when faced with adversity, attempt to problem solve.
5. Learn to reframe: shift your perspective and try to find a positive in the adversity.
6. Adapt your language and outlook: attempt to be more open-minded to new ideas. If you find yourself consistently opposing new ideas, stop and check yourself.
7. Focus outside yourself: focus on important people in your life, rather than constantly focusing on yourself.
8. Nurture a culture of optimism: check your expectations of others at work. Expect and encourage success.
9. Cultivate spontaneity: identify and challenge your own comfort zone. Occasionally take the opportunity to let your hair down and enjoy an unplanned and playful moment.
10. Consider the health benefits, such as an enhanced immune system.

NCLS research on leadership also suggests trying the following:

- Move beyond a 'problem focus' in planning, to a 'possibility focus'.
- Generate a climate of encouragement.
- Help everyone to acknowledge and develop their strengths.
- Help people to talk about themselves and others optimistically.
- Create a safe place where people's hopes can be aired and explored.
- Challenge attitudes of helplessness.
- Share stories of hope and small victories.
- Resist naming people as 'problems'.[43]

(See *Optimism: The Hidden Asset – Leadership Training* from MindTools.com.)

Visit the Internet and search for "Optimism" sites.

REFERENCES

Bowlby, J. (1998). *Attachment and loss. anxiety and anger*. London: Pimlico.

Carver, C.S. & Scheier, M.F. (2005). Optimism. In C.R. Snyder and S.J. Lopez. *Handbook of positive psychology*. New York: Oxford University Press, p. 231-243.

Chang, E.C. (2001). *Optimism & pessimism: Implications for theory, research, and practice*. Washington, DC: American Psychological Association.

Erikson, E. (1968). *Youth: Identity and crisis*. New York: WW.

Ferguson, R. & Kelly, M. (2005). *Enhancing emotional intelligence. Leadership tips from the executive coach*. Raleigh, NC: Mark Kelly Books.

Fitzgerald, T.E., Tennen, H., Affleck, G. & Pransky, G.S. (1993). The relative importance of dispositional optimism and control appraisals in quality of life after coronary artery bypass surgery. *Journal of Behavioural Medicine, 16*(1), p. 25–43.

Fox, E. (2012). *Rainy brain, sunny brain: How to retrain your brain to overcome pessimism and achieve a more positive outlook*. New York, NY: Basic Books.

Hefferon, K. (2013). *Positive psychology and the body: The somatopsychic side to flourishing*. Maidenhead: McGraw-Hill Education.

Lane, R.D. (2000). Levels of emotional awareness: Neurological, psychological, and social perspectives. In R. Bar-On & J.D.A. Parker (eds.). *The handbook of emotional intelligence: Theory, development, assessment, and application at home, school, and in the workplace*. San Francisco: Jossey-Bass, p. 186.

Martinuzzi, B. (2010). *Optimism: The hidden asset*. [Online] Available at: www.mindtools.co./index.html [Accessed April 30, 2010].

Multi-Health Systems Inc. (2011). *The complete EQ-i 2.0 experience*. Toronto: Multi-Health Systems Inc.

Multi-Health Systems Inc & Jopie van Rooyen Psychometrics. (2011). *The complete EQ-i 2.0 experience*. Toronto: Multi-Health Systems Inc.

NCLS Research. (2016). *Lead with your Strengths; Optimism: Build a Culture of Optimism*. [Online] Available at: http://www.ncls.org.au/default.aspx?sitemapid=6171 [Accessed March 6, 2017].

Peterson, C. & Seligman, M.E.P. (1984). Causal explanations a risk factor for depression: Theory and evidence. *Psychological Review, 91*(3):347–374.

Plomin, R., Scheier, M.F., Bergeman, C.S., Pedersen, N.L., Nesselroade, J.R. & McClearn, G.E. (1992). Optimism, pessimism and mental health: A twin/adoption analysis. *Personality and individual differences, 13*(8), p. 921-930.

Seligman, M.E. (1991). *Learned optimism*. New York: Knopf.

Seligman, M.E. (2011). *Flourish: a visionary new understanding of happiness and well-being*. New York: Free Press.

Sharot, T. (2011). *The optimism bias: a tour of the irrationally positive brain* (1st ed.). New York: Pantheon Books.

Snyder, C.R. (1994). *The psychology of hope: you can get there from here*. New York: Free Press.

Snyder, C.R. & Lopez, S.J. (2007). *Positive psychology. The scientific and practical explorations of human strengths*. Thousand Oaks, CA: Sage Publications.

Stein, J.S. & Book, H. (2011). *The EQ Edge: Emotional intelligence and your success* (3rd ed.). San Francisco: Jossey-Bass.

ENDNOTES

1. Chang, 2001.
2. Sharot, 2011:xii.
3. Sharot, 2011:xv.
4. Sharot, 2011:43.
5. Sharot, 2011:57.
6. Chang, 2001.
7. Seligman, 2011.
8. Carver & Scheier, 2005.
9. Sharon, 2011.
10. Martinuzzi, 2010:55.
11. Stein & Book, 2011:208.
12. Hefferon, 2013.
13. Ferguson & Kelly, 2005:92.
14. Stein & Book, 2011:210.
15. Carver & Scheier, 2005.
16. Lane, 2000.
17. Seligman, 2011.
18. Peterson & Seligman, 1984.
19. MHS & JvR, 2011.
20. Carver & Scheier, 2005.
21. Fitzgerald et al., 1993.
22. Stein & Book, 2011:210-211.
23. Hefferon, 2013.
24. Fox, 2012.
25. Carver & Scheier, 2005.
26. Sharot, 2011:58.
27. Seligman, 2011.
28. Hefferon 2013.
29. Seligman, 2011.
30. Ibid.
31. Hefferon, 2013.
32. Scheier & Carver, 1992.
33. Snyder & Lopez, 2007.
34. Martinuzzi, 2010.
35. NCLS Research, 2016.
36. Martinuzzi, 2010.
37. Bowlby, 1988; Erikson, 1968; Plomin et al., 1992; Snyder, 1994; Snyder & Lopez, 2007.
38. Carver & Scheier, 2005.
39. Hefferon, 2013.
40. Seligman, 1991.
41. Martinuzzi, 2010.
42. Ibid.
43. NCLS Research, 2016.

SECTION F: WELL-BEING

The model further allows for a Wellness Indicator. Happiness is indicative of emotional health and well-being, and is not a specific subscale of any one of the areas. It is characterised by feeling satisfied and the ability to enjoy different facets of one's life. It does not contribute directly to the total EI score. Associated subscales include assertiveness, optimism, interpersonal relationships and self-actualisation.

The following skills are discussed:

Chapter 18   Well-being and happiness

Chapter 18

WELL-BEING AND HAPPINESS

Annette Weyers

Happiness is not a destination. It is a method of life.
–Burton Hills

SECTION 1: OVERVIEW

What is the nature of happiness and how do we achieve it? Would the basis of happiness simply be to minimise suffering and maximise pleasure? These are the eternal questions contemplated by philosophers and sages throughout history, and to this day the pursuit of happiness is one of the most compelling and enduring goals in life.

A major focus in positive psychology is the scientific search for the sources of healthy human functioning and ways in which healthy functioning can be promoted. Within this context there is a drive to find an "empirically based conceptual understanding of happiness".[1] A current finding of happiness research suggests that there are practical steps that we can take to increase our happiness and contentment to create a meaningful life.

After completing this chapter, you should be able to:

- define happiness/well-being;
- understand the theory informing happiness;
- describe the rewards of happiness;
- identify individuals who epitomise happiness;
- reflect on ways to improve your own level of happiness; and
- implement individual and group activities to enhance happiness.

DEFINITION OF WELL-BEING AND HAPPINESS

The following definitions of well-being/happiness denote the various ways in which the concept is delineated:

- Happiness is the ability to feel satisfied with one's life, to enjoy oneself, to have fun and to express positive emotions. It is the experience of self-satisfaction and contentment; the sense that one's life is good.[2]

- Happiness is a by-product and/or barometric indicator of your overall degree of emotional intelligence and emotional functioning.[3]

- Happiness (subjective well-being) is a combination of cognitive judgement of satisfaction with life, the frequent experience of positive moods and emotions, and the relatively infrequent experience of unpleasant moods and emotions.[4]

- Well-being is a global combination of emotional well-being, psychological well-being and social well-being.[5]

- Well-being is a broad term, which includes aspects such as happiness, life satisfaction, positive affect, optimism and hope.[6]

- Well-being is the subjective experience of contentment and satisfaction as an outcome of positive and optimal functioning in the physical, psychological, social and spiritual life domains.[7]

THEORY INFORMING THE WELL-BEING AND HAPPINESS CONSTRUCTS

As part of the growth in positive psychology, there is an increased interest in happiness and well-being in order to understand what accounts for a satisfying life and how to assist people to achieve optimal well-being.

Positive psychology: A focus on well-being

Inspired by classical philosophy, psychology has distinguished two major approaches to happiness: the hedonic and eudaimonic perspectives. The hedonic view of happiness in its purest form can be described as the pursuit and enjoyment of life and its pleasures. The hedonic basis of happiness is described in terms of one's own experience of life (subjective well-being). Subjective well-being captures the major elements of what is meant when using the everyday term "happiness". The current subjective well-being research mostly comprises three primary components: life satisfaction, positive affect and negative affect.[8]

The eudaimonic view of happiness is described in terms of the fulfilment of one's inner potential and expression of one's true self (daimon). Eudaimonic happiness is principally associated with "activities that create feelings of challenge, competence, and effort, and that offer opportunities for personal growth and skill development".[9] The two perspectives on happiness motivate two distinct lines of research in psychology, however it is acknowledged that although these conceptions of happiness appear to be mutually exclusive, they are complementary. Therefore, researchers concede that both hedonic and eudaimonic happiness seem to reflect what people consider to be essential components of a good life. Thus, the assessment of well-being includes broad aspects of both hedonic and eudaimonic happiness. Jointly, these two seemingly disparate notions of happiness provide a representation of well-being and happiness that is more veritable than either could provide alone.[10]

The happiness and well-being research projects are diverse and represent different perspectives, however all are aimed at the promotion of optimal human functioning. One of the pioneers of positive psychology, Martin Seligman, also focused on the development of a theory on well-being. Initially, Seligman concluded that authentic happiness presents itself in three guises, positive emotion, engagement and meaning (this was extensively discussed in the previous edition of this book). However, further reflection and research have led him to conclude that the authentic happiness theory is inadequate.[11] The new theory on well-being postulates that various elements contribute to well-being, moreover these elements are chosen not primarily to increase happiness, but for their own sake. The five elements are:

- **Positive emotion**: this equates with the pleasant life of the authentic happiness theory. However, in the new model it is not the goal of the theory, but rather one of the factors that contribute to well-being.

- **Pleasure:** this is the experience of positive emotions derived from enjoying things such as fine food, money, expensive clothes, dancing, and sex. The art lies in discovering the pleasures that bring the most satisfaction in one's life, and to take the time to savour and enjoy them.[12] We can benefit from building pleasure into our everyday lives, as pleasurable experiences can be fun and can add positive experiences to life.[13]

- **Engagement**: this implies to be engrossed in an activity to such an extent that you forget time. People flourish when they are absorbed in activities that demand their full attention and involvement. Activities that captivate people are diverse, for example they could be anything from cooking to taking part in a good conversation, performing a challenging task at work, gardening, reading a good book, teaching a child or listening to music.

- **Meaning**: to belong to or to serve something you believe transcends yourself and which gives meaning to life.

- **Accomplishment**: to pursue success, accomplishment, achievement or mastery in whichever field you may choose. Achievement includes both momentary achievement as well as a life dedicated to accomplishment.[14]

- **Positive relationships**: positive relationships have a profound influence on well-being, as human beings are social beings, with an intrinsic need to connect to others. Therefore, the "pursuit of relationships is a rock-bottom fundamental to human well-being".[15]

In addition to the elements deemed crucial for well-being, Seligman proposes that the daily employment of the 24 signature strengths (Values-In-Action) underpins all five elements, which leads to "more positive emotion, to more meaning, to more accomplishment, and to better relationships".[16] Thus, when signature strengths are improved, they further enhance optimal functioning and well-being: (In this chapter character strengths are discussed as a strategy to improve happiness.)

The following are two further examples of the different views of scholars as to which factors are associated with happiness.

1. Life-satisfaction and happiness are generated by:
   - close social ties;
   - religious faith; and
   - adequate resources to progress towards one's goals.[17]

2. The six core variables that are the best predictors of happiness are:
   - positive self-esteem;
   - a sense of perceived control;
   - extroversion;
   - optimism;
   - positive social relationships; and
   - a sense of meaning and purpose in life.[18]

As the research about happiness and well-being has gained momentum, it has become clear that more research is needed to formulate the most useful and accurate measures of happiness. In addition, theories about happiness, which explain the process of happiness and the identification of factors underlying happiness, need further refinement and exploration.[19]

EMOTIONAL INTELLIGENCE, WELL-BEING AND HAPPINESS

It has been argued in this book that the whole range of the emotional intelligence subscales greatly affects the ability to be happy. However, although it still confirms that all subscales advance happiness, the new EQ-i 2.0 model presents happiness in a different way, i.e. happiness no longer forms part of the 15 subscales; rather, it is included in a new concept referred to as the Well-being Indicator.[20] Happiness differs from the other subscales in that it both contributes to and is a product of emotional intelligence, therefore it is considered a barometer of emotional health and well-being.

Happiness is interrelated to all EI competencies but is mostly associated with optimism, inter-personal relationships, self-regard and self-actualisation. Together, these subscales are presented as a composite picture of well-being,[21] thus balance between these subscales greatly contributes to happiness. The alliance between these subscales and happiness is also endorsed by other theorists who consider these factors as essential to well-being, for example Compton[22] stresses the importance of optimism and self-regard; Seligman[23] regards self-actualisation as important; and the value of positive interpersonal relationships is endorsed by Compton, Bernstein and Seligman.[24]

The interrelationship between the subscales means that gains in one subscale contributes to gains in other areas, which in turn enhances the experience of well-being.

> ## *Myths about happiness*
>
> People often erroneously believe that:
>
> - material wealth will make them happy;
> - the higher their education, the happier they will be;
> - those with high IQs are happier;
> - younger people are the happiest;
> - climate - living in an area with a pleasant climate will make them happier; and
> - a high social standing will make them happier.
>
> *What is your view?*

THE REWARDS OF HAPPINESS

Amongst others, happiness positively influences your ability to be resilient, your health and your performance at work.

Resilience

Happy people experience emotions that are more positive, and positive emotions play a key role in expanding one's resilience, according to Professor Barbara Fredrickson.[25] Fredrickson developed the broaden-and-build theory, which explains how positive emotions can expand resilience by broadening people's momentary thought action repertoires and building enduring personal resources. Thus, the broaden-and-build theory postulates that positive emotions such as joy and contentment help one to open one's thinking and actions to explore novel possibilities, and "this expansion can help to build physical, psychological, and social resources that promote well-being".[26] Durable resources are built through positive emotions by:

- advancing the formation and maintenance of positive relationships and attachment to others;
- promoting creativity and a more creative approach to problem solving;
- expanding intellectual resources such as critical analysis;
- boosting physical health;
- fostering the ability to cope with stress;
- bolstering psychological resources such as optimism, hope and confidence; and
- making it less likely for one to feel threatened by criticism, or to deny or distort information that differ from one's own beliefs and convictions.[27]

The resources that are accrued during states of positive emotion serve as essential and valuable reserves to be drawn upon when needed.[28] It seems that those who are generally more optimistic, cheerful and content reap greater physical, social and psychological benefits than those who tend to be negative, humourless and constantly miserable.

Health

The contribution of positive emotions in advancing physical health is well documented. These health benefits serve as an important physical resource. The following are examples of the distinct relationship between positivity and measurable health benefits:

- Cardio-vascular disease: positive emotions are a valuable resource in the arsenal of factors that guard against cardio-vascular disease (negative emotions such as anger and depression are directly associated with strokes and heart attacks).
- Immunity: happier people are more likely to have an enhanced immune system.
- Blood pressure: positive affect can help to buffer against high blood pressure. In contrast, negative emotions such as anxiety and anger are associated with high blood pressure.
- Zest and vitality: positive emotions boost energy levels.
- Longevity: there is an explicit correlation between positive emotion and longevity.[29]

Work performance

Positive emotions broaden the scope of employees' intellectual and social resources, resulting in improved functionality and better work performance.[30] Therefore, happiness is an important predictor of success as is evidenced by findings that:

- happy employees are generally more energetic, affable, creative, healthy and self-confident; and
- employees high in positive affectivity will have improved and quicker strategies to process information.[31]

Positive emotions are infectious in the workplace; leaders who exhibit positive emotions are more likely to have happy employees, as people flourish in a positive work climate. A positive work environment engenders higher morale, greater job satisfaction, and lower staff turnover.

In summation, Lyubomirsky and Layous[32] observe that, "happiness not only feels good, it is good. Happier people have more stable marriages, stronger immune systems, higher incomes, and more creative ideas than their less happy peers".

DEVELOPING HAPPINESS

Every individual has an average lifetime level of emotionality, which is primarily inherited.[33] Thus, the differences people experience in well-being are influenced by genetics. This may be a disheartening fact, as it implies there is nothing we can do to increase our happiness, however current evidence suggests that genes do not entirely determine the level of happiness a person experiences, but rather that "much of people's happiness is under their control".[34] The strategies discussed below are informed by evidence that positive emotions and enduring levels of happiness can be raised by engaging in intentional activities.

Strategies to increase happiness

Signature strengths

Signature strengths are personal traits associated with a particular virtue, and according to Seligman,[35] when individuals use their signature strengths on a daily basis, they will advance their sense of well-being. The 24 signature strengths identified by Seligman and Peterson[36] emanate from six core virtues that are universally supported by most religious traditions and moral philosophers. The six virtues are wisdom, courage, humanity, justice, temperance and transcendence. Twenty-four character strengths were identified which, when they are utilised, will give expression to a particular virtue, for example the virtue of wisdom can be acquired through a strength such as curiosity or love of learning.[37]

The Values-In-Action Classification (VIA Classification) organises the signature strengths and are used to help with the identification of domains of human excellence or signature strengths.

You can also visit Martin Seligman's website: www.authentichappiness.org and complete the VIA Strengths Survey online.

VALUES-IN-ACTION CLASSIFICATION SYSTEM[38]

Virtue	Defining feature	Character strength	Activities
Wisdom	*Acquisition and use of knowledge*	Curiosity/interest in the world	Take up new hobbies and read about new subjects.
		Love of learning	Take courses on subjects that interest you.
		Judgement/critical thinking	Appraise events in your life – what went well and what would you do differently?
		Creativity, originality	Find new ways of approaching tasks.
		Social and emotional intelligence	Be empathetic in your response to others.

Virtue	Defining feature	Character strength	Activities
		Perspective – seeing the big picture/wisdom	Clarify your views about the world and how people live.
Courage	The will to accomplish goals in the face of opposition	Valour and bravery	Campaign for a cause you believe in.
		Perseverance and diligence	Complete the projects you planned.
		Integrity and honesty	Be honest and true to yourself. Identify situations where you fail to act honestly.
Humanity	Positive social interaction	Kindness	Help others – acts of kindness; voluntary work.
		To love and be loved; intimacy	Tell those whom you care about that you love them.
Justice	Administering justice	Citizenship, loyalty, teamwork	Organise an event to raise money for a charity.
		Fairness and equity	Admit mistakes and apologise.
		Leadership	Identify a leader you admire and list their leadership qualities.
Temperance	Mediate excess	Self-control	Set yourself a goal and take care not to be side-tracked.
		Prudence and discretion	Listen carefully before you react or make a decision.
		Humility and discretion	Work in a team and give credit where it is due.
Transcendence	Connect to the larger universe	Appreciation of beauty and excellence	Spend time in nature or your garden to admire the beauty of nature.
		Gratitude	Keep a journal and list at least three things you are grateful for every day.
		Hope and optimism	Reflect on how you dealt with difficulties in the past, and be able to move on.
		Forgiveness and mercy	Forgive those who have wronged you. Do not nurture a grudge.
		Spirituality	Make a list of spiritual practices that brings peace and contentment.
		Playfulness and humour	Spend time with a person with a good sense of humour.

Enhancing your happiness

An important first step in advancing happiness is to set goals that will motivate actions allowing you to achieve your goal. For example, identify areas in your life where you could use your signature strengths to generate positive affect and engagement.[39] We experience greater levels of well-being when we see ourselves as moving towards a goal we value. The pursuit of goals is an indication that we are engaged in life, and our needs for autonomy and competence are met. However, Stein and Book[40] caution us not to set unrealistically high goals, as we may fail to achieve our aspirations and fall into unhappiness; "one's perception and the ability to set a realistic frame of reference are key to achieving happiness".

What are your goals for the promotion of happiness?

....

....

The theorists Lyubomirsky and Layous[41] contend that through regular, simple and intentional activities people can become significantly happier. The following are empirically tested positive practices that can help you to improve well-being:

- Writing letters expressing your gratitude.
- Counting your blessings.
- Performing random acts of kindness.
- Cultivating your strengths.
- Visualising your ideal future self.
- Meditation.

Activities are positive when they engender an increase in positive thoughts, positive behaviours and need satisfaction. Furthermore, activities are more effective when they are freely chosen rather than following someone else's instructions. A further characteristic of positive activities is that they may differ in time orientation, for example they can be focused on the past (expressing gratitude), present (counting blessings) or future (visualising ideal self).[42]

More ways to build happiness

Professor Ed Diener of the University of Illinois proposes the following three steps to generate more positive affect:

- **Attending**: When one constantly focuses on the negative, it becomes easy to overlook the positive in one's life. Unhappy people tend to dwell on their problems and there is a danger of becoming cynical when one is pre-occupied with the negative. Cultivate the habit of paying attention to all the good things that happen to you. Count your blessings.

- **Interpreting**: Happy and unhappy people tend to interpret life events differently; happy people generally interpret events more positively, and have fewer thinking errors. Thinking errors such as catastrophising, black-and-white thinking and over-generalising generate negative emotions. Pay attention to the way in which you interpret events.

- **Memorising**: Unhappy and happy people often remember events differently. Unhappy people remember negative events in detail and tend to dwell on these memories, which have a powerful effect on their emotional well-being. In contrast, happy people generally choose to nurture and recall good memories. Build good memories by savouring all the wonderful and happy moments. Go over the good events and add more details, including all the positive emotions you felt at the time. Replay your memories frequently and share them with good friends.[43]

Individuals epitomising these skills

Dalai Lama
Barack Obama
Others?

A FINAL WORD

The good news about happiness is that it is not as unattainable or elusive an ideal as we once believed it to be. Although we have a set range for positive emotions, our genetic pre-disposition is not the only factor that determines our level of happiness or well-being. As discussed throughout this book, each of the subscales, when attended to, can increase a sense of satisfaction and contentment. Thus, with the right attitude and through concrete action you can become the architect of your own well-being and happiness.

SECTION 2: ACTIVITIES FOR SKILLS DEVELOPMENT

Self-assessment

Individual activities

 Activity 1

Spend a few moments assessing your level of happiness. Answer the questions below honestly.

1 = Very seldom or not true of me
2 = Seldom true of me
3 = Sometimes true of me
4 = Often true of me
5 = Very often true of me or true of me

For the most part I am happy with my life.				
1	2	3	4	5

I seldom get depressed.				
1	2	3	4	5

I am mostly a cheerful person.				
1	2	3	4	5

I like having a "good time".				
1	2	3	4	5

People say that I have a "sunny" personality.				
1	2	3	4	5

Multiply your score by 4 to arrive at a total out of 100.

Happiness Scale									
10	20	30	40	50	60	70	80	90	100

 **Activity 2**

Reflect on ways to increase your daily experience of positive emotions.

For example:

- Make a list of the things that you enjoy doing.

  ....

  ....

- How many of these things have you done in the last month?

  ....

  ....

- Which positive activities (e.g. writing a letter of gratitude, counting your blessings) would you like to participate in?

  ....

  ....

- Who are the people with whom you have fun? Do you share your sense of fun?

  ....

  ....

Group activity

Activity 3

In your groups, discuss your company's work climate:

- How would you describe the work climate?

  ....

  ....

- Does it promote employee well-being?

  ....

  ....

- How would you go about improving the work climate to be more positive?

....

....

Own work for personal growth: a to-do list for the next fortnight

 Activity 4

1. *Reflect on your life and do a life audit: what do you need to change in your life to achieve more positive affect and happiness?*

   Make a list of things that prevent you from experiencing happiness in the following areas of your life:

   For example:

   - Physical health – what are the healthy habits you can create to experience more life satisfaction?
   - Psychological – do you pay attention to the sources of joy in your life?
   - Social – do you nurture relationships?
   - Spiritual – do you have a sense of purpose?

REFERENCES

Bar-on, R. & Parker, D.A. (2000). *The Handbook of Emotional Intelligence: Theory, Development, Assessment and Application at Home, School, and in the Workplace.* San Francisco: Jossey-Bass.
Baumgardner, A. & Crothers, M. (2014). *Positive Psychology.* Essex: Pearson.
Bergh, Z. & Theron, A. (2007). *Psychology in the Work Context.* Cape Town: Oxford University Press.
Bernstein, D.A., Penner, L.A., Clark-Stewart, A. & Roy, E.J. (2006). *Psychology* (7th ed.). New York: Houghton Miffen.
Compton, W.C. (2005). *An Introduction to Positive Psychology.* London: Thompson Wadsworth.
Fontana, D. (2008). *Psychology, Religion, and Spirituality.* Oxford: Blackwell.
Fredrickson, B.L. (2004). Gratitude, Like Other Positive Emotions, Broadens and Builds. In R.A. Emmons & M.E. McCullough (eds.). *The Psychology of Gratitude.* New York: Oxford University Press.
Hughes, M. & Terrel, J.B. (2012). *Emotional Intelligence in Action* (2nd ed.). San Francisco: Pfeiffer.
Leimon, A. & McMahon, G. (2009). *Positive Psychology for Dummies.* Chichester: Wiley.
Lyubomirsky, S. & Layous, K. (2013). How Do Simple Positive Activities Increase Well-being? *Current Directions in Psychological Science, 21*(1), p. 57 -62.
Peterson, C. & Park, N. (2004). *Classification and Measurement of Character Strengths: Implications for Practice.* In P.A. Linley & F. Joseph (eds.). *Positive Psychology in Practice.* Hoboken, NJ: John Wiley & Sons.

Seligman, M.E.P. (2004). *Authentic Happiness.* London: Nicholas Brealey Printing.
Seligman, M.E.P. (2011). *Flourish.* New York: Free Press.
Stein, S. & Book, H. (2011). *The EQ edge: Emotional Intelligence and your Success* (3rd ed.). San Francisco: Jossey-Bass.
Weyers, A. (2013). *A Social Work Programme for the Development of the Spiritual Strengths of Midlife Women.* PhD Thesis. University of the Free State, Bloemfontein.

ENDNOTES

1. Baumgardner & Crothers, 2014:9.
2. Bar-On & Parker, 2000:18.
3. Stein & Book, 2011:219.
4. Bernstein, Penner, Clark-Stewart & Roy, 2006:425.
5. Baumgardner & Crothers, 2014:32.
6. Fontana, 2008:214.
7. Weyers, 2013:20.7
8. Baumgardner & Crothers, 2014:20.
9. Baumgardner & Crothers, 2014:21.
10. Baumgardner & Crothers, 2014:37.
11. Seligman, 2011:13.
12. Leimon & McMahon, 2009.
13. Seligman, 2004; Compton, 2005.
14. Seligman, 2011:21.
15. Ibid.
16. Seligman, 2011:24.
17. Bernstein et al., 2006.
18. Compton, 2005:48.
19. Baumgardner & Crothers, 2014:36.
20. Hughes & Terrel, 2012:113.
21. Ibid.
22. Compton, 2005.
23. Seligman, 2011.
24. Compton, 2005; Bernstein, 2006; Seligman, 2011.
25. Fredrickson, 2004.
26. Baumgardner & Crothers, 2014:44.
27. Baumgarner & Crothers, 2014.
28. Fredrickson, 2004.
29. Seligman, 2004; Compton, 2005; Leimon & McMahon, 2009; Hughes & Terrel, 2012; Baumgardner & Crothers, 2014.
30. Bergh & Theron, 2006.
31. Lucas & Diener in Bergh & Theron, 2006.
32. Lyubomirsky & Layous, 2013:57.
33. Compton, 2005.
34. Lyubomirsky & Layous, 2013:57.
35. Seligman, 2011.
36. Seligman & Peterson, 2003.
37. Peterson & Park, 2004.

38 Seligman, 2004; Peterson & Parker, 2004; Bergh & Theron, 2006; Leimon & McMahon, 2009.
39 Bernstein et al., 2007.
40 Stein & Book, 2011:224.
41 Lyubomirsky & Layous, 2013.
42 Lyubomirsky & Layous, 2013:59.
43 Leimon & McMahon, 2009:33.

Chapter 19

CONCLUDING REMARKS

Annette Prins

Human beings are not only motivated by reason and intelligence, but are also subject to passions, desires, and a range of other feelings which can motivate them strongly, often in a direction different from that of reason.[1]

For 20 or so years, the cognitive paradigm dominated the field of psychology and its sister discipline, organisational psychology. At the same time, affective experiences were considered secondary. The lack of research in this field left a vacuum in respect of the value and functional aspects of affect in the work context. The past 20 years has, however, witnessed an increased interest in the role of affective experiences (both emotion and mood) in psychology,[2] due to a number of theoretical developments including the Affective Events Theory,[3] the conceptualisation of emotional intelligence, and new knowledge coming to light from the field of neuroscience. Organisational research on emotions has since accelerated its interest and pace in a bid to more fully understand the role and function of emotions in the workplace.

In a fluctuating, competitive and increasingly complex and dynamic environment, organisations are required to position themselves competitively and seek new ways to survive. Employees form an essential core in business success and often provide a competitive edge. The rules of the game have changed and excellent employees are sought and bought; employees no longer remain loyal for extended periods in an organisation, but seek out environments and opportunities that suit their desires. For this reason, organisations have to be vigilant in competing to retain their staff in the global environment. One of the aspects enhancing the attractiveness of an organisation is its approach to the well-being of employees.

It seems that, at the corporate level worldwide, pressure is increasing in terms of taking care of employee well-being. This results, *inter alia*, from legal pressures, such as the Basic Conditions of Employment Act 75 of 1997 and the Occupational Health and Safety Act 85 of 1993 in South Africa. Modern day workers are much more alert to their rights and seem more intent on leading a balanced life, increasingly seeking a balance between work, leisure, and family life. As work satisfaction and well-being have become important issues in a competitive market within organisations, companies are therefore increasingly coming under scrutiny in terms of how well they cater for their employees.

An organisation's focus on well-being has become a key branding issue. In an attempt to attract and retain better staff, it therefore seems that organisations will do well to monitor their psychological climate and resultant affective experiences[4] in order to reap the many benefits thereof in their organisations.[5]

The seismic response engendered by the popularisation of the EI construct resulted in many jumping on the bandwagon and publishing books on the topic. This resulted in numerous texts, many of which lacked solid research to substantiate their expansive claims, promises, one-sided arguments and unproven points of view. Such unsubstantiated claims contributed to questioning and even eroding confidence in the then fledgling construct.

The current text, however, builds on the interest of one of the authors in the concept of EI and her journey to ascertain whether the construct indeed holds true.[6] Research was conducted against the background of the many claims made on behalf of the construct and the criticism levelled by its opponents. The author conducted a PhD in which a literature review thoroughly explored the underlying affective concepts and the neurological basis for both the existence of the EI construct and the possibility of learning and enhancing the underlying skills.

A careful in-depth review of related literature served to advance an argument in favour of the existence of the emotional intelligence construct, unfolding convincing arguments from the field of neuroscience; competing constructs and concepts (such as emotional competence); other influential psychological factors, including the role of the primary caregiver; and the individual's dual task ability to consider simultaneously one's own and others' needs. It was further revealed that the development of emotional intelligence is dependent upon the ability to represent emotions symbolically by means of language.

The importance of neural plasticity was highlighted, supporting the argument in favour of growth as a continual process even in adulthood, allowing for neurogenesis and change. This holds the implication that new skills, such as those predicated in terms of the emotional intelligence construct, may indeed be acquired with practice. In addition, neural plasticity further holds the implication that an individual may undeniably be positively influenced by a salubrious environment and its resultant effects.

The broaden-and-build theory serves to highlight the possible gains in the workplace when experienced positive affect, on the whole, supersedes negative affect. Such gains include, for example, the building of "a variety of enduring personal resources".[7] These comprise enhanced physical, intellectual, social, and psychological resources. Research has clearly demonstrated that positive emotions broaden the thought-action repertoires and the scope of attention, cognition, and action, all virtues that may serve the workplace well. Positive emotions may furthermore serve to undo the effects of negative emotions, protect health, and fuel emotional resilience, all of which contribute to freeing up employee energy that may be channelled into work and other activities, thereby enhancing work engagement.

In addition, the affective events theory was used to demonstrate the influence of affective experiences on both job satisfaction and performance. Individuals react to work events that drive their affective states, mediating attitudes and judgement, as well as affect-driven behaviours. This influences performance and, as has been demonstrated in this particular study, indices of well-being.

The literature review reiterated the important consequences of emotions and moods at work and, more specifically, the important influence thereof for the general well-being of employees, as reflected in both positive and negative work-related outcomes. The primary aim of this study was not to ascertain the predictive value of EI with regard to work success, as this has been successfully researched elsewhere. Research conducted in relation to the EI construct and experience with the construct has validated its importance as an important factor in both personal and business success.[8] It has further been confirmed that EI competencies play "an increasingly important role at higher levels of organisations, where differences in technical skills are of negligible importance".[9]

Rather, the focus of the study fell on the process by which EI may accomplish such outcomes. The variables of interest included, as depicted in the model below, EI as a mediator of psychological (work) climate; experienced job affect; and indicators of work wellness, including work engagement and health, burnout, and contemplated quitting. Positive emotions and well-being are, of course, not singularly an end in and of themselves, but are also important in terms of their relation to performance.

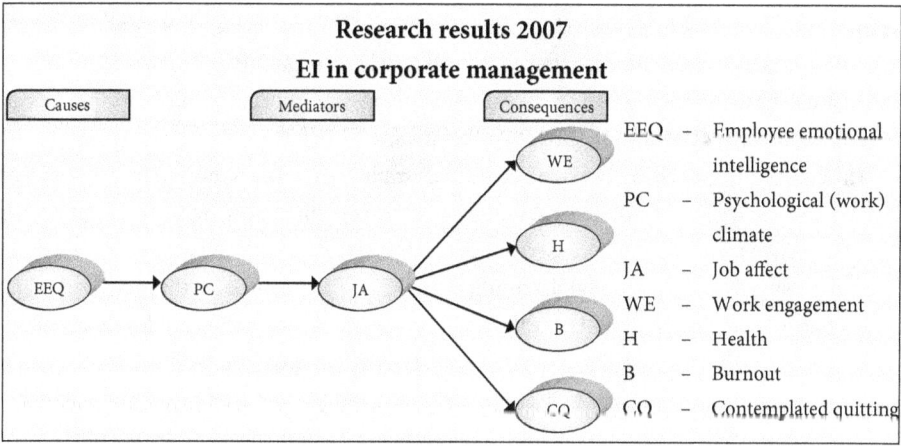

Figure 20.1: Making sense of the evolving EI construct

In order to promote employee well-being and efficacy, we need to align knowledge about optimal human functioning with organisational effectiveness and outcomes. How do different work practices and processes contribute to creating more positive workplaces?

The researcher further reflected on disparities inherent to the different theorists' competing definitions, conceptualisations and psychometric measures of the evolving EI construct . (For purposes of brevity this overview has not been included in the current text since it had appeared in the first edition).

Empirical research, using stringent measures as part of a PhD, put the arguments in the literature review to the test, and the results indeed verified the important role of EI in the work situation. Therefore, despite a flurry of negative views on the existence of the construct (and possible shortcomings in the measuring instruments applied), emotional intelligence, in the referred-to-study, contributes to the way in which the individual experiences his or her work environment, i.e. employees with enhanced EI scores experience their work climate significantly more positively. In addition, the psychological work climate and job affect clearly demonstrated their significance as mediators in relation to the indices of well-being at work. This research demonstrated a significantly positive relationship between the experience of positive job affect, work engagement, and health, and a significantly negative relationship with burnout and contemplated quitting. Factors influencing and mediating similar outcomes therefore require careful consideration in the workplace.

The results again serve to emphasise the important influence of affective experiences in the workplace. This creates a platform for the notion of EI and its possible influence as depicted in the literature, and has of late been supported by neurological evidence. In a quest to understand organisational behaviour better, leaders and managers will do well to consider how best to manage the affective climate at work effectively and to enhance emotional intelligence.

Organisations have long believed that positive emotions are linked to performance, and therefore attention was paid to aspects such as positive reinforcement, positive affect, and humour, all of which are well described elsewhere.[10] By contrast, experiencing negative emotions may serve to create a downward spiral in which negative or depressed moods and pessimistic, narrow thinking reciprocally influence one another, sapping individual energy and redirecting energy and thought processes inward.[11]

The cost of the escalation in burnout among employees needs to be carefully considered. Burnout and its well-described consequences increase exhaustion, with both mental and physical absence from work; decreased levels of both resilience and meaning derived from a lack in the experience of personal accomplishment; and depersonalisation and callousness that may have a detrimental effect on the level of service delivery. Higher levels of burnout may also coincide with an increase in contemplated or real quitting, with an accompanying loss of expertise that may again negatively influence the performance and management of an organisation. Ill health may also have stark monetary implications in terms of escalating medical expenditures for the organisation.

Against the background sketched in relation to emotional intelligence and its important influence on effective functioning at work, home, and in the broader community, this text was prepared and revised at the request of the publishing house. It reflects the EI model refined by Reuven Bar-On and revised together with MHS[12] to incorporate continuous research, adding further value to the most recent model, the EQ-i 2.0.

The authors wish to help individuals acquire this influential group of skills via both knowledge and experiential practice in individual, group and extended self-exercises. The model of choice, as was explained, is the model refined by Reuven Bar-On .

We hope that you have enjoyed this fascinating journey with us.

REFERENCES

Aspinwall, L.G. (1998). Rethinking the role of positive affect in self-regulation. *Motivation and Emotion*, 22:1–32.

Aspinwall, L.G. (2001). Dealing with adversity: Self-regulation, coping, adaptation, and health. In A. Tesser & N. Schwarz (eds.). *The Blackwell handbook of social psychology* (Vol 1.). Malden, MA: Blackwell, p. 159–614.

Goleman, D., Boyatzis, R. & McKee, A. (2013). *Primal Leadership*. Boston: Harvard Business Review Press.

Fredrickson, B.L. (2001). The role of positive emotions in positive psychology: The broaden-and-build theory of positive emotions. *American Psychologist*, 56(3), 1–8.

Hughes, M. & Terrell, J.B. (2012). *Emotional Intelligence in Action*. San Francisco: Pfeiffer.

Luthans, F. (2002). Invited essay. The need for and meaning of positive organisational behaviour. *Journal of Organizational Behavior*, 23:695–706.

Multi-Health Systems Inc. (MHS) (2011). *The complete EQ-i 2.0 experience*. Toronto: Multi-Health Systems Inc.

Prins, A. (2007). *Emotional intelligence and leadership in corporate management: A fortigenic perspective*. (Unpublished PhD thesis). Bloemfontein: University of the Free State.

Prins, A. (2010a). *Emotional intelligence and leadership: A work wellness perspective*. Saarbrücken: VDM Verlag Dr Müller.

Prins, A., Van Niekerk, E. & Weyers, A. (2011). *Emotional Intelligence: Tipping Point in Workplace Excellence*. Randburg: Knowres.

Sing, D. (2006). *Emotional Intelligence at work: A professional guide* (3rd ed.). London: Sage Publications.

Weiss, H.M. & Cropanzano, R. (1996). Affective events theory: a theoretical discussion of the structure, causes, and consequences of affective experiences at work. *Research in Organizational Behavior*, 18:1–74.

ENDNOTES

1 Singh, 2006:53.
2 Prins et al., 2011.
3 Weiss & Cropanzano, 1996.
4 Ibid.
5 Fredrickson, 1998–2001.
6 Prins, 2007; 2010.
7 Fredrickson, 2001:239.
8 Hughes et al., 2012.
9 Goleman, 2013:250.
10 cf Luthans, 2002.
11 cf Aspinwall, 1998; 2001.
12 MHS, 2011.

INDEX

A

abuse, 22, 38, 170, 203, 274, 277
acceptance, 8, 38–40, 53, 69, 141, 144, 185, 197, 211, 234, 258
action tendencies, 20, 181
adapting emotions, 16
adaptive excusing, 277
adaptive response, 255–256
addiction, 41, 202
ADHD (Attention Deficit Hyperactivity Disorder), 38, 215
adults, 211, 215
  illiterate, 172
adversarial relationships, 140
affective concepts, underlying, 302
affective events theory, 301–302
affirmative action, 131
aggression, 107–108, 210
aggressiveness, 103–104
aggressor, 108, 113
alcoholics, 200, 202
alexithymia, 21–22, 67, 157
alpha response, 39
alpha waves, 257
ambitions, 57, 189, 212
anger, 2–4, 37, 40, 67, 70, 94–97, 104, 106, 108–109, 116, 181, 201, 209, 211–214, 220–221, 223, 247, 256–258, 291
antagonism, 91, 140
anxiety, 3–4, 9, 41, 43, 103–105, 107, 109, 199–200, 230, 233–234, 246, 248–249, 252–253, 257-258, 260, 269, 273, 278
APA (American Psychiatric Association), 199, 242
appraisal, 21, 223, 246, 276
approach behaviour, 12–13, 89, 210
aspirations, 57, 123, 125, 127, 294
assertive behaviour, 37, 103, 110–112, 117, 120
assertiveness, 15–16, 37, 52, 68, 90, 103–115, 117–119, 124, 127, 143, 278, 285
assessment, 14, 17, 71, 150, 204, 246, 287, 298
attachment behaviour, 20
authentic happiness theory, 288
authority figures, 231, 272

automatic thoughts, 252–253, 255–256, 278
avoidance behaviours, stimulate, 89
avoidance responses, 12
awareness of negative emotions, 12, 271

B

barometric indicator, 287
Bar-On, 7–8, 14, 17–18, 25, 150, 183, 298
  model, 5, 34, 52
  test, 88
behaviour, 8, 12–13, 18–19, 22, 66–68, 104–107, 112, 158–159, 211–212, 216, 219–220, 228–229, 233–235, 254, 271
  abusive, 144
  adaptive, 67
  aggressive, 103, 107–108
  appropriate, 20
  clinging, 126, 131
  competent, 8–9
  constructive, 182
  dependent, 123
  dysfunctional, 216, 233
  explosive, 112
  impulsive, 211, 216, 218
  inappropriate, 218, 260
  independent, 123–124
  intelligent, 12
  interpersonal, 17
  irresponsible, 210
  non-assertive, 104–105
  passive, 104, 106
  passive-aggressive, 140
  pessimist's, 278
  positive, 294
  self-defeating, 69, 276
  unassertive, 112, 125
  unpredictable, 210, 214
behaviour patterns, 145–146
beliefs, 9, 16–17, 35, 37, 41, 68, 75, 104, 109, 114, 144, 146, 174, 199, 201, 204, 231–232, 252
bioregulatory response, 19
brain, 18-20, 22, 128, 156, 203, 215, 249, 253, 255, 257, 260, 269, 273

intuitive right, 206
rational left, 206
burnout, 24, 65, 69, 234, 247, 303–304
business ethics, 171
business strategy, 140

C

capabilities, 54, 58, 71, 237
  latent, 49
  learned, 8
  natural, 55
  non-cognitive, 8, 14
  unique, 55
capacity, 18, 20–22, 49–51, 56, 123, 129, 154, 162, 180, 184, 206, 210, 229, 250, 257
  cognitive, 181
  emotional intelligent, 127
  intrapsychic, 7
  self-reflective, 20
cardio-vascular disease (CVD), 245, 249, 258, 275–276
catatonic behaviour, 199
catatonic negativism, 230
CBT (Cognitive Behaviour Therapy), 255
change, 14, 34, 40–41, 72, 74–75, 112–114, 118, 145–146, 227–229, 232–235, 237–241, 247, 261–262, 275–276, 278
  behavioural, 246
  envisaged, 234
  execute, 240
  rapid, 233, 247
change behaviour, 269
changing thinking habits, 255
character strength, 288, 292–293, 298
chemical messengers, 249
childhood dependence, 38
childhood trauma, 21-22, 277
circuitry, 18
  amygdala's, 203
  distinct, 18
  limbic, 18
circulatory response, pathological, 275
client-centred therapy, 167
coaching activities, 242
cognitive abilities, 13, 180–181, 231, 247
Cognitive Behaviour Therapy (CBT), 255
cognitive intelligence, 6–7, 14, 18–19, 69, 181

communication, 69, 89, 91–92, 97, 145–146, 156–157, 160, 173, 232
  digital, 149
  healthy, 119
  non-verbal, 92, 96, 143
  skills, 143
  social, 9
  verbal, 91
compassion, 41, 53, 69, 137–138, 211
competence, 140, 287, 294
  emotional, 8–9, 95, 270, 302
competencies, 8–9, 11, 14, 52, 54, 69, 71, 136, 143, 183–184, 278
  associated, 69
  core, 77, 95, 127
  emotional, 14, 66
  epitomise, 136
  important emotional intelligence, 262
  self-management, 209, 220
concentration, 81, 219
conceptualisations, 12, 301, 303
conflict, 79, 90-91, 99, 103, 105, 107–108, 111, 120, 140, 155-156, 170, 195, 246–247, 270, 280
confrontation, 3
consciousness, 75
  clouded, 203
  increasing, 69
contentment, 52, 55, 126, 141, 286–287, 293, 295
control, 67-68, 72–73, 75, 89, 109–111, 124, 126-127, 210, 212–213, 216, 218–219, 221, 228, 233–235, 239, 246–247, 256, 262, 270, 289
coping, 5, 8, 14, 16, 22, 182-183, 198, 234, 246, 258, 273–274, 276
cortisol, 249, 257, 275
counselling, 36, 161
counsellors, 153, 233
creative leadership, 231
creative thinking, 195
creativity, 46, 53–54, 80, 91, 129, 189–190, 232, 241, 290, 292
CSR (Corporate Social Responsibility), 171–172, 178
culture, 9, 53, 92, 94, 124–125, 129, 137, 157, 201, 207, 234, 272
  collectivist, 94-95, 124-125

foreign, 238
individualistic, 94–95, 124
Cybernetic Cycle Adapted, 186

D

decision-making skills, better, 4
decisions, 18–19, 34, 37, 110, 114, 125–128, 130–131, 181, 188–190, 194, 202, 204, 206, 209–210, 234
defence mechanisms, 200
defensiveness, 237
deficits, 18
  psychological disorders highlight, 6
demoralisation, 170
dependability, 139
dependent personality disorder, 125–126
depression, 37–38, 41, 43, 61, 221, 234, 247, 249–250, 253, 257–258, 273, 275–276, 278, 291
destruction, 96, 111, 209, 212
development, 18, 20–22, 38, 40, 45, 137, 143, 149–150, 215, 217, 219, 273, 277, 288, 298–299
  abnormal, 5–6, 17, 21
  cognitive, 20–21
  healthy emotional, 19
  optimal, 138
  professional, 146
  sustainable, 172
developmental challenges, 52
developmental status, 174
diet and nutrition, 250
dignity, 50, 109, 119
diligence, 233, 293
disciplinary hearings, 213
disease, 43, 141, 249, 258, 275
  cardio-vascular, 210, 245, 249, 258, 275, 291
  coronary, 141
disorders, 199, 215, 249
  attention deficit hyperactivity, 215
  immune-related, 3
  mental, 199, 242
  oppositional defiant, 214
  physical, 38, 249
disrupted sleep patterns, 248
distorted thoughts, 255
distress, 3–4, 19, 58, 214, 258, 273, 278

diversity, 47, 137
domineering characteristics, 69
drinking problems, 254
drug addicts, 158, 200
drugs, 174, 202
duel task ability, 20–21
dysfunctional expectations, 254
dysfunctional thoughts, 112, 253

E

EC (Emotional Competence), 8–9, 95, 270, 302
effective verbal response, 161
effects
  immobilising, 229
  negative, 108–109
  significant, 23
  transforming, 277
elevated feelings, 37
embracing change, 232
emotional abilities, 19
emotional alignment, 161
emotional arousal, 21
emotional awareness, 20–22, 67, 90
emotional breakdowns, 213-214, 217
Emotional Competence, *see* EC
emotional consequences, 252
emotional control, 67, 69, 222
emotional conversations, 96
emotional dependency, 16, 123
emotional deprivation, 22
emotional experience, 20–22, 55, 246
emotional expression, 5, 15–16, 88–90, 92, 94–97, 182, 185
emotional expression scale, 98
emotional-focused coping, 183
Emotional Intelligence (EI), 1, 5-6, 3–9, 11–14, 17–20, 22–25, 50–52, 67, 150, 155–156, 170, 195, 229, 237, 242, 262, 289, 298–299, 301–304
  developing, 65, 242
  development of, 17, 23, 302
emotional intelligence capacities, 180
emotional intelligence competencies, 5, 8, 52, 143, 184–185
emotional intelligence models, 11, 13
emotional intelligence skills, 2, 55, 228, 262
emotional intelligence subscales, 289

emotional intelligence test, 183
emotional literacy, 65, 68, 96, 242
emotional reactions, 12, 65, 73, 109, 182, 215, 223, 264
emotional response, 89, 191, 194, 252
  managing negative, 271
  subjective, 181
emotional self-awareness, 2, 15-16, 18, 35, 55, 65-66, 69, 72, 76-77, 79, 104, 158, 185, 209, 216
emotional self-awareness scale, 78
emotional self-expression, 88
emotional skills training, 20
emotional sobriety, 156, 166
emotional state, 19-20, 23, 69, 73, 88-89, 91-92, 210
emotional values, 94
emotion and mood, 3-4, 301
emotion and problem solving, 181
emotions, 2-8, 15-16, 18-25, 35, 65-68, 70-75, 77-79, 81-82, 88-96, 98-100, 154-158, 166, 179-182, 211-215, 251-252, 301-302
empathic communication, 160
empathic engagement, 159
empathic individuals, 155-156, 158
empathic response, 158, 165
empathic understanding, 65
empathy, 2, 4, 12, 15-16, 18, 20, 22, 65, 67-68, 88, 90, 142-143, 153-159, 160-164, 166-167
employee morale, 270
employees, 24, 54, 69, 75, 91, 96, 140, 142, 146, 232, 234, 291, 297, 301, 303-304
Employment Act, 301
empowerment, 103, 127
energy levels, 245, 251, 291
equilibrium, 256
  emotional, 252
ethics, 75, 169, 171
evaluation methodology, 172
executive coach, 242
exhaustion, 246-247, 304
expectancy-value models, 271
expression, 37, 56, 69, 89-90, 92-95, 97, 126, 158, 201, 213, 220, 287, 292
  disgust, 93
  external, 15, 87

  honest, 182
  non-verbal, 89-90, 97
  observed, 89
  physical, 89
  verbal, 91-92

F

facial expressions, 74, 89, 92-93, 97, 99, 108, 117, 155-156, 159-160
fairness, 138, 211, 293
fair treatment, 117
family conflict, 3
family history, 276
fatal flaws, identifying, 190
fatigue, 109, 217, 257
feedback, 34, 68, 70-71, 74, 79, 82, 92, 98, 106, 109, 118, 142, 145-146, 198, 202-203, 207, 213, 223, 229-230
fight-and-flight response, normal, 213
flexibility, 4, 8, 16, 125, 143, 185, 228-238
  cognitive, 181
  downside of, 231
  enhanced, 229, 236
  individuals epitomising, 237
  level of, 112, 229, 238, 241
  personal, 36
  psychological, 230-231, 234, 242
  scale, 238
  skills, 236
frustration tolerance, 210, 214
fulfilment, 49, 51, 53, 56, 73, 125, 155, 287
functional interactive skills, 65
functionality, 250, 291
functional thoughts, 112

G

gender equality, 171
genetic pre-disposition, 295
goals, 10, 12-13, 15, 35, 42, 45-46, 49, 51-53, 55, 57-58, 68, 111, 124-125, 170, 184, 186, 188, 190, 215, 220, 234, 236, 260-261, 271, 278-279, 286, 288-289, 293-294
grief, 153, 158
gross negligence, 144
group activities, 45, 49, 99, 103, 131, 136, 149, 154, 164, 176, 180, 193, 197, 207, 209

growth, 49–51, 58, 125, 203, 276, 287, 302
  intellectual, 8
  optimal, 5
growth goals, 57
growth model, 242
gut feeling, 69, 72, 203, 211, 223

H

habits, 39-40, 70, 153, 157, 166, 207, 216, 229, 235, 239, 251, 257, 294, 298
happiness research, 286
happiness scale, 296
health, 8, 24, 42, 57, 69, 95, 137, 141, 150, 156, 248, 251, 258, 290–291, 302–304
  emotional, 16, 95, 156, 285, 289
  good, 40, 250
  improved, 250
  positive, 275
  psychological, 71
  subjective, 9
health benefits, 95, 282, 291
healthy relationships, 119, 144
helplessness, 38, 108, 126, 273, 282
  learned, 170, 271, 277
  passive, 275
high beta waves, 257
highly effective people, 153
HIV/AIDS, 171–173, 200
holistic approaches, 258
honesty, 47, 69, 91, 139–140, 202, 293
hyperactivity, 215
hypersensitive, 108
hypertension, 249, 258, 275

I

imagination, 230, 235
immune system, 43, 95, 156, 249, 258, 275, 282, 291
impulse, 2, 12, 15–16, 41, 73, 104, 143, 179, 185, 209–211, 214-216, 218–221, 223, 228, 231, 236-237, 271, 276
inadequate self-regard, 38
incompetence, 273
  emotional, 9
independence, 15–16, 52–53, 69, 87, 94, 123–127, 129, 130-133, 216, 228, 231, 237
individualism, 50, 124, 132
individualistic European-American cultures, 95
individuals, 8–10, 14, 18–19, 22, 37–38, 49, 54, 67–68, 72, 89, 92–96, 103, 106-108, 113–114, 124, 169–170, 177, 182–183, 198, 210–211, 216–217, 219–220, 228–236, 245, 257, 270, 273, 278–279, 282
individual's dual task ability, 302
Information Fatigue Syndrome, 247
innovation, 184, 228, 231–232, 240, 277
insecurity, 38, 40, 108, 211, 213, 277
intact neurological system, 21
intellectual ability, 18–19
intellectual capacity, 8, 170
intelligence, 6–7, 9–11, 13–14, 17, 19–20, 22, 72, 181, 183, 301
interdependence, 94, 138–139
interpersonal effectiveness, 68
interpersonal negotiation strategies, 90
interpersonal relationships, 15–17, 42, 52–53, 96, 136–139, 145, 148–149, 153,
interpersonal skills enhancement, 143

J

job disengagement, 261
job dissatisfaction, 247
job insecurity, 247
job satisfaction, 23, 54, 80, 139, 142, 265, 291, 302

K

knowledge, 6–7, 10, 17, 21, 37, 47, 51, 68–69, 97, 138, 140, 144, 177, 182, 184, 189, 220, 303–304

L

leaders, 4, 69, 130, 202–203, 207, 212–213, 231, 240, 242, 291, 293, 304
  effective, 277
  female, 141
  healthy, 277
  high-performing, 54
  inspired, 58
  resonant, 96

successful, 211, 232
leadership, 23, 67–68, 132, 137, 169, 230, 234, 270, 276–277, 279, 282, 293
leadership styles, 202
learning, 20, 24, 38, 71, 155, 203, 231, 255, 292, 302
learning disabilities, 172
lifestyle, 40, 53, 190, 247, 250-251, 263
listener, 2, 58, 82, 143, 147-148, 155, 161, 163
listening, 91, 157–159, 162, 288
logical thinking processes, 216
long-term behavioural change, 255
loyalty, 69, 139–140, 144, 170, 293
   customer, 9

M

managing change, 232
managing destructive emotions, 210
managing emotions during team problem solving, 195
manipulation, 92, 107, 109, 119
marital instability, 39
mastering impulsiveness, 216
measuring emotional intelligence, 17
meditation, 41, 45, 259
memory functions, 245, 249
mental alertness, 235, 257
mental health, 23, 40, 150, 279
millennials, 91
mind's ability, 155, 198
moods, 3–4, 7, 66–67, 71–72, 76, 82, 155, 157, 182, 217, 265, 287, 287, 301–302, 304
motivation, 2, 18, 23, 49-50, 54-55, 81, 140, 145, 233, 249, 269, 271, 276
Multi Health Systems (MHS), 14, 35, 243

N

narcissism, 41, 154, 157
National Church Life Survey (NCLS), 276
negative consequences, 213–214, 271
negative emotional space, 217
negative emotions, 12, 19, 68–69, 91, 93, 95, 209, 212, 220–221, 271, 273, 291, 295, 302, 304
negative mental cycles, 259
negative self-defeating thoughts, 255

negative thinking, 39
negative thoughts, 251
negotiating confrontations, 189
neocortex, 18, 22, 212
neurological basis, 302
neurology, 18–19, 23
neuro-psychologists, 154
neuroscience, 6, 18–19, 269, 301–302
non-cognitive intellective, 6
non-cognitive intelligences, 10, 17
non-intellective intelligences, 8, 9–11
nuancing self-awareness, 71

O

obedience, 69, 124
objective reality, 203, 269
observation, 51
Occupational Health and Safety Act, 301
opinions, 14, 66, 79, 96–97, 99–100, 103, 105, 109–110, 115, 117, 125, 127, 130, 206, 238, 250, 275
optimism, 2, 16–17, 52–53, 141, 227, 269–279, 281–282, 285, 287, 289–290, 293
optimism scale, 280
optimistic viewpoint, 190
optimists, 269–276, 279–280
organisational climate, 4, 139, 142
organisational effectiveness, 303
organisational psychology, 301
organisational research, 301
orientations, 51, 53, 124, 229
outbursts, 92, 117, 214
over-aroused nervous system, 247

P

panic attacks, 257
parental alcoholism, 38
parental over-protectiveness, 38
passive individuals, 105
passive observers, 235
performance, 8, 23, 54, 70, 166, 182, 236, 260, 290, 302–304
   effective, 139
   occupational, 23
   poor, 200
   successful, 261
personal abilities, 39

personal competence, 68
personal goals, 12, 20, 42, 52
personal growth, 38, 45–46, 49, 51–52, 58, 61, 81, 132, 138, 177, 183, 241, 246, 276, 281, 287
personal identity, 40
personal intelligences, 7, 22
personalities, 13–14, 53–54, 57, 106, 119, 150, 167, 210–211, 247
  balanced, 261
  dependent, 125–126
  healthy, 261
  independent, 125–126
  strong, 131
personality characteristics, 214
personal relationships, 40, 58, 136, 143
perspectives, 6, 15, 21, 71, 135, 154–155, 167, 169-170, 184, 189, 203–204, 206–207, 269–270, 282, 287–288, 293
pervasive feelings of helplessness, 126
pessimism, 258, 269, 272–273, 275, 277–278, 280–281
pessimists, 189, 269–276, 278–279
physiological changes, 92
plasticity, 22, 24, 229, 237
positive affirmations, 129
positive ambiance, 142
positive attitude, 16, 269–270, 279
positive attributions, 144
positive emotions, 126, 146, 194–195, 213, 216, 270, 273, 275, 279, 286, 288, 290–292, 295, 297–298, 302–304
positive expectations, 143, 270
positive feelings, 41–42, 260
positive focus, 190
positive impact, 184, 270
positive psychology, 5, 51, 137, 150, 195, 286–288, 298
Positive Psychology for Dummies, 150, 298
Positive Psychology in Practice, 298
positive qualities, 38, 42, 276
positive reinforcement, 304
positive relationships, 91, 138, 141, 144, 273, 288, 290, 304
positive self-regard, 37, 40, 45, 47, 97, 127
positive social interaction, 293
positive thoughts, 259, 294
power, 42, 70, 109–111, 113, 124, 234–235

distribute, 140
implicit, 90
perceived, 23
personal, 73
psychological, 90
role of, 109–110
powerlessness, 108, 153
power relations, 109, 114
practical intelligence, 6, 10, 17
practice gratitude, 42
practice intuition, 204
predisposition, 106
  individual's biomedical, 8
pre-empting consequences, 217
prefrontal cortex, 21
  left, 273–274
  ventromedial, 19
pressures, 8, 14, 71, 157, 212, 214, 223, 232, 246–247, 262, 301
  environmental, 124
  legal, 301
  social, 125
primitive neurological survival system, 213
problem solving, 15–16, 37, 54, 180–188, 191, 193–194, 206, 228, 231, 237, 257, 278, 281, 290
productivity, 4, 23, 80, 91, 139, 142, 156, 184, 218, 236, 249, 270
projects, 18, 93, 111, 171–172, 211–213, 217, 260, 281, 293
  community-based developmental, 172
prosocial peer relations, 20
prospective mentors, 173
psychiatrists, 199, 215
psychoanalysis, 50
psycho-historians, 200
psychological adjustment, 141
psychological afflictions, 247
psychological benefits, 291
psychological disorders, 195
psychological science, 298
psychological wellbeing, 8, 46, 258
psychologists, 3, 6, 24, 38, 162, 199, 215
psychology, 5–6, 37, 50-51, 150, 181, 195, 269, 287, 298, 301
psychometric measures, 9, 303
psychopathology, 5, 199, 212
psychopaths, 155

psychopathy, 154
psychosocial, 210
psychotherapy, 36

R
rash behaviours, avoiding, 210
rational analysis, 254
reactions, 72-73, 75, 89–90, 94-95 99, 118, 155, 189, 212-214, 216, 218, 256, 262
realisation, 51, 252
reflective reasoning, 129
regression, 200
rehabilitation, 276
rejection, 38, 146
relationship building, 90, 173
relationships, 15–18, 23, 67-68, 70, 73, 90, 92, 94–97, 107, 109–111, 125, 127-128, 131, 135–144, 146–147, 149, 155, 162, 210, 213-214, 234, 272, 276, 304
relationship trauma, 166
relaxation, 39, 257-260, 262
religious background, 158
religious traditions, 292
repetitive thoughts, 81
reprogramme thoughts, 41
research, 14, 17–20, 23–25, 181, 183, 234, 247, 249, 251, 258, 270, 274, 276, 287–289, 301–304
  contemporary, 269
  continuous, 304
  empirical, 24, 303
resentment, 40, 105–107, 109
residual feelings, 41
resilience, 8, 166, 217, 234, 250, 261–262, 270, 290, 304
  emotional, 302
  increased, 53, 141
resources, 246, 289, 291
  expanding intellectual, 290
  individual's, 246
  inner, 41
  material, 246
  psychological, 290, 302
  required, 90
  social, 290–291
responsibility, 76, 105, 124, 126–127, 170, 173, 185, 200, 209, 211, 214, 216, 254

restlessness, 74, 215
rewards, 13, 19, 52, 126, 141, 170, 215, 219, 286
rights, 39, 90, 103–105, 108–110, 112, 114–115, 117–119, 124, 170, 204, 237, 301
risks, 42, 59, 126-127, 129, 170-171, 190, 201, 210, 220, 231, 247, 249, 275–276
road rage, 9, 213, 217
role model, 175

S
sabotaging ourselves, 217
Safety Act, 301
sarcasm, 105, 160, 214
SC (Social Competence), 8
scale
  composite, 15
  following, 82
  interpersonal relationship, 148
  problem-solving ability level, 192
  self-perception, 15, 87
  testing, 206
schizophrenia, 199
schizophrenic, 230
self-absorption, 41, 50
self-acceptance, 37, 39–40, 53
self-actualisation, 15–17, 35, 49–60, 230, 285, 289
self-affirmations, 39, 129
self-alienation, 170
self-assertiveness, 37, 114
self-assessment individual activities, 43, 59, 69-71, 77, 97, 114, 130, 147, 163, 175, 191, 205, 221, 230, 238, 262, 279, 296
self-awareness, 18, 52, 65–77, 81, 88–89, 96, 104, 109, 145, 155, 158, 216–218, 265
self-blame, 39, 273
self-centredness, 106
self-confidence, 15, 36–37, 69, 71, 111, 125-126, 234, 257, 291
self-control, 68, 107, 182, 209–211, 213, 216–217, 293
self-critical attitude, 248
self-critical dialogues, 39
self-criticism, 37, 41, 128, 254
self-deception, 197
self-defeating, 129, 242, 255
self-delusion, 197, 202

self-denial, 197
self-determination, 235
self-development, 71
self-discipline, 216, 234
self-disconnect, 40
self-doubt, 37, 39-40, 109
self-efficacy, 8, 174, 246
self-efficiency, 127
self-esteem, 36-37, 43, 47, 104, 106, 109, 111, 125, 141, 174, 201, 228-229, 254, 247-248, 250, 289
self-evaluation, 202, 216
self-fulfilling prophesy, 269
self-improvement exercise, 45
self-indulgence, 50
self-management, 18, 127, 155, 217
self-motivation, 12, 126, 128
self-perception, 15, 34-35
self-persuasion, 81
self-realisation, 53
self-regard, 3, 16-17, 35-47, 52, 127, 218, 272, 289
self-regulation, 21, 182, 209, 220
self-reinforcement, 128
self-rejection, 41
self-renewal, 217
self-respect, 37, 109, 119-120
self-responsibility, 209
sensationalism, 12
sensations, 20, 66-67, 73-74, 181, 248
setbacks, 16, 41, 47, 153, 209, 220, 227, 246, 252, 263, 270-271, 273, 279-280
sexual expression, 46
sexual feelings, 104
short-tempered, 248
skills, 8-9, 14, 25, 72, 76-77, 97, 126-127, 143-144, 147-148, 155-157, 172-173, 184, 191, 228-229, 232-233
  basic, 4
  cognitive, 17
  critical, 156
  distinct, 25
  emotional, 14, 69
  empathic, 162
  fundamental, 155
  intelligent, 34
  interpersonal, 7, 137, 140, 234
  learned, 158

meta-cognitive, 230
non-verbal, 97
problem-solving, 41, 52, 235
reality-testing, 197, 201
technical, 303
testing, 201-205
skills development, 43-44, 59-60, 77, 114, 130, 147, 163, 174-175, 191, 205, 221, 238, 279, 287, 296
sleep deprivation, 40, 203, 250-251
social and emotional intelligence, 292
social awareness skills, 18
social competence (SC), 8
social consciousness, 16
social effectiveness training, 143
social intelligence, 6, 10, 14
social media, 149
social psychology, 150
social relationships, 14, 58, 137, 289
social responsibility, 15-16, 69, 124, 135, 169-172, 174-176
social sciences, 137
social skills, 4, 14, 22, 143, 145, 148, 219, 278
social support, 22-23, 42, 138, 142, 150, 182, 246, 270
social work programme, 299
society, 8, 24, 36, 41, 53, 59, 69, 141, 169-171, 174, 176-178, 184, 198-200, 203, 250, 261
solving complex problems, 186
spiritual awareness, 46
spiritual qualities, 235
steps in empathic communication, 160
steps in mental rehearsal, 128
stress, 4, 38, 107, 111, 142, 183, 199, 203, 209, 214, 217-220, 245-251, 258, 260-265, 269-270, 275, 278
stress management, 16, 34, 216, 227, 257, 262, 264
stressors, 6, 246, 251, 263-264
stress symptoms, 109, 248
stress tolerance, 2, 16, 39, 41, 245, 250, 262-263, 265
strong value system, 228
subscales, 15-17, 52, 90, 185, 285, 289-290, 295

T

teams, 15, 69, 80, 88, 90, 135, 137, 140, 145, 182, 184, 211–213, 223-234, 230, 240, 242, 293
tension, 74, 106, 120, 140, 214, 218, 246, 248, 257
theory, 7, 14, 17, 21, 65, 72, 150, 154, 197–198, 209–210, 245–246, 252, 270–271, 286–288, 298
  broaden-and-build, 290, 302
theory informing independence, 124
theory informing interpersonal relationships, 137
theory informing problem solving, 181
theory informing self-actualisation, 50
theory informing self-regard, 37
theory informing thinking, 66, 89, 104, 230
therapeutic process, 153
thinking, 18, 76, 78, 82, 105, 108, 181–182, 189–190, 201, 205, 217-218, 221, 232, 235–236, 245, 251–255
  black-and-white, 295
  catastrophic, 235
  constructive, 274
  critical, 69
  dysfunctional, 253
  independent, 132
  informing, 103, 229, 270
  irrational, 217
  narrow, 304
  person's, 155
  rational, 182
  right-brain, 188
transforming relationships, 139
trust, 15, 23, 38, 47, 92, 112, 126, 129, 135, 137–140, 144, 146, 149, 174, 202, 204, 277

U

unarticulated life goals, 248
unassertiveness, 104
unfavourable comparisons, 254
untreated sufferers, 199

V

values, 66, 68–70, 75, 123–126, 140–141, 144, 157–158, 183–184, 201, 204, 206, 228, 231, 301, 304
Values-In-Action, 288, 292
ventromedial prefrontal, 19
verbal fluency, 18
verbal responses, 161, 220
victim manipulator, 113
victims, 37, 105, 107, 111, 119, 170, 200, 202, 205, 214, 253
violence, 170, 174, 218, 277
vulnerability, 59, 92, 217, 264, 270, 276

W

weaknesses, 10, 37, 40, 44, 47, 71, 155, 234, 271, 282
well-being, 14, 37, 249, 286, 302
well-being indicator, 17, 289
wellness indicator, 16, 285
work environment, 6, 142, 149, 247, 291, 303
workforce, motivated, 142
work performance, 276, 291
work wellness, 303
worthlessness, 37

[Created with **TExtract** / www.Texyz.com]

www.ingramcontent.com/pod-product-compliance
Lightning Source LLC
Chambersburg PA
CBHW080357170426
43193CB00016B/2745